Physical Expressions
of
Intelligence

Physical Expressions of Intelligence

BRYANT J. CRATTY

University of California, Los Angeles

Prentice-Hall, Inc., *Englewood Cliffs, New Jersey*

ISBN: 0–13–668723–7

Library of Congress Catalog Card Number: 71–179621

10   9   8   7   6   5   4   3   2   1

Prentice-Hall International, Inc., *London*
Prentice-Hall of Australia, Pty. Ltd., *Sydney*
Prentice-Hall of Canada, Ltd., *Toronto*
Prentice-Hall of India Private Limited, *New Delhi*
Prentice-Hall of Japan, Inc., *Tokyo*

*This work is dedicated to my colleagues
in other nations*

CONTENTS

II
Individual Differences

III
Exercise, Attention, and Motor Skill

IV
Improving Academic
and Intellectual Abilities

PREFACE

This book examines the current interest in mental-motor relationships, both statistical and causal, and attempts to put these relationships, in a proper context with regard to their impact on education. It is essential for educators to have an understanding of mental-motor relationships because:

1. Movement abilities have a potentially more useful role in the educational program than has been traditionally assigned to them.

2. Poorly planned participation in programs of movement activities that fail to achieve their goals are likely to block rather than further the insertion of motivating movement tasks into school programs.

3. Research efforts, if expanded, could lead to even more useful applications of movement skills to general education and, conversely, to the use of intelligence within the practice of motor skills.

Although I first intended to write a short paperback, combining a selected model of the intellect with appropriate movement activities, Walter Welch, Physical Education Editor at Prentice-Hall, persuaded me to attempt a rather comprehensive coverage of what came to be termed "The Physical Expressions of Intelligence." It has also been my intent in this volume to summarize information dealing with "Intelligent Expressions of the Physical."

I am indebted to Mr. Gaston Vandal, of Cegep College in Canada, who helped me to translate the work of the French writer, Le Boulch. Mr. Ernst Kiphard, of Westphalian Institut für Jugendpsychiatrie in Cologne, Germany, has sent me numerous publications that opened up to me new directions within the general problem area. I am grateful to Professor Torbjörn Stockfelt, of the University of Stockholm, and to his students, for providing me with the results of their studies. Professor Iwao Matsuda, of the University of Tokyo's School of Education, met with me to discuss the work being done there on exercises and intelligence. I am also grateful to Professor Willie Railo, from the Norwegian Sports School, for permitting me to utilize his work. Mr. Maketo Sakamoto helped me translate some of the work of Japanese researchers on relationships between physical activity and psychological processes. Professor Miroslav Vanek, Ph.D., of Charles University in Prague, made it possible for me to perceive new dimensions in the intellectual training of athletes —many of the ideas in Chapter 5 arose from my discussions with him during our collaboration on *Psychology and the Superior Athlete* in 1968 and 1969. Numerous people helped me to obtain data on the effects of learning games upon various academic competencies. At least twenty school principals and twice that number of teachers within Los Angeles schools in the Catholic Archdiocese have permitted me and my staff to use their facilities to teach children in the ways described in Chapters 11, 12, and 13. During the four years of research on this project, I had the help of two Catholic nuns, Sister Margaret Mary Martin, OSF, and Sister Mark Sczcepanik, OSF. Both performed energetically and competently in their roles. Sister Margaret Ann and Father John Mihan of the Los Angeles Archdiocese helped us to formulate objectives and overcome administrative difficulties. The lovely children with whom we worked during these years provided constant inspiration.

Members of my office staff, Miss Barbara Gien, Brian Tash, and Miss Nancy Laskow, suffered nobly through this effort, as they have through others, with notable aplomb, editing, typing, and somehow unraveling the words and pages.

Despite my indebtedness to the people named, and to numerous others unnamed, the conclusions, confusions, and conundrums contained in these pages are solely my responsibility.

B.J.C.

Physical Expressions
of
Intelligence

I

INTRODUCTION

1

Introduction and Overview

Historical Trends

Physical activity may be an aid as well as a detriment to the educational processes. Some educators feel that the physical education period helps children to release tensions and thus makes them more responsive to the classroom sessions that follow. On the other hand, many teachers view an excess of physical activity within the classroom as a handicap to intellectual efforts.

Throughout history educators considered vigorous bodily actions as a somewhat mixed blessing when combined with academic exercises. Although the development of the physique enjoyed high status within the ancient Greek and Roman civilizations, during the Middle Ages the body came to be regarded as evil, and spiritual and intellectual assets became paramount.

The Renaissance saw a reawakening to some of the ways in which the movements of children might be used within the instructional context, as can be seen in the writings of Rousseau and others. The naturalists of the middle 1700s and early 1800s believed that the physical needs of children and youth should be properly expressed in school; some schools of this period went beyond the restrictions of the traditional desks and slates to include important lessons taught while the children were at play.

A historical review of the educational systems in America also reflects some of these same trends relative to relationships between the physical and the intellectual side of children. The Puritan's work ethic branded all play and recreational activities as evil influences working upon the nature of basically wicked humans. The school masters during the expansion of the West began to some degree to permit children to escape the confines of their one-room schools for at least a brief period each day.

Just before the turn of the present century the scientific mood seen in other areas began to be adopted by many scholars interested in the schools. Psychologists began, with varying degrees of success, to examine educational processes in an attempt to measure the extent to which academic goals might be reached. However, during the first decades of the 1900s, relatively little emphasis was given to the activity needs of children. Instead, a separate group of studies reflected an interest in the physical side of the child in isolation from the intellectual, dealing with such subjects as age changes in movement capacities and focusing upon measures purportedly basic to abilities to play games well.

After World War II, however, and particularly during the 1960s, scholars from various disciplines began to illuminate the many possible interactions between the child's physical "self" and his ability to perform academically and cognitively. Some optometrists, for example, began to prescribe visual-motor exercises that might enhance the visual-perceptual abilities upon which a number of academic competencies purportedly rest. Others devised schemas in which basic walking and crawling activities were the primary training exercises; if followed faithfully, it was claimed, they would "neurologically re-order" the defective nervous system, or "better organize" the average nervous system, thus permitting more effective listening, seeing, and thinking.

Others began to find that if one apparently enhanced the self-concept of certain atypical children through helping them to gain physical skills that lead to success in games, the scores they achieved on intelligence tests sometimes reflected their heightened feelings about themselves.

Still others began to combine motor activity and academic operations in more direct ways. "Learning games" were devised in an effort to improve spelling, letter recognition, mathematic operations, and similar activities.

From 1950 to 1970, theoretical speculations were often followed too rapidly by changes in educational strategies, without obtaining data to substantiate the usually logical hypotheses put forth.[1] By the beginning

[1] It is sometimes lamented that new "discoveries" in education are followed by a fifty-year "lag" before they are put into practice, rather than being

of the 1970s, however, a number of reasonably sound studies were producing data that aided in the sorting out of speculation from truth and fantasy from fact. These studies established practices that would prove helpful to the achievement of important goals.

For example, the simplification that "movement is the basis of the intellect" was answered by findings from studies that employed the armless and the cerebral palsied as subjects. These studies indicated that the subject afflicted with severe movement problems often evidenced intellectual abilities that were intact and at times superior to those of children with normal capacities for action. Other research showed that the therapy that advocated creeping on the floor by children with average or slightly below average intellectual deficiencies did little but cause physical discomfort to the youth involved.

An initial and a most promising group of studies seemed to be that in which intellectual and academic operations became an integral part of the program of movement activities. Well-controlled studies of retarded children, in which only traditional physical education and exercise activities were employed, indicated that only their physical capacities had been positively influenced; whereas, when similar subjects were exposed to movement games in which they were required to think at the same time about some facet of the educational program, whether it be counting, spelling, recognizing letters and words, or similar operations, their academic improvement ranged from measurable to startling! However, research during the 1960s also pointed to ways in which foreign language learning could be improved by accompanying the attempts to recognize phrases with the actions that these phrases suggested, much in the same way that a normal child learns his native language. From this program emerged concepts designed to improve the linguistically deficient child's abilities in speaking and understanding his native language.

A second category of research also expanded during the decades following World War II—studies that had little to do with movement abilities. In ways more scientifically precise than their predecessors (Binet, Dewey, Thurston, and others), Bruner at Harvard, Guilford at the University of Southern California, and others began to explore the sub-abilities comprising the mozaic referred to as the intellect.

Their computers enabled them to examine identifiable clusters of abilities that were obtained by contrasting innumerable tests designed to

---

incorporated immediately into classrooms. However, it is probably healthy if at least a ten- to fifteen-year period is devoted to testing out theoretical speculations concerning variables that influence educational processes before they are adopted wholeheartedly.

reflect processes contributing to intelligence, creativity and problem solving. The results supplied pieces of information important to educators. Their findings, however, while scientifically precise, are sometimes not immediately helpful to the classroom teacher. One researcher, for example, demonstrated the existence of about 145 intellectual sub-abilities, a number too large for the teacher to translate into processes and then incorporate into her daily lesson ("How about working 47 cognitive strategies into your mathematics lesson today, Mrs. Jones?").

A third trend in the literature, often divorced from the studies covered above, is the theme "movement education," which appears in many texts. Often helpful, these guides suggest groups of activities that purportedly aid in developing creative abilities by giving children choices in the exercise of physical capacities. These activities eliminate the usual restrictions of traditional physical education classes in which games contain a relatively limited number of skills that are confined within even more restrictive systems of rules.

Within such a movement education system, children are exposed to movement problems such as, "How many ways can you get into that circle on the ground?", and then are given the freedom to make up solutions to the problem. The stated goals usually include expanding the child's ability to solve problems, to act in a creative way, and to provide the kind of "flexible" approach to motor activities that will result in a broad base of abilities and skills. These programs are widely practiced in England, and are more often found in elementary schools than in institutions for older children.

Although the enthusiasm the movement education approach engenders in children is obvious to outside observers, there has been little sound research carried out over a prolonged period with the same children as subjects to confirm or deny the validity of the claims made. The authors of these programs, while sometimes well versed in how to motivate children to move in a variety of ways, often display little understanding of the research dealing with cognition, creativity, intelligence, and problem solving, themes that nevertheless are recurrent on the pages of their writings.

In this text, the practices that have been well researched will be identified as such, and those that are more speculative than scientific will also be noted. The activities described are not movement cures; they must be artfully applied by sensitive, perceptive, and innovative teachers. The child's mind moves faster than his larger muscles. For many children an overuse of the activities described may indeed prove wasteful of time, while it is obvious that the facilities may be costly and will certainly take up more space than does a school desk within an average classroom.

It is one of the purposes of this book to advance examples of the manner in which movement activities enhance certain types of intellectual traits. Thus, it brings together some of the literature described above: the studies in cognition and creativity, as well as the work dealing with just how incorporating the impetus to think into situations that encourage and require vigorous bodily activity does change intellectual, academic and language capacities.

I do not propose here to pave a magic avenue along which all educational goals may be reached. The tendency today to engage in what might be termed "educational overkill" is as abhorrent to me as it may be to the reader. Rather, I intend to present helpful ways in which a child may, in a manner obvious to the observing teacher or parent, act out his thoughts and, hopefully, modify the quality of his thought processes.

Why Movement Education May Work

Although it was perhaps suggested in the previous paragraphs that the "evidence is in" regarding the case for incorporating movement into educational processes, indeed this is not true. The number of studies upon which the following material is based are few. And, while their results are encouraging, sorting out the reasons behind the often positive results is difficult indeed. The authors of this research, however, present the following reasons why a child or youth in action often learns more quickly and efficiently.

MOVEMENT IS MOTIVATING

The author of the studies of retardates that were carried out at the end of the 1950s in England and researchers of more recent work at Stanford cite the fact that motor activities, when molded into academic games or when simply introduced into the curriculum, may prove motivating to the children to whom they are applied. We have carried out research that indicates that the self-confidence of children is blunted in a variety of ways if they lack the capacities to play well, while findings of other studies have confirmed the fact that children with above average physical capacities are not only more confident as children, but grow up into adults who are also more at ease with themselves and with others. It is a common observation that children have fun in games; they can act out adult roles, can find happiness in joyful release, while at the same time testing out at rudimentary levels various types of personal aggressive-competitive-cooperative interactions. It is not surprising to find that this kind of aura surrounding vigorous games seems at times to "spill over" into academic exercises that are incorporated into, or closely accompany, these games.

PERSONAL NEEDS TO MOVE ARE MATCHED TO CURRICULUM

It is a well-researched fact that even from infancy the human animal varies widely in his tendency to move. At birth some infants are more than 150 times as active as others, while well-controlled studies using the same subjects from birth to the age of 40 document the fact that passive versus active children of nursery school age become adults who are different in rather marked ways from each other.

Despite these apparently innate differences, it is usually observed that the vast majority of classrooms are largely those in which little obvious physical activity is tolerated. Some children, as they enter school, easily accomplish the channeling of activity needs into the passivity required by their teachers, others simply fidget in their seats, failing to learn, while still others become emotionally upset and evidence even more heightened activity levels. This last group often comprise at least a percentage of those judged "hyperactive" and thus difficult to educate by their teachers and by the school psychologist who is finally called to their side.

Some researchers who have found that various movement games seem to work suggest that they provide avenues through which the more active children—the active ghetto child or the boy who needs excessively to prove his toughness or bravery for a number of reasons—may engage in an educational program that better matches his natural behavioral tendencies.

One researcher produced findings that some of us are sensitive, perceptive "augmenters"; we put together what comes into us through our visual and kinesthetic senses, and are highly sensitive to all the subtleties of the education program. On the other hand, this same researcher discovered the "reducers," those who prefer to move, rather than to sit and "soak up" what is placed before them. The scholar who has provided a movement channel through which learning may take place may have thus provided a way for the "reducer" to accept somehow some of the education lessons that society demands for efficient functioning within its complexities. The "augmenter" is provided for daily in thousands of school rooms in each city; perhaps the more active "reducer" may also be aided to learn better by exposing his teachers and parents to some of the teaching strategies found within the following chapters.

MOVEMENT ACTIVITIES FOCUS ATTENTION

Children participating effectively in learning games must focus their complete attention; their bodies and minds, as well as their visual attention, are directed toward the task, according to some scholars. Unlike classroom learning passivity, disinclination to learn and to participate are easily discernible by the observing teacher; the children may not act attentive when jumping into lettered squares and in reality may be as inattentive as they are at their school desks when practicing spelling. At the same time movement games tend to raise the activation level of the more lethargic child; vigorous movement arouses children who are habitually "sleepy" to optimum learning levels, while, when movement games require prolonged attention, the duration of attention given them may be accurately observed and at times lengthened when the task is further prolonged by the clever teacher.

Total body movement, according to some authorities, is a kind of synthesizing experience toward which the other senses of touch, kinesthesis, vision, and auditory perception contribute. Thus, it is conceivable that the active games described on the pages that follow contribute in positive ways to the important processes of attention and the gaining of optimum activation levels, both critical to school achievement.

Preview of What is to Follow

The material that follows has been divided into four sections that, to some degree, are not mutually exclusive. In Section I, Chapters 1 to 4 attempt to provide the reader with a rather broad view of movement-motor relationships, ranging from the historical review of intelligence testing and theories of the intellect found in Chapter 2 to views of how movement and intelligence are intermeshed within the developing infant and child. Chapter 3 deals in some detail with some of the contemporary writings of scholars throughout the world who have perceived various causal relationships between movement and other components of the human personality. The final chapter in this section gives a brief look at the manner in which movement and early indices of intelligence seem to pair within a developmental context.

Section II contains three chapters that indicate how movement activities may be applied to individuals within various mental and physical ability groupings. The role that intellectual training plays in the preparation of the superior athlete is covered, for example, in Chapter 5, while important and stimulating new work with retarded children is outlined in Chapter 6. The final chapter of this section contains a summary of representative studies from researchers who have attempted to determine whether motor activities aid in the remediation of learning difficulties in children within the normal I.Q. range.

Section III contains data that describe the manner in which movement activities, physical skills, and muscular tensions are shaped and modified by intellectual processes; conversely, the ways in which tension change, physical exercise, and motor skills learning may change intellectual output are also examined. Perhaps in no other section of the book are the data so sparse and, at the same time, so suggestive of the important studies to come, hopefully, from the young and able researchers emerging in the behavioral sciences.

The final part of the text, Section IV, outlines how one may potentially modify various academic and intellectual abilities by exposing children and youth to various kinds of movement experiences. Throughout the text, but particularly within these final sections, the reader is cautioned to be skeptical of claims that suggest that too much transfer may be occurring between activities within movement education programs and traditional learning tasks, when the former are highly dissimilar from the latter. These cautions are again emphasized in the concluding chapter (14).

BIBLIOGRAPHY

ASHER, JAMES J. "The Learning Strategy of the Total Physical Response: A Review." *The Modern Language Journal* 1 (February, 1966).

———. "The Total Physical Response Approach to Second Language Learning." *The Modern Language Journal* 53, (January 1969).

———. "The Total Physical Response Technique of Learning." *The Journal of Special Education* 30(1969).

———. "The Strategy of the Total Physical Response: An Application to Learning Russian." *International Review of Applied Linguistics* 3 (1965).

ASHER, JAMES J., and PRICE, BEN. "The Learning Strategy of the Total Physical Response: Some Age Differences." *Child Development* 38 (December, 1967): 1219–22.

BLOOM, BENJAMIN S., *Taxonomy of Educational Objectives, Handbook I, Cognitive Domain.* New York: David McKay, Inc., 1956.

BRUNER, JEROME S., *Toward a Theory of Instruction.* Cambridge, Mass.: Harvard University Press, Belknap Press, 1966.

CRATTY, BRYANT J. *Active Learning.* Englewood Cliffs, N. J.: Prentice-Hall, Inc., 1971.

CRATTY, BRYANT J. and MARTIN, M. M. *The Effects of a Program of Learning*

Games Upon Selected Academic Abilities in Children with Learning Difficulties. Washington D.C.: U.S. Office of Education, Bureau of Handicapped Children, 1970.

CRATTY, BRYANT J.; IKEDA, NAMIKO; MARTIN, M. M.; JENNETT, CLAIR; and MORRIS, MARGARET. *Movement Activities, Motor Ability and the Education of Children.* Springfield, Ill.: Charles C. Thomas, Publishers, 1970.

GUILFORD, J. P. *Intelligence, Creativity and Their Educational Implications.* San Diego, Calif.: Robert R. Knapp, Publishers, 1968.

HUMPHREY, JAMES. "Comparison of the Use of Active Games and Language Workbook Exercises as Learning Media in the Development of Language Understanding with Third Grade Children." *Perceptual and Motor Skills,* 21 (1965): 23–26.

KUNIHIRA; Shirou; and Asher, James. "The Strategy of the Total Physical Response: An Application to Learning Japanese." *International Review of Applied Linguistics* (IRAL) 3 (December, 1965): 277–89.

PHARNES, JOAN S. "The Relationship between Whole Body Movement and the Retarded Child's Ability to Learn Selected Geometric Forms." Master of Science thesis, University of North Carolina, 1968.

POPHAM, JAMES W., and BAKER, EVA L. *Systematic Instruction.* Englewood Cliffs, N. J.: Prentice-Hall, Inc., 1970.

ROSS, DOROTHEA. "Incidental Learning of Number Concepts in Small Group Games." *American Journal of Mental Deficiency,* 74 (1970): 718–25.

———. "The Use of Games to Facilitate the Learning of Basic Number Concepts in Pre-School Educable Mentally Retarded Children." Final report, Project # 6–2263, Washington, D.C.: U.S. Office of Education, December, 1967.

2

Intelligence and Intelligence Testing

Introduction

The beginnings of interest in intelligence and provision for its measurement seem almost to parallel the first use of written language. It has been reported, for example, that both in ancient China as well as in early Greek and Roman civilizations, tests were employed to ascertain those who might be the most able participants in civil government. The relative stability of the Chinese and Roman civilizations has been attributable to the objective manner in which their administrators were selected. The philosophical writings of Aristotle, Hippocrates and other Greek scholars are also replete with attempts to define the intellectual, personal, and physical qualities of the "ideal" member of these societies.

Several scientific, philosophical, and social threads discernible during the beginning of the 1800s spawned an interest in the definition and evaluation of human intelligence. The thrust of humanism, for example, extending into the educational realm, prompted several foresighted scholars in France to propose the then rather radical hypothesis that mentally sub-normal children might indeed be changed through exposure to special tutoring. In England during this time Sir Francis Galton, stimulated by the orderliness discovered by his contemporaries when investigating genetic inheritance in lower animals and in plants, began to hypothesize that perhaps human intellectual abilities might be subjected to the same laws uncovered by Mendel and others of that time.

Thus by the middle of the 1800s scholars began to perceive the need for reasonably exact evaluation devices to better deal with practical as well as theoretical problems. Experimental psychology emerging in Wundt's laboratory at Leipzig also nurtured some aspects of the intelligence testing movement during the latter part of the same century.

By the turn of the century, workers with the retarded, such as Alfred Binet in France, in order both to classify feeble-minded children and to verify any improvement thought to be as a result of training, also began to search for tests that discriminated, in rather exact ways, between the intellectually unfit and the normal and the varying degrees of retardation within the former group.

By the first decade of the 1900s, tests developed by Binet were discovered by American workers and translated into English. The testing movement in the United States flourished after this time and joined with the new factor analytic techniques pioneered by Spearman and his co-workers in England. This was an expansion not only of intelligence tests, but also of discussions relative to the basic concept of intelligence itself.

Thorndike and Terman, students of Stanley Hall, provided meaningful tests and testing concepts that forever wedded intelligence tests with educational practices in the U.S. Not only were the feeble-minded accorded attention during the second and third decades of the twentieth century, but normal and gifted children also were exposed to the questioning of psychologists who attempted to place scores upon their intellectual abilities and potentials. Terman's classic studies of genius, to be continued with the help of his co-workers into the last part of the twentieth century, provided the main impetus for programs for intellectually superior children, beginning in schools following World War II.

At the same time, perhaps given impetus by the testing of draftees supervised by Terman, Otis, and others, research dealing with intelligence flourished. Bruner, whose research at Harvard concerning the subtle subdivisions of intellectual functioning, and Guilford, who published sophisticated factor analyses, are some of the more important contemporary names whose work will be discussed in sections that follow.

Thus, several historical trends can be seen as contributing to and interwoven with the study of intelligence and the development of tools for its appraisal. Such progenitors of psychology as Stanley Hall, in America, and Wundt, the father of experimental psychology, in Germany, left the stamp of their philosophical speculations upon the testing movement in direct ways and indirectly through their students. Similarly, the general scientific awakening of the late 1700s and 1800s, reflected in a search for more objective ways of evaluating the universe as well as evaluating man's place in it, resulted in the development of statistical tools that played an important part in the first tests developed, as well as in applications and objectification of later efforts.

Two other groups of men played a not inconsequential part in the realization during the nineteenth century that human behavior was not only measurable but perhaps modifiable. Charles Darwin's writings on evolution provided evidence, to those willing to listen, that, in rather predictable although slowly moving ways, human destiny is undergoing change. And the efforts of Itard and his able pupil Sequin, working with retarded children shortly after the time of Darwin, demonstrated to the surprise of many that the capabilities of the "idiot" could be improved even if normalcy could not always be achieved.

Moreover, the social consciousness, perhaps triggered by the French Revolution, prompted Esquirol as well as other scholars in Middle Europe to plead for more exact ways of placing the feeble-minded, not only to identify those in need of special help, but to avoid misplacing children who might have fair to good intellectual potential but who evidenced behavioral problems within the schools. Coupled with the desire of educators to identify more precisely than had been done by physicians using physical measurements or classifications of mental deficiency were the commendable goals of ferreting out the more capable children and of providing them with challenging programs to help them make their maximum contribution to the betterment of themselves and of mankind in general.

In the sections that follow, I will attempt to take a closer look at these operational, historical, and sociological trends that undergirded concern about, and provision for, measuring the intellect.

Galton, Cattell, and Binet

The rumblings of scholars who found order in nature and man are evident in writings produced even before the beginning of the nineteenth century. For example, Linnaeus, the Swedish botanist and physician began formulizing his system for classification of plants during the latter decades of the 1700s; while Albrecht von Haller presented his classification for the groupings of diseases for the consideration of the scientific world in 1785.

By the middle of the next century, various workers had begun to extend the order seen in nature to various characteristics of man. The much discussed work of Darwin was preceded in 1846 by the speculations of a Belgian astronomer and statistician, Quetelet, who demonstrated that the laws of probability previously outlined by Gauss and Laplace could be applied to the physical measurements of man, and he proceeded to arrange the magnitude of body weights and heights taken from French soldiers to demonstrate his hypothesis. He further hypothesized that there is truly no normal or average individual, and suggested that the average seems to be an ideal toward which nature is working.

Although not in complete agreement with Quetelet's assumption, Galton became intrigued with the idea that an individual's measurements need not only be expressed in exact terms, but also could be expressed as the frequency with which the characteristic might be expected to occur in a given population. He at once realized the implications for not only biological, but also psychological measurement.

In England, France, and the United States in the late 1800s and early 1900s scholars were giving voice to the need for the crystallization of concepts of intelligence in the form of reasonably precise assessment devices. After receiving his doctorate with Wundt, J. McKeen Cattell returned to America and wrote the first article mentioning mental testing, which contained outlines for a test that he suggested would be helpful in evaluating the intelligence of college students and in planning more meaningful programs based upon their scores.

To investigate these proposals the then new American Psychological Association formed a committee. The first tests produced by Cattell, like the early attempts of Binet, contained sub-tests that evaluated sensation, reflecting the influence of the early psychophysicists under whom the former had studied.

In France, the brilliant Binet began, shortly after the turn of the century, to devise tests that were a marked improvement over the imprecise methods and often vague questioning commonly employed by physicians of that era to assess the intelligence competence of individuals who were being considered for residence in institutions for the mentally incompetent.

It was primarily from the speculations and searchings of these three men that the later more refined research and concepts revolving around human intelligence were based. The polished factor analyses of Spearman and more exact I.Q. scores of Terman and Wechsler emerged from ideas formed initially in the minds of Cattell, Binet, and Galton.

GALTON

Nineteenth-century England contained a number of notable figures, some of whom contributed either directly or indirectly toward illuminating and objectifying various facets of human intelligence. Erasmus Darwin and his illustrious grandson Charles, introduced the concept of evolution to the world; while Galton, wealthy cousin of Charles, was struck by the fact that illustrious fathers were likely to have eminent sons, and published his *Heredity Genius* in 1869. This initial text was followed by others, including the book titled *Inquiries Into the Human Faculty and Its Development* in 1883.

Some of the questions Galton raised in these and other books still plague the scientific community, while his contribution to mental testing primarily centered around his attempts to objectify and organize various indices of intellectual behavior.

By some, Galton has been labeled the "Father of Mental Testing." As early as 1882 he had established a laboratory in London, to which individuals might come for a series of physical and psychological measurements. Although most of the measures he used were not new, having appeared in the laboratories of Wundt and others, what was unique was the concept that the scores he derived would be of interest to the individuals being tested.[1]

Although most of Galton's tests involved evaluating rather simple sensory functioning, including reaction time tests and the like, he did speculate that processes of mental imagery were not only capable of being measured, but led to insights into the functioning of the human mind. Thus, although he cleaved to a "faculties theory," which held that the evaluating of the basic sensory and motor facilities of an individual were a direct line to the assessment of higher mental processes, Galton was already showing the way toward the evaluation of more subtle mental processes.

Most important, however, was Galton's contribution to the objectification of human psychological characteristics, and the fact that scores obtained from behavioral tests might be arranged on a continuum, upon a scale of normal distribution, and compared with their deviation from the mean, as well as expressed in absolute terms.

This concept was a forerunner of the computation of I.Q. scores based upon deviation of intellectual functioning from that considered normal by a child of a given age. Galton's support and encouragement of his young assistant Karl Pearson, gave birth to the computations and concept of correlation, a precursor of the more elaborate and helpful factor and analytic techniques to follow in the twentieth century.

---

[1] . . . . and worth money, as they were charged a small fee for exposure to his batteries of tasks.

CATTELL

In the 1840s, two unrelated but important events occurred that planted the seeds of interest in mental processes in the United States. In 1844 the *American Journal of Insanity* was founded, and although, as its name suggests, the majority of its articles reflected an emphasis upon mental disease, even the earlier volumes contain writings that include references to mental subnormality. The creation of this professionally recognized outlet for those interested in mental retardation and subnormality brought attention to the need for research on the several controversial issues voiced during the first part of the nineteenth century.

The second milestone was the immigration of Itard's gifted student, Seguin, to the United States in 1848. Though Seguin had studied under Itard and Esquirol, he did not share their beliefs in the irrevocability of mental retardation, but voiced the then radical suggestion that mentally retarded children could be changed for the better with exposure to proper educational methods. When only twenty-five years of age and still in France his missionary zeal led him to establish, in 1837, a school for mentally retarded children. Upon coming to this country he stimulated the establishment of similar institutions.

During the next decades an increasing number of schools for the feeble-minded were founded in this country and in European countries, but at the same time, many of the mentally retarded were too frequently consigned to prisons instead of to facilities that might enhance their intellectual capabilities. Similar to the imprecise and often somewhat mystic methods used to classify the retarded in Europe, the evaluation of the mentally incapable in the United States was carried out by those who depended upon invalid medical signs or even more spurious bodily conformities: head shape, and the like.

Not until the year 1890 does Cattell's first mention of mental testing appear, as an article in the journal aptly named *Mind*, in which he called for the institution of mental tests that, he advanced, would fulfill a number of purposes.[2]

To unravel these high level processes, Cattell brought with him the finely-honed experimental tools borrowed from Wundt, but at the same time rejected the tendency of those in the Leipzig laboratories to group scores obtained from a number of individuals, preferring rather to concentrate upon individual differences in the measures he obtained.

---

[2] He also predicted that "Experimental psychology is likely to take its place in the educational plan of our schools and universities"!

The worth of intelligence testing, Cattell pleaded, would result in (a) discovering the constancy of mental processes, and (b) the inter-dependence of mental processes; (c) permitting comparison of scores taken at different times and places, (d) aiding in self-assessment by the individuals tested, and finally (e) helping individuals with their education, mode of life, or even in the diagnosing of various diseases.

As would be expected, the content of the first test batteries emerging from Cattell's laboratory at the University of Pennsylvania contained a preponderance of the types of sensory and motor tests one would expect from a student of the German father of experimental psychology (Wundt). His list included tests of reaction time, ability to maintain grip pressure against a dynomometer, rate of movement, detecting slight differences in hand-held weights, bisecting lines, time judgments, and various tasks involving tactual sensitivity. One of his tests resembled many contemporary tests of intelligence and involved short-term memory for letters "once heard." The tests were administered largely to the college population within the purview of Cattell. No attempt was made to average scores, and the modern student of psychology will not be surprised to learn that no correlation was found between the scores he obtained and college success measured by inspecting the grades of his subjects.

Although most of the tests employed by Cattell have been long excluded from tests of intelligence, his primary role was that of a stimulant to succeeding psychologists in the United States. Jastrow, in 1882, used similar tests with students at the University of Wisconsin, and a decade later set up an exhibition at the World's Columbian Exposition in Chicago. These same tests were applied to school children by Jastrow and by Boas and Gilbert before the turn of the century. Unfortunately the scores obtained evidenced only a chance relationship to estimates of academic success made by teachers of the children tested.

It was not until the importation of the work of Binet, from France, in the following decades, that mental measurement and the concepts of intelligence and intelligence quotient began their steady and scholarly progression toward the more elaborate and exact testing methods generated by Thorndike in 1910 and by Terman in the 1920s, and the sophisticated theory building by Kelley and Guilford in the 1930s and 1950s.

BINET

For centuries prior to the time of Binet, men had relied upon various means with which to detect intelligence and to separate the able from the less able. A favorite strategy of the ancients was to employ measures of bodily conformations when classifying individuals based upon mental ability. During the middle and last parts of the nineteenth century this method was still in vogue. Even such scholars as Galton and Cattell were still basing the selection of the sub-tests contained within their batteries upon the supposition that simple tests of sensory awareness, which purportedly evaluated the soundness of a person's basic "faculties," were indices of the quality of higher level intellectual processes which that same individual might evidence.

Binet's concepts might have stemmed from the writings of a number of scholars during the nineteenth century. Esquirol's classic book appearing in 1838, for example, may have influenced Binet, particularly the emphasis Esquirol placed upon the concept that "idiocy" was not a single category but that actually there existed various types of mentally deficient individuals. Esquirol's chapter on idiocy represents the first systematic attempt to organize available information on mental deficiency and to begin to formulate a scientific vocabulary on the subject.[3]

Taine's often cited work titled "On Intelligence," appearing in 1870, may also have found an interested reader in Binet. This treatise on the subject of the intellect suggested, among other things, that by studying the less able minds, one might gain new insights upon the workings of more capable intellects. Taine's writings had considerable impact upon French psychology of the period, and are likely to have found their way into the hands of the Parisian psychologist Binet.

Leading directly to the writings of Binet, which included *Psychology of Rationality* in 1886 and *Alternations of the Personality* in 1891, were the books by Theodule Ribot, in the 1870s. (*Contemporary English Psychology*, and *Contemporary German Psychology*). The writings of Ribot contained suggestions that a search be made for principles that would gather the groupings of signs of intellectual malfunction into workable categories.

Binet's approach to intelligence testing, on the other hand, was a rather marked departure from these previously used assessment strategies. It was espoused by this able Frenchman because of several observations he recounts in his several texts.

Repellent to Binet's sensitive social conscience were the inexact medical examinations and questioning used by contemporary physicians to place individuals in homes and/or schools for the feeble-minded. He pointed out that not only were the assessment techniques inexact and probably invalid, but that from physician to physician the questions and criteria were rarely similar. Moreover, he was struck with the fact that some of the tests of intelligence formulated by his contemporaries

---

[3] Six years later, an *American Journal of Insanity* evidenced the beginnings of scientific interest in this same subject, on the other side of the Atlantic.

contained items that had not been tested with children in schools, an oversight that he rectified when formulating his first testing batteries.

He also observed that one must not only take into account a child's intellectual capabilities when evaluating his intelligence, but must also consider as important the chronological age of the child when making an assessment. He was the first to introduce the concept of "mental age" into the literature, although the early tests he formulated did not produce the rather precise arithmetic ratio that later emerged from the more refined tests designed by Terman, Thorndike, Wechsler and others.

While admitting that severely retarded children and youth usually evidenced rather serious sensory-motor impairments, Binet pointed out that (a) in the case of the more severely retarded, even the most casual observer could make the necessary discrimination between their functioning and that of normal children; (b) basic tests of sensory functioning (i.e., reaction time measures) are of little help in discriminating among individuals evidencing the higher levels of retardation; and (c) the existence of such individuals as Helen Keller was ample evidence that even people having rather serious sensory impairmight might indeed possess the ability to make high quality intellectual judgments.

Binet was a practical man, not a theorizer. His contribution was the introduction of the concept that different types of tests must be used at several age levels to measure intelligence accurately. He cared not why an individual earned a score indicating that he was stupid or smart, but only that the evaluation was carefully carried out and that it was a true indication of what he termed "judgment," "good sense," or "the faculty of adapting one's self to circumstances."

Moreover, he entered the schools to try out his tests to see if they significantly differentiated between normal children and those consigned to schools for the retarded, and to determine what test items discriminated against normal children of various chronological ages. He characterized an individual who might devise a test of intelligence based solely upon his own speculations, as "making a colonizing expedition into Algeria, advancing always only upon the map, without taking off his dressing gown."

Binet's aim was to make scales that were simple, rapid, convenient, precise, and heterogenous, and he was one of the first writers to emphasize the importance of the testing environment when obtaining a valid score. One must hold the subject in "continued contact" with the test, he admonished those giving this type of test.

Binet was sensitive to the fact that he was a critic of the testers of the day, and felt obligated to improve upon the prevalent methods of assessment. "We do not destroy an erroneous idea when we do not replace it by another," he wrote in 1907.

In 1897 in an article published with his colleague, Henri, Binet described tests with which they purposed to measure eleven qualities in children, including (a) memory, (b) mental imagery, (c) imagination, (d) attention, (e) suggestibility, (f) aesthetic appreciation, (g) comprehension, and (h) moral sentiments. Two other categories contained tasks involving muscular activity, including one type termed "force of will," evaluated by requiring an individual to sustain muscular effort for a period of time, and another category named "motor skill."

Through the next fifteen years, Binet and his co-workers, exposing his tests to school children of various ages and contrasting their scores with the efforts of obviously abnormal youngsters, produced several revisions of their original battery. Moreover, Binet was not always interested in quantitative scores or measures, but in qualitative differences in the strategies employed by children of various ages when attempting to solve the tasks he placed before them. He observed, for example, that extremely young children could often not define, in any terms, the nouns they frequently used in their speech. By five or six, they gave definitions based upon usage, while still older children could define nouns with reference to the categories into which they fell. To cite another example, his testings in the schools near Paris revealed that younger children could only enumerate objects while older ones could describe actions that were occurring in pictures.

His early searchings also revealed that the perceptual-motor performance of various ages differed in interesting and predictable ways. Copying a square, to cite one example, appeared easier than drawing a diamond or triangle.

Even simpler perceptual tasks were included in some of Binet's earlier batteries, such as "le regard," or whether a child will follow a lighted match with his eyes. However, Binet pointed out that such tests are only to determine whether or not a child is severely retarded, and do not help in assessing intelligence at the higher levels.

The memory tests contained in Binet's batteries (repeating three or more figures) as well as tests of visual memory (copying a design after the stimulus figure had been removed), had their counterparts in texts devised by Ebbinghaus at about this same time. However, the latter scholar was primarily interested in memory as a psychological phenomenon in its own right, and was not interested in the more practical ramifications of intelligence testing, as was Binet.

Binet professed an interest only in the higher mental processes, and most of the tasks contained in his batteries reflect that interest. However, it is also interesting to note the possible influence of contemporary German psychophysicists upon his test formulations. For example, he placed in his early batteries such tasks as requiring a child to judge differences in hand-held weights and similar measures of kinesthetic perception, which resembled the experimental protocols employed decades before in Leipzig by Wundt and his colleagues.

Binet's contribution to intelligence testing and his indirect contribution to the concept of intelligence itself, was marked and profound. His 1911 test, with revisions, is presently employed in all parts of the world.[4] He was the first, as has been pointed out, to introduce the concept of mental age, and moreover he was also one of the first to attempt to validate his speculations with the collection of carefully acquired test scores from children themselves.

The Twentieth Century

RESEARCH AND THOUGHT ABOUT THOUGHT

Two separate trends manifested themselves within the early years of the twentieth century both in the United States and in Europe. On one hand, an expansion and sophistication was seen in the methods employed to test intelligence. Verbal as well as performance tests were developed, the latter included the devices formulated by Porteus and by Goodenough. On the other hand, there was also an increased speculation concerning the manner in which the human mental ability manifested itself. The specificity and generality of the concept of intelligence occupied the writings of a number of theoreticians. Those in England generally favored the thesis that there was a single general fact (G) surrounded by a number of more specific sub-abilities. The Americans, notably Thorndike, Kelley, Terman, and later Guilford, opted more for the marked specificity of human intellectual abilities.

Other movements relative to the study of the intellect developed in the first decades of the twentieth century. The developmental approach to the study of the intellect, introduced by Galton in the first co-twin control studies [5], which he had carried out in the previous century, proliferated and was employed by numerous investigators between the world wars. A number of investigators, including Binet, were aware that different tests were appropriate in the evaluation of intelligence at various

---

[4] Including the 1910 translation into English by Henry Goddard, who subsequently tried out the test at the Vineland School for Retarded Children in New Jersey.

[5] These studies attempted to differentiate between the influence of nature versus nurture in the developmnt of abilities by exposing one of two identical twins to some kind of intellectual and/or academic stimulation, and then comparing the progress of the twin who had not been afforded this additional stimulation.

ages. However, it remained for Hofstaetter in 1954 to objectify the three types of abilities that alternately emerge and then withdraw in the changing intellect of children as they mature.[6] Piaget, during the previous decade, began his classic observations of emerging intellectual strategies and "schemata," which resulted in numerous texts published first in French and then in English translations in the 1950s.

Despite the less desirable outcomes of world conflict, the world wars provided great impetus to the testing movement, particularly in the United States where thousands of young men were exposed to assessment procedures that seemed to predict rather well how they might perform jobs they would perhaps meet in the service of their country. This coming of age of intellectual tests carried over into the problem of the job classification of factory workers, and similar problems in education, government, and industry. Another example of this kind of "spin-off" is the classic longitudinal study of gifted children initiated by Terman at Stanford, which is not due to terminate until the year 2010.

Conceptually there has been an increased attempt to define intelligence within several possible frames of reference during the twentieth century, with varying degrees of success. Some have attempted to define intelligence by outlining the type of mental operations purportedly carried out well by individuals assumed to be mentally capable. Some theoreticians have only searched for the meanings of words denoting some aspect of intelligence, and others have seemed to probe deeper and seek the "essence" of intellectual activity, while still others have apparently been mired in the supposition that intelligence is composed of qualities that thousands of psychologists agree upon as emanating from purportedly "valid" tests of I.Q.

In the early years of the twentieth century, perhaps influenced by Galton's earlier speculations concerning the inherent nature of the intellect, many theoreticians assumed that intelligence was rather fixed and unaffected by environmental conditions. Binet states quite succinctly in his 1916 text (*The Development of Intelligence in Children*), that he has little concern, when testing intelligence, with the child's "past history" or with his future, and refuses to differentiate between what he terms acquired and congenital "idiocy" in this same reference.

By the 1940s and 50s however, there was a more enlightened view of the marked influences of environmental conditions, levels of culture, and ethnic situations upon measures of I.Q. The classic studies by Gor-

---

[6] Hofstaetter was influenced by previous studies by Bayley and others, which demonstrated that there was little correlation between early measures of infant and childhood intelligence and later achievement in I.Q. tests, when the same children were in middle and late childhood and adolescence.

don on canal-boat and gypsy children in England began to illuminate the fact that cultural opportunity was at least as important a modifier of intelligence test scores as whether the child had a gifted uncle. In both these groups of children lacking adequate educational opportunities, it was found that there was a steady decline in I.Q. scores with age, while there was a positive correlation obtained when years of schooling and I.Q. scores were contrasted. Studies that followed similarly produced data that confirmed the stultifying effect of a bland culture upon measures of intelligence. By the 1960s, with increased effort, a number of I.Q. tests that are purportedly culture-free became available.[7]

In summary, interest in human intelligence during the first six decades of the twentieth century was marked by several trends: (a) increased sophistication in the analysis of data from intelligence tests resulting in the identification of various components of human mental abilities; (b) increased application of a variety of tests suited to discover aptitudes in the more "practical" (i.e. mechanical), as well as more academic pursuits; (c) an appreciation of the marked influence of a number of variables upon the measures of intellect obtained from children and youth, including not only biological maturation, but also the unique social-cultural variables to which each child is inevitably exposed; and finally, (d) an intense interest in, and pursuit of, the various qualities of human intellectual functioning, instead of focusing only upon quantitative aspects as had been the case previously. This final trend was not only manifested in complex statistical analyses afforded by data collected by Spearman, Kelley, and Guilford, but also stimulated by the insightful observational analyses formulated by the prolific Piaget.[8]

ADVANCES IN THE TESTING OF INTELLIGENCE

Upon the death of Binet in 1911, a number of translations of his tests were undertaken in the United States and in Europe. As was mentioned, Goddard translated the Binet to English, but his version was followed by others at about the same time. Kuhlmann translated two versions of the Binet, while Bobertag also translated the Binet into German in 1911.

[7] The first of these included the Goodenough draw-a-person test and Porteus's maze tests, both of which were initiated in the 1920s.

[8] Piaget's theorizing has obvious relevance to the content of a text dealing with relationships between mental and motor functioning due to his emphasis upon the importance of the sensory-motor period in the early intellectual development of the human infant. However, a separate chapter (4) has been devoted to the discussion of movement within a developmental context.

In 1912 Terman and Child published a report of their preliminary work on the Stanford revision of the Binet, which was later to appear in 1916. The 1916 revision contained many new items and changed the scoring of so many others that essentially it became a new scale that received widespread acceptance. The primary innovation introduced by Terman was the introduction of the concept and computation necessary to formulate the intelligence quotient as the basic method of expressing results. The ease with which it could be computed and the fact that it supplemented the less precise "mental age" concept of the previous tests resulted in widespread acceptance of the Stanford-Binet by psychologists throughout the world for a period of twenty-one years. For the first time also, precise instructions for the administration of each test were presented. Terman covered in detail the manner in which supplementary questions might be asked of a child, the manner in which unusual or marginal responses should be scored, and similar points that were left to the discretion of the testers in previous tests of intelligence.

Terman took care to suggest that the I.Q. was only a general guide, not a precise ruler to measure intelligence. Unfortunately many people, then as now, overlooked or forgot these cautions and became too ready to accept the I.Q. as a final criterion upon which a child's potential abilities might be evaluated for all time.

The 1937 revision of the Binet by Terman resulted in even more helpful refinements. The extreme "ages" on the test were standardized further, while the scores from a large population composed of both rural and urban children were used as norms—as contrasted with the 1916 standards, which were based only upon the scores of middle-class urban children. For standardization children were also chosen with reference to sampling an accurate percent of the various occupations of their parents, due to the realization that factors such as these were important modifiers of the achievement by their children.

Immediately after the declaration of war in 1917, a committee of the American Psychological Association, headed by R. M. Yerkes, set to work building a scale of mental tests to be used for the armed services selection system. The results of this were the institution of the Army Alpha Test, and a second test (the Beta), which could be used for illiterate recruits. Psychologists who used these tests and sensed their success were soon unleashed upon school populations following the war. Truly the decade of the 1920s may be characterized as the "Golden Age of Testing" within the schools of the country, a period of time during which the I.Q. test score of a child was religiously collected, but unfortunately was not often as carefully interpreted to teachers and parents.

Employing his revision of the Binet, Terman at Stanford in the

1920s began to conceive and initiate perhaps the most ambitious and longitudinal study ever carried out within the comparatively short history of psychology. He identified over 1500 children between the ages of seven to eleven years, who purportedly represented the top one percent of those in school on the West Coast during this decade. Obtaining a variety of data on these children, Terman then proposed to follow their progress through life and to determine the manner in which their high potential was either realized or failed to reach fruition. Follow-up testings and questionnaires continued into the 1950s. Since Terman's death, his colleagues are continuing the study with the termination scheduled for the 2010s, when it is predicted that the final subject will have expired.

Terman's primary objective was to identify the variables that seemed to stimulate the achievement of reportedly superior youngsters and, with the data, to improve educational programs that might enable all so-called gifted youngsters to make their maximum contributions to the betterment of society. His findings indicated that children identified as gifted in this manner do succeed in a variety of educational, governmental, and scientific fields. Though their achievements were found to be less dramatic in the arts, questionnaire data regarding their personal adjustment, rates of suicide, and drinking habits, indicate that as a group they are no more stable or unstable than would be expected in a normal population. Medical appraisals of their vigor and health as children also tended to belie the common supposition held by many that scholarly children are marked by frail physiques and less than average good health. Moreover, the I.Q. test scores administered throughout the subjects' lives suggested that their intellectual potentials remained consistent, around 150 on the average, into their fifties and beyond. Although a few of their lives are not found to be marked by high achievement, it was suggested by Terman and others interpreting the data that the academic achievement of a percentage of the underachievers was blunted by parental apathy toward the goals of higher education.

Although Terman's data collection techniques were marked by all the controls and safeguards usual in studies of intelligence, and are superior to most, both in the amount of data collected and in the duration of time during which the subjects were studied, there might be at least two variables biasing the interpretations that have been found in several volumes describing this fascinating investigation. For example, Terman took a great personal interest in his subjects, calling them "my children" even in questionnaires he periodically sent to their homes. One may read into his writings his own high needs for them to achieve and one wonders whether these personal feelings and interest may have molded the efforts and directions taken by the subjects, who learned from him at an early age that they possessed unusual intellectual qualities. One might also be a little skeptical of the objectivity of the questionnaire data collected from the subjects themselves, in which *they* were asked to indicate the degree of emotional stability, marital happiness, and freedom from alcoholism they evidenced as they matured.

Terman's contribution to the understanding of intelligence, however, was and is a substantial one. To his credit must go many of the programs for gifted children that appeared in the schools before and after World War II, programs that continue to proliferate today.

The testing movement in the United States was similarly stimulated by World War II, but the psychological community did not emerge from this conflict with the same assurance that its tests were the "last word in evaluating human capabilities and potential." Rather, this conflict and the large number of subjects that could be tested, had the effect of producing tests that sampled individual abilities in a variety of tasks. This expansion in the scope of the testing movement was reflected in the careful factor analyses of Fleishman, that dealt with psychomotor abilities and sub-abilities and stemmed from testing of Air Force personnel shortly after World War II.

Most important, psychologists interested in evaluating school children became more careful and guarded in their interpretations of the I.Q. scores they obtained.

The number and type of tests available with which to measure various aspects of human abilities continued to expand, with scales constructed to sample personality, mechanical abilities, and similar qualities proliferating during the 1940s and 1950s. For example, the Wechsler Intelligence Scales for children and for adults came into wide use.[9] The Children's Scale contained sections evaluating short-term memory (via digit span sub-tests, i.e., "Repeat back to me these three or more numbers."), vocabulary similarities ("How are a cat and mouse the same?"), information ("What must you do to make water boil?"), comprehension ("The train will be wrecked due to a broken track. What can you do?"), as well as sub-tests evaluating spatial abilities, in which a child is asked, via colored blocks, to duplicate various designs increasing in complexity (The Kohs Block Test), and object assembly tasks. The Adult Scale contains more verbal than perceptual-motor items.

[9] The advantage of using the Wechsler versus the Binet is that the former yields separate performance vs. verbal I.Q. scores, while the latter does not. Essentially, however, the total scores from each will generally correlate quite highly with one another.

A recently developed Wechsler Preschool and Primary Scale of Intelligence (WPPSI) has been available for too short a time, as of this printing for proper interpretation.

In the 1970s, the types of levels of scales available, with which to test children and youth, are numerous and varied in their intent. Lacking, however, were really valid tests for ethnic minority groups. Most of the scales available, even by the early 1970s, contain items that are so culturally related as to make a large percent of the responses from ghetto children "wrong ones." [10]

PERFORMANCE TESTS OF INTELLIGENCE

In the previous pages the preponderance of sensory-motor items on the early tests for evaluating intellectual functioning were pointed out. During the twentieth century these items were modified, made more complex, standardized and either remained as sub-tests of the available batteries, or appeared as separate batteries of tests of intelligence. The latter were usually developed as an effort to construct "culture-free" non-verbal measures of I.Q. that would not punish a child from a deprived background, and that also would allow comparisons of the abilities of children from various countries.

The establishment of the initial tests of this nature in the 1920s was prompted also by the need to evaluate the potential job capabilities of the numerous immigrants who came to America immediately following World War I. Knox, meeting these immigrants at Ellis Island, composed one of the first batteries of non-verbal or performance tests, and many of the items he used were incorporated into later tests, developed by Pinter and Paterson, as well as in the batteries of the Cornell-Coxe series and the Arthur Point Scale appearing in the 1930s.

At the time Binet was formulating his tests in France, Stanley Porteus was at work attempting to evaluate the "practical trainability" of retarded children in Melbourne, Australia. While he acknowledged the usefulness of the Binet, he felt that its ability to predict the potential of a child to perform various manual tasks within workshops was limited. From these speculations he devised a test that he felt would evaluate what he termed "planability" or "planfulness." The Porteus Maze Tests consisted of line mazes, increasing in complexity from the easy to the difficult, which required a child to draw from the "beginning

---

[10] For example, the Peabody Picture Vocabulary Test, designed as a non-verbal test of I.Q., presents pictures to children that they must name in order to achieve a "correct" answer to one item. The child must name it a "wiener," not a hot dog, as would most central city children. This often-used test has been standardized on a group of 4,000 children near Atlanta, Georgia, even though it is not infrequently used to test Negro youngsters in the central cities of our metropolitan areas.

to the termination point without crossing lines." These tests were brought, in 1917, to the Vineland School in New Jersey for validation and comparison against teachers' ratings of children's learning potential, and against scores from the Binet and other similar tests. Claiming moderate to high positive correlations between what he named "manual planning capacities" needed in simple industrial tasks and emotional adjustment, initiative, and similar observational measures, Porteus has compiled a large bibliography that the interested reader may pursue. He also contacted bushmen in Africa and Australian aborigines, with whom his measuring devices were used to compare the responses from individuals of these primitive cultures with those from children in more "advanced" societies.

In the middle 1920s, Florence Goodenough also devised a performance test that she hoped would prove to be relatively free from various cultural contaminations. Her object was to evaluate the quality of a child's drawings of human figures, and, by carefully evaluating the presence or absence of fifty-two details, to arrive at a score that would prove to be a valid index of intellectual functioning.

It was her intent to look not at artistic quality, but at the presence or absence of conceptual development as expressed in the relative completeness of a child's rendition of a person. Her initial scale was devised by first collecting and then ennumerating various items to determine which were scorable and which significantly differentiated between about 3500 children of various ages. The first scale underwent five revisions with subsequent changes in the 1960s carried out by Harris. In general, the scoring points are derived from inspection of such items as: Are the head, arms, and trunk present? Is the hand shown distinct from the fingers? Are motor coordinations shown? What about the presence of eye details of four types? Is the profile correct? The addition of the chin is an additional point.

In general, research carried out with this instruction reveals that general art training, as usually received by younger children, does not influence test results; while specific training towards the test—teaching children to draw the specific characteristics that are contained in the test—will positively influence the final scores obtained.

In numerous studies it was found that a moderate to high positive correlation will be obtained when comparing the Goodenough scores to those from the Binet and similar verbal measures of I.Q. At the same time, the correlations, as would be expected, are higher between nonverbal items of the more used scales and the scores obtained from the Goodenough test. Interest in this test continued high, used in conjunction with other measures of I.Q. by many clinicians.

Contemporary Theories of Intelligence

Since the beginnings of written records, men have speculated about the human brain, intelligence, and thought. Writings in the last century appearing in such journals as *Mind*, indicate the same preoccupation with such topics as the ingredients that make up mental imagery, conceptualization, and "practical" intelligence.

With the development of testing procedures and, more important, the statistical tools necessary to assess their reliability and validity, one might have hoped that some of the theoretical arguments concerning the nature of human intelligence might have been, if not solved, at least illuminated to some degree. However, this has not been entirely the case. Correlational techniques available before the turn of the century convinced nearly all who would heed them that simple tests of basic faculties (seeing, hearing, reaction time, kinesthetic awareness, etc.) did not discriminate in the same way among and between individuals who were obviously well endowed in their ability to engage in higher thought processes and the less able. At the same time, these same correlation coefficients, refined and elaborated upon in the form of factor analyses in the 1920s and 1930s, perhaps created even more controversy than existed in the previous century.

The most prevalent theoretical argument revolved around whether human intelligence was a single quality (or at least a single quality about which were grouped lesser abilities), or whether there were separate and equal qualities, discrete factors that contained no overall base of mental functioning common to all the scores obtained.

SPEARMAN

Advocates of the first position were primarily the group at Cambridge University, whose champion was Spearman. His writings, which covered the period from 1904 to 1926 revealed not only a passionate interest in human intellectual abilities, but also a thorough analytical mind capable of grappling with and honing sharp the new tools of correlation through the use of the even more complex "correlations-of-correlations" factor analyses. In his earlier writings he pointed out the fallacies of suggesting that basic tests of sensory functioning emanating from Wundt would in any way correlate with measures of higher level judgments.

In his later writings, Spearman pointed out the apparent existence of what he named a G factor, (general) factor, in intelligence, common to a number of tests. Additionally, however, he gave heed to the prevalent supposition that was developing within the scientific community that man's ability structure was quite complex. Thus his data also revealed that in addition to some general factor prevalent in many tests, there were a number of specific abilities covering such sub-qualities as sensory acuity, mechanical ability, verbal ability, psychological ability, imagination, memory, and mathematics. Although many in England, including Burt and Vernon, generally supported Spearman's interpretations of the data, there were more, particularly in the United States, who took issue with the G and s doctrine advanced by the group at Cambridge. Kelley, for example, pointed out in 1928 that Spearman's G is really composed of separate qualities involving retention, a verbal factor, memory, accuracy, abstract thought, and others. Additionally, Kelley correctly pointed out that Spearman did not factor out age in many of his studies; thus maturity could be the G factor that Spearman had identified.

This kind of controversy continues and its reconciliation depends upon the philosophical biases of the scholar who selects the test to place in his battery the type of analytic techniques he chooses to employ, and the insight used when naming the factors once they have been "clustered" by the computer.

GUILFORD

Perhaps the art and science of searching for and identifying the complex processes, sub-abilities, and operations contained within the boundaries of the human personality labeled intelligence has been raised to its high level in the studies of Guilford in the 1950s and 1960s. Not only did Guilford identify 120 primary mental abilities, but also suggested that there may be another 20 or 25 subdivisions to intelligence that are not only independent of each other but separate from the initial 120! Helpfully, however, Guilford attempted to coalesce his findings into the three-dimensional model shown in Figure 2.1.

Through this model, Guilford suggests that unique or primary intellectual abilities may be organized into a single system called the "structure of the intellect." One classification or dimension of abilities Guilford names "operations," and subdivides these into five components: (a) memory: retention of what is learned; (b) divergent thinking in which the individual must think in new directions, searching and seeking for variety; (c) convergent thinking in which new information is developed from new or remembered information; (d) evaluation: reaching decisions concerning correctness, suitability, or adequacy of what is known; and finally (e) cognition: which means the discovery or rediscovery of information.

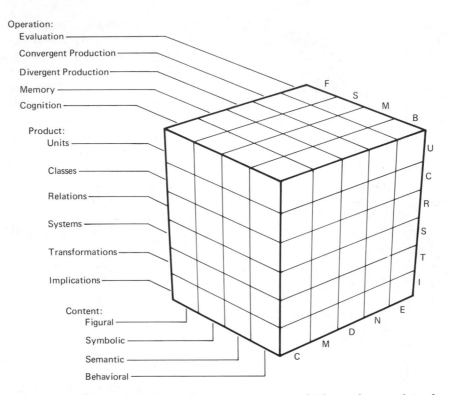

Operation:
Evaluation
Convergent Production
Divergent Production
Memory
Cognition

Product:
Units
Classes
Relations
Systems
Transformations
Implications

Content:
Figural
Symbolic
Semantic
Behavioral

F S M B
U
C
R
S
T
I
E
N
D
M
C

Reprinted from J. P. Guilford, *Intelligence, Creativity, and Their Educational Implications*. Robert R. Knapp, Publisher.

FIGURE 2.1

The structure-of-intellect model, representing the intellectual
abilities classified in three intersecting ways.

Additionally, Guilford suggests that intellectual factors may be classified according to the type of sensory information with which the individual is dealing. Thus, the information may be gained through vision, touch or hearing in which such properties as size, location, color or texture are dealt with. Guilford terms this *figural content. Symbolic content* refers to letters, digits and other conventional signs such as the alphabet or numbers. *Semantic content* refers to the meanings or ideas, while *behavioral content* means information derived from observing or interpreting the behavior of other people.

The third dimension of Guilford's model refers to the products or outcomes of various intellectual activities. Into this dimension, Guilford's research indicated, may be placed the *classes,* the simple classification of one or more of the products previously outlined: *relations,* dealing with relationships and drawing inferences from information; *units; transformations; implications;* and *systems.*

Guilford states that, although the structure he has suggested indicates the possibility of at least 120 separate intellectual abilities, his research generally resulted in the isolation of "only" fifty. In other terms, according to Guilford, there are at least fifty ways of manifesting one's intelligence. He points out that his model has practical implications as well as theoretical ones. Future study of intelligence, he explains, could well explore further facets of the sub-abilities he has identified, while from a practical standpoint more efficient placement of individuals in jobs could be achieved by first analyzing the qualities needed in various lines of work and then evaluating prospective candidates. From a pedagogical standpoint, Guilford suggests, educators might well take the viewpoint that all the learning strategies or operations he has identified, as well as the ability to acquire various of the contents he has also pointed to, are modifiable by exposing students to the proper experiences. To concentrate solely upon operations to the exclusion of material, or upon simple memory of content, will result in a less than fully educated individual, Guilford implies.

BRUNER

Jerome Bruner's thoughts about thinking have had considerable impact upon educational strategies and philosophies during the 1960s. Stemming from investigations carried out in the 1950s dealing with intellectual strategies, his writings offer theoretical guidelines that aid in the elucidation of thought processes and contain tutorial processes that might maximize the expansion of the former.

Bruner views intelligent behavior as a process taking place over time, characterized by the arrangement and interpretation of stimuli unique to an individual's experience, and proceeding toward the internalization of events into a "storage system," and concluding with the resolution of conflicts found in the environment or contrived by a teacher. Intellectual growth, Bruner postulates, comes about when an individual has to utilize symbols well and form the symbols internally in order to subtly test future actions and possible outcomes. Moreover, Bruner continues, intellectual development is characterized by an increasing capacity to deal with more than one alternative in a given situation and to allocate one's time and attention in appropriate ways in the presence of these multiple possibilities and demands. In his several texts Bruner has attempted to combine these concepts of intelligence into helpful theoretical guidelines through which one may enhance the intellect through constructive teaching strategies. Bruner's recent work which explores the manner in which manipulative behavior in early infancy forms as well as reflects intellectual abilities, is likely to prove one of the most helpful contributions since those of Piaget in explaining the nature of early developmental processes.

GAGNE AND BLOOM

In the late 1950s and early 1960s, both Gagnè and Bloom derived what are essentially hierarchies of intellectual functioning, or as one has labeled his, a taxonomy of levels within the cognitive domain. The inference they both seem to make is that there are levels of intellectual functioning from the more simple processes or operations to the more complex. Gagnè specifically points out that, in order to reach the higher levels, one must first master the more basic ones within his framework. At several points in the remainder of the text, the stages within these two models will be referred to.

Benjamin Bloom's six levels are as follows:

Knowledge: The recall of specific information or the recall of methods, patterns, or structures of settings. There is little more than "bring to mind" within this stage, with no manipulation or interpretation of material implied.

Comprehension: The lowest form of understanding the use of material without the necessity of relating it to other material, or finding out its fullest implications.

Application: The use of abstractions in specific situations. The abstractions may be in the forms of procedures, ideas, or generalized concepts from one situation to another. The application of theories is also placed within this category.

Analysis: The breaking down of information into component parts, so that relationships between ideas are made more clearly.

Synthesis: The building up of elements, or the combining of parts into wholes, evolving a structure or a pattern not present before.

Evaluation: The judgments about the value of materials and methods, as related to their purposes. Both quantitative or qualitative judgments may be made about the degree to which methods or materials meet some criteria, criteria designed by others or evolved by the learner himself.

Gagnè arranges his levels within his hierarchy from the more simple to the complex and specifies that mastery of the upper levels depends upon acquisition of abilities in the more basic ones. Similar to the levels outlined by Bloom, Gagnè's levels were given considerable attention by educators and as a result, classroom tasks were more carefully analyzed, educational objectives were more clearly worked out, and most important, instructional methodologies were given clearer direction and more meaningful outlines.

1. *Response differentiation:* The simple copying of a stimulus by a learner, that is, an exact replication of the stimulus figure presented by the instructor. An A is shown by the teacher, the child finds the same A on his paper.

2. *Association:* A response on the part of the learner, which is the only one possible, but may not be the exact stimulus presented by the teacher. If asked which is the largest state of the union, the learner may only respond correctly by saying "Alaska."

3. *Multiple discrimination:* The differentiation of a "correct" stimulus when presented with two or more potentially confusing stimuli, i.e., underlining a triangle when presented with a square, circle, triangle, and rectangle.

4. *Behavior chains:* Upon presentation of a stimulus, the recalling of a chain of stimuli that are logically attached to the one presented. For example, if asked to recite the pledge of allegiance the student would proceed to do so.

5. *Class concepts:* The ability to form classifications based upon their similarities upon presentation of a number of stimuli having common qualities. For example, the ability to call a configuration the letter "A," despite the variety of ways in which it can be written or printed, would constitute this level of behavior.

6. *Principles:* The application of a rule within several situations. The ability to see similarities in situations and to apply rules learned in one situation to another.

7. *Problem solving strategies:* The discovery of content principles for a series of novel situations, providing intermediate (mediating) responses in a sitmulus response situation, necessary to meet a specified goal.

As can be seen, Gagnè's terminology was influenced by Skinner and other S-R learning theorists. This framework and that by Bloom elicited widespread interest within the educational community and will be referred to at several points in the chapters that follow.

Summary

The history of man's concern with the processes of his mind is as extensive as the history of civilization itself. It has been recorded that civil service tests were given in ancient China and Rome, while the writings of the golden era of Greece contain numerous speculations concerning the nature of human intelligence.

During the past 200 years this interest coalesced into the extensive theorizing found in contemporary literature, together with the formulation of the numerous batteries of tests to measure intelligence in children, youth, and adults.

The beginnings of attempts to objectify intellectual processes via tests are found in France during the last century, when the socially conscious psychologists became apprehensive lest they commit the wrong individuals to homes for the feeble-minded. Although initial intelligence testing was guided by the rather simplistic faculty theory, later efforts contained tasks aimed at sampling intellectual processes at a higher level than were obtained when simple reaction time tests were administered by Galton and Cattell in the 1890s. These early scholars were given direction and guidance by Binet, who, in the first decade of the twentieth century, devised a battery of tests that were both educationally and scientifically defensible. After his death in 1911, Binet's concept of mental age was objectified further by Terman, Thorndike, and others. In England, the early statistical concepts illuminated by Galton and his student Pearson, with reference to intellectual abilities, were similarly expanded by Spearman, in England, and by Kelley and later by Guilford, in the United States.

The theoretical argument most heard during the 1920s and 30s was whether one could consider valid the concept of a central general quality surrounded by sub-abilities, or whether the intellectual powers were fragmented and specific, without collecting around some central ubiquitous factor. Spearman, Vernon, and Burt, in England, held for the former interpretation, while the Americans led by Kelley and others, held out for the latter framework.

Stimuli for research in intelligence testing and classification were provided by both world wars, during which thousands of soldiers were tested, and by the studies of gifted children initiated by Terman and his colleagues in the decade following World War I.

Later the most attention was directed toward the theories advanced by Bruner and Guilford, while Bloom and Gagnè provided hierarchies of intellectual functioning. Piaget's writings, when translated into English in the 1950s, similarly inspired many to research the manner in which the infant engages in intellectual behaviors of increasing complexity as he matures.

Overall, both theorists and test makers seem to indicate that the following are valid generalizations concerning the nature of human intelligence:

1. The human intellect is not a single quality, but is multi-dimensional. Not only does evidence from various factor analyses indicate this truism, but the subsequent multi-dimensional content of test batteries

also confirms this principle. Just how many dimensions it contains is still the object of further research.

2. Intelligence is being studied within at least four contexts:

a. Intellectual functioning and change in intellectual endeavor and strategies may be viewed developmentally from birth to maturity.

b. Intelligence may be considered with reference to a time dimension, as an ongoing process, beginning with the individual's attention to a situation, proceeding through an examination by him of alternative solutions, and ending with some resolution of the conflict he perceives.

c. Human intellectual activity may be illuminated by evaluating the outcomes of thought. Such consequences of mental functioning as problem solving, theory building, classification and/or re-classification, and similar results, may be considered within this third category.

d. Thought processes may be arranged in hierarchical order from the easy-simple to the hard-complex; from processes like recognition and categorization of events, people, behaviors, and symbols to the more difficult undertakings labeled by several theoreticians as problem solving, synthesizing, analyzing, evaluating, and the like. Intellectual activity is usually conceived of as dealing with complexities, resolving ambiguity, as a kind of "sorting-out" process. Basic to these higher level processes are simpler ones involving memory, classification, and the like.

In the chapters that follow, I will attempt to determine how various intellectual processes, strategies, and developmental processes are reflected in, and in some way may be influenced by, observable muscular activity.

BIBLIOGRAPHY

Bayley, Nancy. "Mental Growth in Young Children." *Thirty-ninth Yearbook of the National Society for the Study of Education,* 2:11–47. Bloomington, Ill.: Public School Publishing Co., 1940.

Binet, Alfred. *The Mind and the Brain,* London: Kegan Paul, Trench, Trubner & Co., Ltd., 1907.

Binet, Alfred, and Simon, Th. *The Development of Intelligence in Children.* Baltimore: Williams & Wilkins Co., 1916.

Bloom, Benjamin S., ed. *Taxonomy of Educational Objectives, Handbook I: Cognitive Domain.* New York: David McKay Co., Inc., 1956.

Bruner, Jerome S. "The Course of Cognitive Growth." *American Psychologist,* 19 (January 1964): 1–15.

———. *Toward a Theory of Instruction,* Cambridge, Mass.: Harvard University Press, 1966.

Bruner, Jerome S., Goodnow, J. J., and Austin, G. A., *A Study of Thinking.* New York: John Wiley and Sons, 1956.

Burt, C. "The Evidence for the Concept of Intelligence." *British Journal of Educational Psychology,* 25 (1955):158–77.

Cattell, J. "Mental Tests and Measurements." *Mind,* 15 (1890): 373–80.

ERLENMEYER-KIMLING, L., and JARVIK, L. F. "Genetics and Intelligence: A Review." *Science,* 142 (1963): 1477–79.

ESQUIROL, JEAN-ETIENNE D. *Des Maladies mentales considérées sous les rapports medical, hygiénique, et médico-légal.* Paris: J.B. Bailliere, 1838.

FLEISHMAN, EDWIN A. *The Structure and Measurement of Physical Fitness.* Englewood Cliffs, N. J.: Prentice-Hall, Inc., 1964.

GAGNÈ, R. W. *The Conditions of Learning.* New York: Holt, Rinehart & Winston, Inc., 1965.

GALTON, SIR FRANCIS. *Hereditary Genius.* London: Macmillan & Co., Ltd., 1869.

———. *English Men of Science: Their Nature and Nurture,* London: Macmillan and Co., Ltd., 1874.

———. *Inquiries Into Human Faculty and Its Development.* London: E.P. Dutton & Co., Inc., 1883.

———. *Natural Inheritance.* London and New York: The Macmillan Company, 1889.

GLASSER, ALAN J., and ZIMMERMAN, IRLA LEE. *Clinical Interpretation of the Wechsler Intelligence Scale for Children (WISC),* New York: Grune & Stratton, Inc., 1967.

GOODENOUGH, FLORENCE L. *Measurement of Intelligence by Drawings.* Cleveland: The World Publishing Company, 1926.

———. *Mental Testing,* New York: Holt, Rinehart & Winston, Inc., 1949.

GORDON, H. *Mental and Scholastic Tests Among Retarded Children,* Education Pamphlet No. 44. London: Board of Education, 1923.

GUILFORD, J.P. "Three Faces of Intellect." *American Psychologist* 14 (1959): 469–79.

———. *The Nature of Human Intelligence.* New York: McGraw-Hill Book Company, 1967.

———. *Intelligence, Creativity and their Educational Implications.* San Diego, Calif.: Robert R. Knapp, Publisher, 1968.

HARRIS, DALE B. *Children's Drawings as Measures of Intellectual Maturity.* New York: Harcourt Brace Jovanovich, 1937.

HOFSTAETTER, P.R. "The Changing Composition of Intelligence: A Study in T-technique." *Journal of Genetic Psychology* 85: 159–64.

HUMPHREY, GEORGE, and HUMPHREY, MURIEL. *The Wild Boy of Aveyron.* New York: Appleton-Century-Crofts, 1932.

ITARD, JEAN-MARC GASPARD. *The Wild Boy of Aveyron.* Translated by George and Muriel Humphrey. New York: Appleton-Century Crofts, 1932.

JASTROW, JOSEPH. "Some Anthropological and Psychological Tests on College Students—A preliminary Survey." *American Journal of Psychology* 4 (1892): 420–27.

KELLEY, T. *Crossroads in the Mind of Man.* Stanford, Calif.: Stanford University Press, 1928.

KUHLMANN, E. "A Revision of the Binet-Simon System for Measuring the Intelligence of Children." *Journal of Psycho-Aesthenics, Monograph Supplement,* 1912.

McNEMAR, QUINN. *The Revision of the Stanford-Binet Scale.* Boston: Houghton Mifflin Company, 1942.

PIAGET, JEAN. *The Child's Conception of the World*. Translated by J. and A. Tomlinson. New York: Harcourt Brace & World, Inc., 1929.

———. *The Early Growth of Logic in the Child*. Translated by E. A. Lunzer and D. Papert. London: Routledge & Kegan Paul, Ltd., 1964.

PORTEUS, STANLEY D. *The Maze Test and Clinical Psychology*. Palo Alto, Calif.: Pacific Books, 1959.

QUETELET, L. A. J. *Letters on Probabilities*. Translated by O. G. Downs. London, Layton & Co., 1849.

RIBOT, TH. *English Psychology*. Translator anonymous. New York: Appleton-Century-Crofts, 1874.

———. *Heredity: A Psychological Study of Its Phenomena, Laws, Causes, and Consequences*. Translator anonymous. New York: Appleton-Century-Crofts, 1903.

———. *German Psychology of Today: The Empirical School*. Translated by J. M. Baldwin. New York: Charles Scribner's Sons, 1886.

ROBACK, A.A. *History of American Psychology*. New York: Crowell Collier and Macmillan, Inc., 1964.

SEGUIN, EDWARD. *Idiocy: Its Treatment by the Physiological Method*. New York: Bureau of Publications, Teachers College, Columbia University, 1907.

SPEARMAN, C. "General Intelligence: Objectively Determined and Measured." *American Journal of Psychology*. 115(1904): 201–92.

SPEARMAN, C., AND JONES, L. W. *Human Ability*. London: MacMillan & Co., Ltd., 1951.

SYMPOSIUM. "Intelligence and Its Measurement." *Journal Educational Psychology* 12 (1921): 123–47.

TAINE, H. *On Intelligence*. New York: Henry Holt and Co., 1879.

TERMAN, L.M., and ASSOCIATES. *Genetic Studies of Genius, Vol I, Mental and Physical Traits of a Thousand Gifted Children*. Stanford, Calif.: Stanford University Press, 1925.

TERMAN, L.M., and MERRILL, MAUD. *Measuring Intelligence: A Guide to the Administration of the New Revised Stanford-Binet Tests of Intelligence*. Boston: Houghton Mifflin Company, 1937.

TERMAN, L.M., and ODEN, M.H. *The Gifted Child Grows Up*. Stanford, Calif.; Stanford University Press, 1947.

THORNDIKE, E.L. *The Measurement of Intelligence*. New York: Bureau of Publications, Teachers College, Columbia University, 1926.

THORNDIKE, E.L., et al. *The Measurement of Intelligence*. New York: Bureau of Publications, Teachers College, Columbia University, 1927.

VERNON, P.E. *The Structure of Human Abilities*, New York: Barnes & Noble, 1950.

WISEMAN, STEPHEN, ED. *Intelligence and Ability*, Baltimore, Md.,: Penguin Books, 1967.

3

Contemporary Theories Linking Movement and Cognition

Introduction

During the 1950s, and particularly during the 1960s, theorists began to suggest that motor activity, if properly applied, might enhance a number of perceptual, intellectual and academic functions in children and youth. The formalizers of these concepts came from several disciplines. An optometrist in the United States, for example, wrote about the role of visual, visual-motor, and motor training in the enhancement of cognitive and perceptual functions. A psychologist from a Midwestern university produced a number of books that elicited a great deal of discussion among educators in which he postulated that movement is the basis of the intellect and that by improvement of motor capabilities one might improve a number of perceptual, cognitive, and academic abilities. A man with a doctorate in school administration in Philadelphia unearthed a recapitulation theory in writings of the seventeenth and eighteenth centuries, and attracted a widespread audience of parents and others who hoped to help severely handicapped youngsters to function better intellectually by exposing them to a building-block type program of locomotor activities, reflex training, and similar activities.

At Rutgers University, Muska Mosston, an Israeli immigrant, outlined a teaching methodology in which cognitive and creative abilities might be enhanced through the gradual shifting of decisions to the learners when they seem capable of making them. Jean Le Boulch, in Paris, produced a book and several articles in which he outlined how the improvement of various educational processes might be achieved by exposing children to the proper movement experiences.

This marked interest in movement as an educational and therapeutic modality through which a rather large range of human capabilities might be improved has had several short-term and possibly long-range effects. On the positive side of the ledger, are the following trends:

1. The writings of the aforementioned theorists, as well as others, prompted numerous scholars to engage in more research in which they explored some of the suppositions advanced. The findings of this research, while not always positively supporting the hypotheses of the theory being tested, at the same time pointed to new helpful directions movement in education may take.

2. A wider variety of emotionally, educationally, and/or physically handicapped children are being worked with in ways that are often constructive.

3. Programs of physical activity, particularly in the United States, are finding their way into programs of elementary education to an increased degree.

4. Some of the movement methodologies advocated, while often not remediating as large a list of academic, perceptual, and cognitive problems as suggested by their formalizers, *do* provide a rich supply of techniques with which to help children with motor difficulties.

Negative ramifications arising from some of the theorizing include:

1. Often the claims for the therapeutic effects of movement activities transcend reasonable expectations; and when the claims are not met, in some cases a type of "backlash" has occurred, similar to that seen in the political arena. For example, a program of movement activities incorporated into a school program, under the assumption that it will remediate reading problems, may be quickly removed when it apparently fails. In truth its components may have had a positive effect upon the emotional and motor functioning of some of the children exposed to it.

2. The sometimes confining and stilted movement activities in certain of the programs are likely to have less effect upon perceptual functioning, social maturity, and motor ability than if the children were left alone to engage in free unrestricted play activities.

3. The harsh methods advocated by some have been demonstrated to have had adverse effects upon children's emotional stability as well as upon their academic functioning and motor abilities.

It is an often-voiced lament within the educational literature that there is usually a fifty-year lag before positive research findings are implemented within school programs.

Due to the widespread publicity some of the methodologies and theories received in the American press, there was not time to "check-out" their veracity before certain educators gave them wholehearted approval and incorporated them into school curriculums. In any case, there has now been time for a number of researchers, not under the influence and/or jurisdiction of those expounding various theories, to test the hypotheses presented with reasonably well-controlled studies. One of the purposes in this chapter is to examine some of the theories, methods, and claims with reference to recent research findings. Additionally, I will attempt to classify the methods and theories into coherent categories and to suggest future research that might further illuminate some of the suppositions of the various authors reviewed.

Theories Emphasizing Intellectual Abilities

The initial theories outlined were formulated by individuals who seem to place major emphasis upon involving the child intellectually when exposing him to motor activities. Mosston devotes his theoretical speculations exclusively toward these ends, while Frostig, Le Boulch and Cratty present frameworks in which a triad of perceptual and motor, as well as academic and intellectual, attributes are explored as ones which are influenced positively by movement experiences. Humphrey, on the other hand, devotes himself to explaining how certain vigorous games may enhance various academic abilities. The ideas of the six theorists that follow are only briefly sketched in; particularly in those sections dealing with specific academic operations, the ideas of several are pursued further by examining in some detail the nature of the experiences they advocate.

LE BOULCH

Dr. Jean Le Boulch is a professor of physical education and doctor of medicine attached to the Bureau of Educational Research of the Chamber of Commerce and Industry in Paris. His interest in movement prompted him to write a book, *Education Through Movement*, and several articles. These have attracted widespread interest within educational circles in French-speaking communities.[1]

His rather comprehensive coverage of the role movement may po-

[1] Unfortunately Le Boulch's book does not appear in an English translation at this writing.

tentially play in the education of children is accompanied by practical suggestions for activities designed to implement his theoretical speculations. Le Boulch appears to be the latest in a chain of French educators dating back to the humanistic philosophies of Rousseau in the eighteenth century, who, within sometimes less elaborate conceptual frameworks, suggested that natural motor experiences will enhance the development of the well-educated youth.

Le Boulch contends that movement experiences will positively influence a rather wide range of human attributes including the organization of time, space, similar perceptual abilities, and motor coordination, as well as higher level intellectual processes. His activities are classified not only according to the type of ability they may enhance, but also according to the ages that are likely to be aided by exposure to specific movement tasks.

Le Boulch places movement experiences on a continuum, from those that are simple and "goal-oriented," through successively more complex categories that are more demanding. These range from *automatic skills*, which have to be learned; *complex automatic movements*, which may have several independent parts such as are sometimes seen in industrial tasks; to *movement activities*, which are more thoughtful and contain a large number of *intellectual and/or artistic creative elements*.

Le Boulch is seemingly appalled at some practices in athletics, in which he feels there is a kind of dehumanizing "knee-jerk" response elicited through fear of punishment.[2] Rather than the stereotype drills in physical activity programs, this French physician-educator maintains that motor activities must be goal-oriented, to be truly effective, and they must require the child to utilize insight into processes needed to solve movement problems. Le Boulch places emphasis upon the encouragement of silent internalization of goals as a helpful process prior to indirect action. Efforts to bypass this process or to submerge it by the teacher, Le Boulch brands as less than helpful. Trial and error learning is thus thought of as more helpful than simple unthinking responses to teacher-presented instructions.

Regarding high level skills, Le Boulch suggests that one should attempt to achieve accurate, automatic-like reactions, and yet provide the child or youth with a variety of responses in his memory store from which to choose. He thus emphasizes educational methods designed to produce "plasticity" of response, rather than those likely to produce rigidity.

[2] At one point Le Boulch cites the practice of a prominent American swimming coach who uses an electric cattle prod to remind his athletes, by touching them on the elbow as they move through the water, that their elbows should not be excessively high in the arm recovery phase of the stroke.

Le Boulch has attempted to classify movement experiences in various ways. For example, he suggests that the following categories represent ability groupings in which movement activities might make a contribution to the education of children:

1. Improving coordination
2. Enhancing the body image
3. Adjusting posture, balance
4. Perceiving time
5. Enhancing the awareness of space
6. Producing a feeling of freedom through play.

Le Boulch's suggestions include the point that teaching by demonstration may produce rather stereotypic movement expressions on the part of the learners. Rather, he believes a more meaningful strategy lies in presenting free-choice situations in which a child, for example, is asked to demonstrate ten ways of walking from here to there. He would, thus, exclude drills from programs of movement education. He believes a teacher should provide time for a child to engage, silently and in an immobile manner, in motor planning prior to acting out his thoughts.

In summary, he suggests that the intellectual, spiritual, emotional, and physical components of man are inseparable. He further points out that movement experiences in schools are equal in importance to reading, writing, and mathematics. He suggests that emphasis should be placed on lessons that permit the individual to establish relationships between the motor, intellectual, and emotional components of his personality, and that participating excessively in the common "drill" methods of instruction will result in the alienation of the human being whose body is being used simply as an object or instrument.

KIPHARD

Ernst J. Kiphard is a physical educator who is associated with the Westphalian Institute for Child Psychology in Cologne, Germany. In his numerous texts, he outlines a rather wide-ranging program of movement activities that, among other objectives, are focused upon the remediation of coordination problems.

At the same time, Kiphard suggests that a properly conducted program of physical education should not only improve physiological functions, but also enhance emotional and intellectual potentials. Furthermore, Kiphard argues for what he calls the "multi-dimensional effects of exercise," which include (1) the functional aspect, (2) the emotional aspect, (3) the social aspect, and (4) the educational aspect. Within the "functional aspects" Kiphard groups, as goals, improving muscular strength-endurance and physical skill; at the same time, the overcoming of clumsiness aids in perceptual organization by permitting the child to perceive visually two objectives simultaneously, instead of concentrating solely upon his bodily movements while engaged in physical activities.

Kiphard believes that motor activities aid a child to learn to relax; additionally, Kiphard's makes numerous references to the lowering of the self-concept that is often the outcome of motor ineptitudes and failure in physical performance situations. He hypothesizes that, with repeated failure and a lowering of the self-concept, a child may eventually incur psychosomatically-based physical illnesses. Kiphard suggests that a child, while exposed to inordinate failure in games, may manifest either (1) inhibition, a refusal or inability to move at all; (2) complete lack of restraint or self-control; or (3) indifference. In all cases, it is implied, he is likely to manifest failure in other aspects of his life.

The activities that Kiphard recommends are too numerous to do justice to here. But, in general, they encompass relaxation training, self-discovery activities, rhythms, music and keeping time with a beat, and exercises in "deliberate gentleness."

Kiphard's contribution also includes helpful test batteries, which aid in the discrimination between children with and without motor problems. With the translation of his work into English, his contribution should become more widely appreciated than is presently possible.

MOSSTON

During the 1960s, the ideas of Muska Mosston, director of teacher training in the Physical Education Department of Rutgers University, had a marked impact upon many educators in the United States.[3] Influenced by the writings of such cognitive theorists as Jerome Bruner, Mosston has outlined in several publications what he terms his "Spectrum of Styles."

He suggests that true education is taking place only if the learner is able to make some decisions within the educational environment. Using motor experiences as content, he proceeds in great detail, to specify temporal, qualitative, and quantitative guidelines that a teacher may follow when attempting to permit students freedom of choice and decision-making opportunities. Mosston's main contribution, in my opinion,

[3] Professor Mosston is presently heading the Teaching Behavior Institute at East Stroudsberg State College in Pennsylvania.

is to present a theoretical and practical structure through which the teacher may gradually transfer decisions to the student.

Although the first step in Mosston's spectrum involves the stimulus-response teaching situation frequently encountered in physical education programs, in which students are expected simply to respond in a reflex-like manner to a teacher's commands, it is not difficult to detect his disdain for this strategy. His views on the animal-trainer approach to teaching physical activities are similar to those expressed by Le Boulch.

However, at this point in his theorizing Mosston does not advocate a simple throw-open-the-doors approach of some educational philosophers around the turn of the century. Rather, Mosston has carefully considered just what kinds of decisions are most appropriate first to permit the learner to assimilate and incorporate into lessons. He concludes that the next step in his "Spectrum," after the command phase, involves "teaching by task." During this second stage, if the learners seem capable of assuming the structure, decisions about the manner and modifications in which a given task may be executed should be extended to them. Thus, for example, quantitative decisions may be extended to the students, as would occur if the teacher said, "Now you may jump as many times as you wish to the music." Perhaps qualitative decisions may also be transferred to the children or youth with whom the teacher is dealing, as would occur if it was requested that pupils "show me different ways of getting from this line to the other one fifteen feet away."

This stage in the "Spectrum" involves permitting the learner to make decisions connected with evaluation, or within a time dimension, after the task is completed. To accomplish this Mosston suggests teaching through the *use of partners*: one child performs and a second observes and evaluates. Within this situation an instructor should not, admonishes Mosston, give direct signs to the performer of whether a performance is good or poor, but rather should ask the evaluator, "Is that skill accomplished well?" or "Did he really jump that far?"

If the children or youth seem capable of taking decisions following the task, or, in other terms, evaluative decisions, without chaos reigning, Mosston suggests that further teacher restrictions be removed and that decisions prior to the lesson be considered next for transfer from teacher to learner. Operationally, this methodologist suggests several strategies that may accomplish this, including the following: students may be asked to construct individual programs around some kind of general goals (i.e., "How can we get our arms stronger?"). Perhaps groups may be involved in how to reach some kind of general goal (i.e., "How may a ball be brought down a basketball court the quickest way?"), prior to guiding students toward floor patterns appropriate to the fast-break offense in basketball.

The final stages in Mosston's schema involved *problem solving through movement,* in which a considerable amount of intellectual involvement is sought in students. Within this phase Mosston discusses in detail his concept of "guided discovery" in which discovery comes finally to the students, but with some meaningful guidelines provided by the more astute teacher-instructor. It is within this critical phase that the crossing of what he terms the "cognitive barrier" occurs; thus this marks the first signs of intellectual awakening and the willingness of students to think about what they are about to do and to engage in silent thought prior to acting.

The last part of the "Spectrum of Styles" is not fully developed in Mosston's book, but involves what he terms "creativity." Perhaps in future publications he may devote more space to creativity-movement relationships than he did in his 1966 text.

Like other cognitive theorists who have devoted their energies to outlining optimum educational strategies, Mosston believes it important to produce what has been termed "cognitive dissonance" in learners, midway in the problem-solving processes. Thus, learning, within Mosston's framework, is not made easy; indeed he was noted for creating intellectual struggles within his own students at Rutgers. Essentially, the concept of cognitive dissonance implies that the instructor should, by voice, deed, and/or through the arrangement of the environment, create a disturbance in the learner, causing him to ponder, to suffer perhaps, while attempting to solve the problem. Then, with the resolution of the dissonance, the gaining of insight and the acting out of the solution in movement, true change of behavior, attitudes, and the acquiring of new intellectual insights should be the new possessions of the learners exposed to this often harrowing teaching-learning situation.

Mosston characterizes himself as a theoretician, a methodologist, perhaps even a philosopher, and prefers to pose problems that he hopes others objectify in the traditional research studies. He confirms his own insights through his clinical explorations. Unlike Le Boulch, who seems concerned about a rather comprehensive range of movement experiences from those designed to correct coordination problems to those requiring intellectual involvement, Mosston cleaves more closely to the cognitive end of the behavioral continuum when outlining his strategies and goals.

CRATTY

Bryant J. Cratty is a professor of physical education at the University of California at Los Angeles. In numerous books and articles, he has outlined several of what might be termed "middle level theories," or models attempting what he conceives of as the relationships between movement and intellectual and academic activities. He might be properly termed a cognitive theorist, as his speculations contain the assumption that one must carefully consider and be cognizant of central thought processes when attempting to relate movement to the intellect. He generally rejects the ideas of those who advance the theory that early movement attributes are the basis of perceptual and intellectual development. Rather, he has outlined in several publications a complex four-channel theory of development in which proliferating intellectual abilities play a central part.[4]

The research he carried out in the latter part of the 1960s was based upon several guiding principles, including the following:

1. Movement is a component, not the sole basis of developing human abilities.

2. Highly structured movement experiences intended to remediate motor problems should be applied only to children who evidence clumsiness, rather than in a blanket manner to all elementary school children.

3. The several areas in which movement programs may assist in the educational process include:

a. Aiding the child with handwriting difficulties so he may better express his intellect

b. Aiding children to gain self-control, improve attention span, and adjust their levels of arousal to levels compatible with classroom functioning

c. Aiding in the improvement, in certain academic functions, if the academic skills it is desired to enhance are incorporated directly into the motor activities to which children and youth are exposed.

Relative to the final principles, Cratty conducted research since the middle 1960s in the central city of Los Angeles, through which it was found that significant improvement can be achieved through learning games in various pre-reading and reading skills, as well as in certain measures of self-control, short-term visual and auditory memory, and spelling. The findings of this work are incorporated into Chapters 12 and 13.

HUMPHREY

James Humphrey is a professor of physical education and health at the University of Maryland. Since the early 1960s he has conducted work on the effects of various learning games upon the acquisition of academic

---

[4] See Chapter 4 for a more thorough exposition of this position.

skills and a number of classroom concepts. Like Cratty, he does not see his work as some kind of educational cure-all, but *is* encouraged by the positive findings emanating from his studies, most of which have been carried out within the normal school setting. Humphrey also believes that his findings indicate that learning games may be of particular help in the education of children with learning difficulties.

Although one of the chapters in Humphrey's latest text is titled "Theory of Learning Through Learning Games," his theorizing is limited to listing examples of how the games may be used to enhance a variety of educational concepts and abilities. At the same time, he points out that from the time of Plato into the Renaissance, some educators emphasized the importance of placing the child in natural situations when educating him, environments that permit free and natural movements. Humphrey believes he is continuing this trend and presents highly persuasive evidence for the effectiveness of his concepts.

Humphrey suggests that three types of factors positively influence learning when children are exposed to his active game approach:

1. *Motivation:* including the suggestion that games are motivating because they possess intrinsic interest to children, motivations as the result of competition in games, and motivation arising from the immediate knowledge of results concerning relative success which games provide.

2. *Proprioception:* sensory experience arising from muscle action acts as a kind of coordinating process that aids in the integration of visual and auditory input, forming a holistic kind of perceptual experience as a child moves his body and limbs in the games he has devised. He coins the term *"motorvation"* to describe the phenomenon that results from the combination of the psychological concept of motivatioin with the physiological factors of proprioception, both purportedly involved as a child participates in active games.

3. *Reinforcement:* active games are helpful, because they are compatible to Premack's reinforcement hypothesis. Although this hypothesis is not developed fully in Humphrey's writings, he suggests that within the reinforcement concept is the tendency of games to provide a kind of focusing situation, one that "reinforces attention to the learning task and to the learning behavior."

His most recent text, co-authored with Dorothy Sullivan, reveals a firm grasp of educational processes, including a highly structured framework for the teaching of language skills. Moreover, the games that are contained in this book are creative to the extreme and should be given careful consideration by teachers of mathematics and science, as well as reading and other academic subjects.[5] Several of the approaches advo-

[5] The concept of electric impulse transmission is, for example, illustrated

cated by Humphrey, together with the findings emanating from his research, are found in Chapters 11, 12, and 13.

FROSTIG

Dr. Marianne Frostig is known within educational circles primarily for her work in the development of a test assessing perceptual abilities in young children together with a training program that is closely linked with this evaluative device. It was not until the publication of her 1970 text titled *Movement Education,* that most educators became familiar with her interest in motor activity as an educational tool.[6]

Like Humphrey and Cratty, Dr. Frostig does not view movement as endowed with magical curative powers, but in her text she points out several ways in which motor activities may be helpful in the enhancement of educational goals and intellectual processes. Dr. Frostig takes the same global look at movement as does Le Boulch and outlines strategies to enhance a wide range of abilities including language development, mathematics, and reading among academic skills and perceptual-motor abilities that include increased coordination, bodily awareness, strength-fitness, temporal sequencing, emotional development, and social adjustments.

Unlike Le Boulch and Mosston, however, Frostig attempts to support her claims with reference to the research literature, which, accompanied by her perceptive clinical speculations, result in a text containing not only a number of theoretical implications for movement experiences, but also an extensive list of highly motivating movement games that are closely integrated with virtually every academic and social goal that has ever been considered as the job of the school.[7]

She ties much of her program containing movement experiences into the theoretical speculations of Piaget: the importance he attaches to the early sensory-motor period suggests its importance particularly when working with the child evidencing learning difficulties. Practical exercises within her text also concentrate upon building various kinds of language abilities, including both expressive and receptive aspects, as well as short-term memory for words and phrases.

---

in a game in which a ball, representing the current, travels through lines of children, and is at one point "short-circuited" as it leaves the aisle of bodies created for it.

[6] Possessing a Ph.D. in psychology, Dr. Frostig also earned a certificate in physical education and dance from the city of Vienna; her first publication in the United States was a paper, written in 1946, "Motion and Emotion."

[7] Frequent references are made, for example, to factor analyses of motor abilities when devising training procedures, a practice not often adhered to by other theoreticians within this general subject area.

Dr. Frostig and her associate, Phyllis Maslow, do not present an original cogent theory illuminating movement-intellectual relationships. Instead they cite theoretical speculations by Piaget, Bruner, and Mosston, as well as Laban, Barsch, Kephart, and Getman, to support the validity of their claims and the worth of the activities they outline. These activities will be referred to in chapters dealing with language, reading, and mathematics.

Summary

As can be seen, the previously reviewed scholars take various approaches to explaining why movement experiences may influence in a positive way various intellectual and academic abilities. Some are rather operational and accompany the activities they discuss with a minimum of theorizing or borrow concepts and theoretical justification from others. Mosston, in truth, concentrates upon the nature of the teaching behavior, which he believes is a key to developing a child's intellectual and creative abilities. Some concentrate upon the qualities inherent in movement experiences themselves. Humphrey is an example of this approach.

Criteria that are valid to apply to a theory are (1) What is the quality of the research upon which it is based? and (2) What research has the theory seemed to inspire in others? In general, the theoretical assumptions formulated by Frostig were based primarily upon the research of others, research often not directly tied into the intellect-motor relationships it attempted to elucidate. A clinician herself, Dr. Frostig was also apparently more amenable to suggestions by other clinicians, notably Kephart, Barsch, and Getman, than others might be.

Mosston's assumptions are also beginning to draw the attention of researchers. Whilden, for example, found that the teaching-by-discovery method advocated by Mosston produced more flexible strategic abilities in children, while teaching by the command method elicited quicker learning of specific skills. It is expected that Mosston's "Spectrum of Styles" will undergo further modifications to correct the obvious inconsistencies that seem to beset it at the present time. For example, a phase that he terms "teaching by team," placed immediately after teaching with a partner, is not congruent with the basic tenants of his method. The final phases involving problem solving, and particularly the one dealing with creative behavior, are superficial to the extreme. However, most helpful, when reviewing Mosston's work, are the highly creative teaching strategies he recommends; the lessons in his 1966 text and particularly those in his more recent efforts are truly classics and should be reviewed by all teachers in all subject fields. Mosston admonishes, however, that in order to work effectively within his "Spectrum of Styles" one must be aware of all the subtle as well as the obvious vicissitudes of the subject matter (in this case, movement) with which one is dealing.

Additionally, Mosston's approach might be criticized in so far as both in personal appearances and in his writings, he rather dogmatically seems to assert that his is the *only viable way* for a teacher to instruct, a tactic that is hardly appropriate in one who, at the same time, advocates flexibility and acceptance in teaching behaviors!

Cratty and Humphrey have produced what might be termed pilot studies that, in part, support the worth of the learning games they advocate. The additional research of Ross and McCormick and his colleagues have produced data that offer support to their statements. However, the justifications for their methodologies, as well as the writings of Mosston and Le Boulch, contain not what might in truth be termed valid theories, but instead the beginnings of *conceptual models*, which may be fleshed out when their statements are tested further by those interested in their ideas. Like other work in this general area, the writings previously reviewed that purport to relate movement to intellectual operations contain few references to data from research dealing with cognitive operations, an oversight that I hope is rectified in Chapter 13 ·

Perceptual-Motor Theories

The following theoreticians advocate principles and practices that are in many ways similar. They concentrate upon building what they conceive of as important perceptual-motor bases of higher level intellectual processes. The writings seem to reflect traditional child development theories emanating from Gesell, Piaget, and others, which suggest that movement capacities precede perceptual abilities, and that, in turn, perceptual capacities are vital supports of children and youth who are "intellectually capable."

All are clinicians and thus in general do not apparently feel put upon to produce their own research findings supporting their claims. At the same time there are some references that allude to studies that contain reasonably "hard" data. All see their ideas and methodologies as helpful to the academic functioning of both normal children and atypical children. However, they have been accused by careful behavioral scientists of oversimplifying educational as well as maturational processes.

Their ideas emerged following World War II, perhaps stimulated in some measure by Strauss and his colleagues dealing with brain-injured children as well as by the manner in which movement plays a role in the development of the normal child, seen in the works of Gesell prior to the war. Getman worked for a time with Gesell, while Kephart was associated with Strauss.

All four might be characterized as peripheral rather than central theorists: they concentrate upon sensory and motor machinations rather than upon more central thought processes. All seem to infer, either directly or indirectly, however, that no perceptual "event" can be engaged in by the individual unless there is some involvement by the expressive (motor) components of the personality. Thus, perceptual awareness is an active not a passive process, while at the same time they believe that perceptual abilities (usually visual-perceptual abilities) cannot develop independently from movement experiences. In their numerous books, films, and workbooks, they take pains to outline just what motor experiences will be helpful in expanding to the fullest the unfolding capacities of the maturing child.

To a marked degree, the theories resemble the "faculties" theories of the last century, in which it was proposed that one must possess sound basic sensory and motor abilities if the intellect was to manifest itself. Just as Cattell and Galton searched diligently, and in vain, for a simple sensory or motor test with which to evaluate intelligence (see Chapter 2), Getman, Kephart, and Barsch seem to be engaged in a similar search for a set of relatively simple sensory-motor experiences that will result in the development of the intellect.

Like all searchers for the truth, it is probable that they have been in part successful, and to some degree they have been misled and misleading. Whether they are purveyors of the truth or merely movement medicine men depends upon what the reader considers "research," "evidence," and in short just what appears to be the philosophical orientation of those considering their writings. I hope that the following reviews will clarify, rather than mislead, will illuminate rather than confuse.

KEPHART

Newell C. Kephart is presently director of the Glen Haven Achievement Center in Colorado. A clinical psychologist formerly at Purdue University in Indiana, he has a long history of interest in children with learning disabilities. With Strauss he co-authored *Psychopathology of the Brain-Injured Child* (Vol. II) and he wrote several books with other co-authors, as well as *The Slow Learner in the Classroom*. However, unlike Strauss who advocated a rather multi-sensory approach to the remediation of the problems of the hyperactive brain-injured child, Kephart has seemingly focused most of his attention upon the motor clumsiness often seen in this type of children. His theorizing is thus based primarily upon the assumption that movement is the basis of the intellect: thus the remedial methodologies he espouses are usually movement tasks of various kinds. Furthermore, he suggests that reading, writing, and arithmetic involve many perceptual-motor skills. Thus, a clumsy child evidences what he believes are basic learning deficiencies that are likely to be reflected in academic deficiencies. Thus, while most authorities would suggest treating children with reading problems by exposing them to practice in sight reading, Kephart would argue for remediating basic motor generalizations upon which he believes the reading act is based.

Most important, according to Kephart, is achieving what he termed a perceptual-motor "match" in which the child is effectively integrating input (perceptual events) with his movements. A lack of congruence in these two aspects manifests itself in the "spillover" of excess motor behaviors seen in hyperactive youngsters.

To accomplish the building of a solid motor base to perceptual and to higher intellectual processes Kephart cautions against the teaching of specific splinter skills; rather, he advocates concentrating upon at least four categories of activities that he terms "motor generalizations." These include:

Posture and Balance. Great emphasis is placed on the importance of balance in the belief that a child who cannot orient his body well to the "only constant in the universe" (gravity) by balancing well cannot be expected to make accurate perceptual judgments because of the unstable base from which spatial judgments are made (i.e., his body).

Further, emphasizing the importance of balance, Kephart states in his 1966 text that since balance is controlled by the cerebellum, a child's balance problem will tend to "short-circuit" thoughts descending through the cerebellum from the cortex.

Locomotion. Locomotor activity aids the child to learn better about the dynamics of his relationships to objects, he hypothesizes. Thus, a child with a clumsy gait pattern may be spending too much time watching his feet, thereby not effectively organizing the world around him and thus evidencing perceptual handicaps of various kinds.

Contact. Deficits in manipulative skills preclude the child's becoming aware of objects, shapes, and textures. Furthermore, as a child becomes aware of near space via manipulative activity, he extrapolates this visual-motor "data" to distant space. This suggests that manipulative ineptitude will also be reflected in problems as the child attempts to organize events some distance away.

Receipt and Propulsion. This fourth generalization is derived from the child's experiences when throwing and catching balls. It is through this type of activity that a child learns about velocities, sizes, and distances in distant space.

Besides the four "motor generalizations," Kephart also mentions in his film series other "generalizations" including body image and laterality. According to Kephart, the body image is a rather all-encompassing group of perceptions formed as the child moves his body in various ways and in various media, and the "laterality generalization" involves the child's ability to coordinate one side of his body with the other and to discriminate perceptually between one side and the other. A deficiency in this second area, Kephart asserts, will result in problems involving directionality in space reflected in letter reversal (strephosymbolia) and in the incorrect placement of letters in words. Laterality, then, is related to directionality as the child must project his body image and its left-right dimensions to space when forming left-right judgments. Stemming from this hypothesis is the suggestion that body-image training will correct problems of letter reversal when reading and printing.

Further, Kephart suggests that it is imperative that these motor generalizations be well established, for they provide the basis from which the child organizes his world perceptually, which, in turn, makes possible sound intellectual functioning. Conversely, a deficiency in motor coordination is thus likely to produce a child who is perceptually disorganized and therefore intellectually incapable.

Kephart's training methods parallel what he terms the "stages of learning development." Enumerated, these include:

1. *The practical stage:* during which the infant manipulates without accurately perceiving the nature of the tasks or the objects he contacts. Important during this phase is the ability to balance, to move various parts of the body in combination with others or separately. During this phase the child does not always evidence an awareness of what is part of him and what is separate from him. Simple balance activities, as well as arm-leg coordination work, are important here, Kephart states.

2. *The subjective stage:* during which the child combines motor and perceptual information. The generalizations of contact and locomotion are important to develop during this phase; the activities suggested, including walking balance beams, manipulative tasks of a variety of kinds, and practice in locomotor activity are important in this stage.

3. *The objective stage:* during which the child begins to associate perceptual data with the concepts. He learns to project beyond his immediate sensory experience into time and space he cannot perceive in an immediate way.

4. *Training activities:* numerous training activities are suggested in Kephart's many publications and nineteen hours of films. Chalk board training similar to that advocated by Getman forms a part of the methodology, as do various kinds of gross motor training activities including balance training, and a "game" called "angels-in-the-snow," in which a child lies on his back and slides his arms and legs separately or in various combinations up and down, to the sides and overhead, while

keeping them in contact with the mat, to heighten an awareness of their location in space.

Training in ocular control and in rhythmic activities form important parts of the procedures Kephart advocates. The former are intended to aid in visual tracking, which Kephart feels is important to a number of perceptual, visual, and academic processes; the latter (rhythmic activities) are intended to aid a child to form concepts of sequencing and timing important in activities such as reading, speaking, and writing. Form boards and various activities to heighten an awareness of the shapes of objects are also important in the total training program he advocates.[8]

Kephart's ideas may be examined indirectly via general theoretical and research evidence or by reviewing research dealing directly with effects of his program on reading and other perceptual-motor attributes. Some research findings, for example, suggested that reversal problems contribute to poor reading on the part of only from 2 to 4 percent of all children with reading deficits. Further, the work of Olin Smith resulted in the identification of five unrelated visual-perceptual attributes, whereas the studies of Fleishman and others pointed to the specificity of motor performance. Thus, the suggestion that motor learning influences perceptual processes is at best imprecise and at worst misleading. In addition, data collected in our laboratory and in a study by Ayres indicates that measures of directionality in children with perceptual-motor deficits are not related to their ability to identify correctly their left and right body parts.

Kephart also suggests that training in visual tracking will positively influence academic success, and in his 1960 text, he advanced methods for evaluation of ocular coordination. (The child is asked to watch a thumbtack fixed to the eraser of a pencil moved by the tester. The failure of the child's eyes to move as smoothly as "ice on a glass of water" is supposedly evidence of an ocular problem.) Again, however, such statements differ from the findings of research conducted over a period of almost 140 years that point out quite clearly that as a child reads his eyes move in rapid starts and stops at a rate too rapid for conscious control (3–8 times per second); and thus problems in fusion or hyperopia, and not binocular tracking, are likely to be found in groups of poor readers.[9]

---

[8] The "Purdue Perceptual-Motor Survey" is a test that has been published by Kephart and his colleagues through which various attributes may be assessed by teachers in a format involving a four-step checklist.

[9] Five discrete eye movements are made as a child follows a line of print with his eyes: among them are micro-movements resembling finite accommodation, rapid throwing movements of the eye across the page at the rate of about

Several researchers have utilized Kephart's techniques in experimental studies to determine their effects on reading. Generally, the results have been negative. LaPray and Ross experimented with two groups of first-graders low in reading, one of which was subjected to visual training and large muscle activities, while the other was exposed to practice in reading. The former group improved on perceptual-motor tasks, while the latter improved more in reading. Roach and Brown similarly found no significant differences in oral reading on the part of groups exposed to Kephart's techniques. Haring and Stables, on the other hand, reported that various perceptual and motor attributes were improved in a Kephart-type program, but no reading measure was obtained in this investigation.

In a 1969 investigation Fisher produced findings that suggest that Kephart's assumptions may be not entirely valid. He found that a program of activities advocated by Kephart for children with learning deficiencies, with two children to a single instructor, elicited no significant changes in academic achievement, perceptual-motor functioning or intellectual ability. (See also, Chapter 7.)

In summary, most of the available data fail to support the contention that, in groups of normal children and in children with reading problems, significant gains in reading competency will be achieved by participation in the techniques outlined by Kephart.

There are facets of the Kephart program that may have value, however. Rutherford studied the influence of Kephart-type activities on scores obtained from kindergarten children in the Metropolitan Readiness test. He found that while the boys had gained significantly, the girls had not. Kephart's rather carefully designed methods of motor training of neurologically impaired youngsters should prove of value when attempting to improve *motor functions*. Brown found that improvement does result from the attributes in Kephart's program that are specifically trained for. Additionally, Kephart's suggestion that motor activities during the preschool years may prove to be good preparation for later learning has not been adequately researched, and thus his hypothesis should not be summarily dismissed without further investigation.

GETMAN

In 1952, Dr. Getman published a monograph titled *How to Develop Your Child's Intelligence*. This publication contained theoretical assumptions with activities to improve classroom learning for the child entering school for the first time. The practices outlined were composed

---

3-8 per second, and micro-scanning movements as the eye encounters a difficult to decipher word configuration.

primarily of motor activities coupled with visual training. This text was followed in 1963 by a workbook of activities titled *The Physiology of Readiness*. This publication contained six sections, three of which contain developmental activities primarily involving movement, while the other three contain tasks that are perceptual-visual in nature.

Like Kephart, Getman proposes that movement is the basis of intellectual development. He states at one point that "this [the development of general movement patterns for action] is a primary process and lays the foundation for all performance and for all learning" and "movement *is* learning; learning *requires* movement". Continuing, he asserts that "foundational to every intellectual activity of the human being is the skill of motor control and coordination." Movement and the efficiency of muscle use are prerequisites to all knowledge and intellectual performance. He says, "Thoughts which do not get into muscles never fully possess the mind!"

Getman, however, also emphasizes the importance of vision. His term "vision" is a rather global concept, at various times seemingly all-encompassing ocular and perceptual, as well as intellectual, processes and attributes. Memory, for a variety of events is equated with vision, for Getman states that "visualization is an ability to ignore time and space . . . visual patterns are substitutes for action, speech, and time." Later he remarks, "Visual-perceptual organization is the ultimate process in the development of the total child."

Claiming that 85 to 90 percent of a child's learning is acquired through visual processes, Getman hypothesizes that deficiencies in some component of the visual mechanisms will lead to learning difficulties. Thus, he outlines practices to lead a child through several levels of visual-perceptual development, including:

> *General Movement Patterns.* Involving primarily locomotor activities and movements of the hands and eyes in concert.
>
> *Special Movement Patterns of Action.* The use of the body and body parts to control and to manipulate things in the world—the combination of hand and eyes in various tasks.
>
> *The Development of Eye Movement Patterns.* The learning of eye movement skills necessary for the quick and efficient visual exploration of the world. Development of these skills will leave the hands free to become "tools," i.e., to learn writing skills, etc.
>
> *Communication Patterns to Replace Action.* Learning to use visual and movement experiences to communicate with others.
>
> *The Development of Visualization Patterns.* Learning visual discriminations, recognitions of numbers and words, and the like. The calling up of visual images constitutes another component of this step.

The Development of Visual-Perceptual Organizations. The ultimate process in the development of the child's intellect, involving the ability to interchange movement for interpretation, understanding, and concept formation.

Getman suggests that each of these six steps, although interwoven with the others, is a stage through which a normal child must pass as he enters school and begins to learn and to read. The motor, visual-motor, and visual activities contained in his texts purport to enhance these various stages of development and thus enable a child to learn better when in the classroom.

He further emphasizes perceptual and visual skills necessary when reading. Although stating that "reading is more than seeing words," he also suggests that ocular training involving visual tracking exercises, as well as tasks intended to improve near-point fusion and accommodation, should aid a child to read better as he enters school. Getman writes that "it is now known that most children, age six, have not adequately acquired the neuromuscular controls necessary for advanced learning tasks . . . eye movement skills, the physiological maturities of the visual mechanisms and the integrations of vision, hearing and speech necessary for ultimate success in the reading load, are not yet available to most first grade children." He further contends that if children are introduced to reading too early in life, it may indeed impair their visual-perceptual mechanisms. He undergirds this claim by pointing to evidence collected by D. B. Harmon and at the University of Chicago Hospital, showing that, although only 2.4 percent of all children are born with visual difficulties, this increases from 20 percent at age five to 40 percent at age eight.[10] The stress of near-point reading in school causes this increase in ocular problems, Getman suggests.

Getman also writes that inadequate movement patterns involving skeletal muscles influence a variety of other attributes in children. At one point he states that "better control of muscles anywhere has an effect on speech" and at another point he contends that "dental problems and communicable illnesses (as well as visual problems) are more prevalent in children who lack full freedom of movements . . ."

A comprehensive evaluation of Getman's theory and practices is made difficult because of the manner in which he blurs distinctions between ocular-visual, visual-perceptual, and cognitive attributes. For example, he states that "reading is more than seeing words," while also stating that "vision is intelligence," and "vision is the dominant factor in

---

[10] D. B. Harmon is an "educationalist" who conducted the study of 160,-000 children in Austin, Texas, published in *Medical Women's Journal* in 1942.

human development." Further difficulties arise when interpreting the available research on this topic as one attempts to separate faulty eye movements when reading from eye movements during faulty reading. At the same time, the degree to which a given measure of ocular malfunction detracts from the ability to read well is not clearly outlined.

There is, however, a considerable amount of evidence from previous research that has clarified relationships between ocular function, motor attributes, visual training, and classroom learning (including reading). Eye movement studies, stemming from the pioneer work of Johannes Muller in 1826, have rather exactly demonstrated just what movements the eyes make as we read. The more contemporary investigations of Eames, Taylor, and Tinker explored, with a great degree of sophistication, relationships between visual function and academic proficiency.

In general, the available evidence does not support the generalizations made by Getman concerning the close, positive, causal relationship between movement, ocular function, and academic success. Good reading, for example, appears greatly dependent on higher mental processes. In every study carried out in which the intelligence of poor and proficient readers is compared, I.Q. differences are apparent. Reading is accomplished with both the eyes and the brain, with the latter probably contributing more than the former to the understanding and interpretation of the printed page.

The close correlation advanced by Getman as existing between ocular function and reading is also not supported by most of the available research evidence. Dingman found that eye movement scores were relatively independent of reading comprehension scores in a factor analysis published in 1958, as did Gruber in 1962. Although it is true that as a child matures he reads more efficiently by engaging in a fewer number of fixations per 100 words, if he is trained to fixate less, it is likely that he must then fixate longer each time his eyes come to rest on a word. Thus, his overall reading speed may not improve. Tinker suggested that improvement of span functions with some training apparatus is no greater than with well-motivated practice in reading itself!

Getman's contention that visual problems are brought on by excessive stress of early exposure to reading is also questionable on consulting the available evidence. The research suggests that the reverse may be true. Fewer ocular problems are found in groups of poor readers of college age than are found in groups of younger children with reading problems. The available evidence thus suggests that exposure to the printed page may train the eyes to engage in better near-point fusion as the child matures.

Difficulty in tracking is not usually found to be related to poor reading. More important is efficient fixation, for the child cannot see anything until the eyes are fixed. The manner in which the child fixates and the ratio of fixations to regressions he evidences when scanning is a highly individualized characteristic, which to a large degree appears to be inherited and remains relatively constant during maturation. Attempting to train eyes to function in a manner at odds with these individual characteristics is not likely to be successful, for the eye fixates, as has been pointed out, at a rate too rapid to be placed under the conscious control of the learner. As Taylor states, "Eye movements are neither the cause nor the effect of good or poor reading. The eyes do not dictate to the mind what it should understand nor does the mind dictate to the eyes where they should look."

Three research studies explored the manner in which Getman's methods may contribute to various parameters of academic performance. One of these is a mimeographed paper mailed with one of Getman's workbooks. Halgren, following a ten-week program with thirty-one control and thirty-one experimental subjects, found that the I.Q.s of the latter had improved seven points, and they had also improved on the average of 2.1 years in reading speed and 2.8 years in reading comprehension. When describing the methods used, however, the writer made it clear that these improvements were gradually modified when individual children's behavior indicated that a change in methods was called for, thus suggesting that the techniques may be effective only in the hands of a clinician well trained in their use. Halgren also failed to treat his data with anything approaching adequate statistical procedures. No distribution scores accompanied the averages he listed, and thus no test can be made of the statistical significance of the changes he reports. Honzik found that the I.Q.'s of 69 percent of the children she studied over a period of years changed fifteen points or more due to some combination of experience and/or maturation, whereas the I.Q.'s of one third of the children she investigated changed by twenty or more points. A change of seven points, then, in I.Q. even if occurring only over a ten-month period as reported by Halgren, may have been due to factors other than visual-motor training. Lyons and Lyons also reported the influence of visual training on three subjects. Improvement was reported in scores of tests evaluating verbal meaning, reasoning, perception, and the SRA Primary Mental Abilities Test.

The research available that is supportive of Getman's procedures is thus sparce indeed, whereas studies containing evidence that groups of children with academic deficiencies may have problems other than those involving eye function are numerous. It is apparent that application of a program of visual training such as that suggested by Getman to large *undefined* populations of children with mild to moderate educational difficulties is less than sound. Additional evidence is needed before a definitive statement can be made concerning the influence of visual training on *ocular* functioning, and the influence of ocular training on academic achievement has received only infrequent and cursory attention.

It is probable that some children are failing to learn because of ocular problems. The usual school evaluation of eye function contains only a test of distance acuity (the Snellen), whereas the ocular problem most frequent in poor readers is near-point fusion. With additional research, therefore, some of the techniques and premises advanced by Getman may prove valid. Even at a later date, however, remedial visual training of this nature should be accompanied by comprehensive pre- and posttests of the ocular capacities of children. An overreaction to the program and techniques that Getman suggests, without additional evidence of their worth, however, could prove wasteful of the time of some of the children engaged in such training, as well as of the school personnel administering it.

BARSCH

Like Kephart, Barsch's early interest in the educational properties of movement arose because of his work with neurologically impaired children. A clinician, similar in background to Kephart, his more recent writings have moved his theorizing toward a total method in education, which he contrasts to the more traditional "intellectual" and "pyschiatric" strategies.

Barsch's theory dwells within a colorful language he has developed that he terms his "movigenic" vocabulary. Containing such terms as "cognitive space," "terranaut" (the human infant moving in space), "milieu time" (the time periods of human development), "physiologic time" (the rate of performance of various physiological systems), and the like, his writings are viewed by some as profound and erudite, while others might term them trite and pretentious.

His methodologies themselves, the "movigenic curriculum," rest upon eleven basic propositions that he has derived from the works of others, as well as from his own clinical observations and experiences. These dimensions include:

1. *Muscular Strength:* The ability to maintain adequate muscular tonus, power, and endurance to meet daily demands, is deemed important.
A number of exercises are given to improve bodily strength in the trunk as well as in the extremities.

2. *Dynamic Balance:* The ability to activate antigravity muscles in proper ways is a second dimension to Barsch's theorizing. Walking

boards and movement around a dark room are some of the approaches recommended to enhance this dimension of perceptual-motor functioning.

3. *Spatial Awareness:* Eight categories of activities are suggested to heighten a child's awareness of his spatial "surround." These include those designed to enhance a child's ability to rotate in space (left-right, etc.); labeling directions in space (up-down, etc.); visualization of space without sight (blindfold identification of objects, etc.); rolling in space; and bodily transport in space (walking, running, jumping, etc.).

4. *Body Awareness:* Various games such as "Simon says" are recommended to heighten a child's conscious awareness of his body, its parts, and its potential movement capacities.

5. *Visual Dynamics:* Rather comprehensive use of the visual apparatus to scan, fixate, and otherwise deal with stimuli near to and distant from the observer. A variety of tracking and accommodation exercises are recommended, together with activities that appear to be more cognitive than visual, such as asking a child to remember a series of objects previously seen and to recall their colors and other characteristics.

6. *Auditory Dynamics:* The capacity of the organism to receive, process, and send auditory stimuli. Moreover, it includes the process of attaching relationships to the "world of sound." Thus, a variety of auditory training techniques are advocated, similar to those seen in language enrichment programs advocated by others.

7. *Tactual Dynamics:* Information derived from active and passive touching of objects in the environment. The identification of shapes via non-visual manual inspection are included within this phase of his training program.

8. *Bilaterality:* Barsch describes laterality as the "interweaving" of two sides of the body, similar to the meaning attached to the term by Kephart. Two-handed drawing tasks, the imitation of bi-lateral movement of a teacher and simalar tasks constitute the training regimen attached to this dimension.

9. *Rhythm:* Similar to the previous concepts, the definition of rhythm is rather global in nature and includes the harmony and grace of movement appropriate to a variety of situations. Barsch proceeds to outline a number of activities using metronomes, tom-toms, clapping, tapping, and similar movements in a program which also includes walking, singing, running, and speaking.

10. *Flexibility:* The modification and shifting of movement patterns to meet situational demands defines this dimension. Exercises to improve muscular ability with other situations in which a child must make decisions concerning appropriate responses might aid the development of this dimension of the child's personality, but Barsch does not detail a program within this realm.

11. *Motor Planning:* The planning of a movement prior to its execution is construed as evidence that a child is able to engage in effective "motor planning." Ayres also discusses this same dimension, which involves both cognitive as well as perceptual-motor abilities.

Barsch presents a global picture of cognitive, perceptual, and motor tasks to which children might be exposed, and, although his language, goals, and evaluative techniques are at times vague, as is sometimes true of clinicians, he has apparently engaged in a rather difficult task of summarizing the nature of the totality of functioning. He seems intent upon being an innovator in situations in which discoveries by others have preceded him. For example, his techniques of auditory training are superficial as compared with predecessors such as McGinnis, Barry, Myklebust, and those with similar orientation.

The techniques he outlines for movement experiences have the advantage of being comprehensive rather than restrictive in nature and encompass the pairing of movement with thought, touch, sight, and verbal behaviors. Barsch's orientation remains one which suggests that movement experiences enhance a wide variety of perceptual and cognitive abilities. The weakness of his theoretical speculations lies in his use of obscure terms to denote behavioral phenomena that have already been given generally agreed upon labels; the strengths of his writings include a rather broad spectrum of human abilities to consider when working in a clinical setting, as well as a rich variety of movement experiences with which one may confront children.

Neurological Organization

DELACATO

The Delacato method has been much maligned by the medical profession and others, although receiving praise in some of the popular press. Essentially, his theory is based on a view of neural function that suggests that specific "layers" of the brain mediate discrete motor functions. Moreover, Delacato believes that training in specific locomotor tasks positively influences various brain centers (the midbrain, pons, medulla, cortex), which, in turn, affect other perceptual and cognitive functions that are advanced as being the exclusive purview of these centers.

The cornerstone of Delacato's theory is that "ontogeny recapitulates phylogeny," in other words, that human development from birth through infancy to adulthood parallels the evolution of the race from invertebrates to vertebrates to mammals and finally to primates. As an outcome of this premise, he suggests that unless infants and children do not evidence the expected stages of normal development, they will not evidence effective communication, receptive competencies, or motor abilities, including mobility.

The early adequate training sequences thus suggested by Delacato for the basic motor development include a stereotyped reflex-like patterning that he terms the "tonic-neck reflex." He assumes that reflex movements not only form the basis for human development, but also the head-neck reflex similar to the back-and-forth movements of the fish, man's early evolutionary ancestor.

Later stages of training include crawling movements, those in which the stomach remains in contact with the floor and progress is made by moving the same-side leg and knee ahead at the same time (homolateral crawling), and those termed "cross-patterned creeping," in which the stomach is off the floor and the regular crawling gait is molded and guided and the opposite hand-knee move forward at the same time.

To check the progress of a child rather extensive check lists are employed (termed the Doman-Delacato Neurological Profile). Clinicians using this profile can diagnose developmental problems in children evidencing a variety of difficulties, and they may check on the progress of children exposed to these types of training techniques.[11]

Critical to the theory is the establishment of hemispheric dominance to improve speech and other sensory functions by training in unilateral hand use and monocular activities and the removal of music and other tonal experiences from the child. Tonality, it is hypothesized, is mediated by the nondominant brain hemisphere, and thus listening to music conflicts with the achievement of dominance by the half of the brain that controls speech functions.

This theory and the resultant practices again can be examined on theoretical or practical grounds. Most neurologists, as well as the bulk of research emanating from the laboratories of those studying brain function during the past seventy-five years, fail to support Delacato's theory. Complex locomotor functions have been found to be controlled by a number of portions of the brain rather than by a single part, as he suggests.

Delacato's theory dwells at some length on the importance of establishing so-called cerebral dominance by encouraging similar arm-hand-eye-ear use. It is, therefore, important to briefly outline pertinent

[11] Keeping abreast of the training methods is a rather difficult undertaking, particularly if one is not in residence at the Philadelphia Center. They have at various times included re-breathing one's own expired air, sight-reading training, as well as ocular training of various kinds. Patterning has been first described as essential in the program, but in more recent writings one of the physicians at the Philadelphia Center suggests that it is omitted in children who crawl and creep well. (E. W. Thomas, *Brain Injured Children*, Springfield, Ill.: Charles S. Thomas, Inc., 1969.)

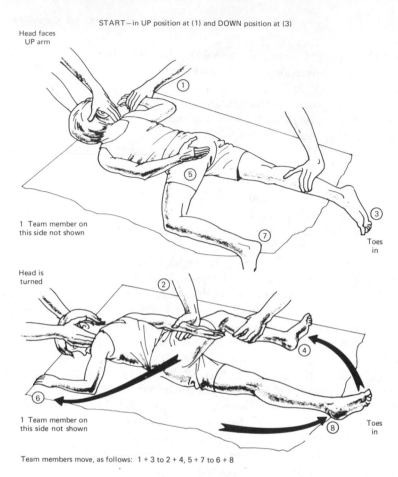

FIGURE 3.1a

findings relative to hand-eye preferences in humans and in lower animals.

Hand-eye preference in humans has been described by Gesell and Ames as a type of functional asymmetry stemming from the tonic-neck reflex in infancy. They further explain that it is not a simple trait, but an ever-changing focal symptom of the human action system. Studies of the development of hand preference in infants support the hypothesis that it is a somewhat inconsistent and irregular trait, not stabilizing until about the age of ten.

It is probable that both hand and eye preference are inherited. Merrell found that 77 percent of the offspring of right-eyed parents tend also to prefer their right eye, while only about 46 percent of all children of parents both of whom are left-eyed tend to be right-eyed. Hecaen

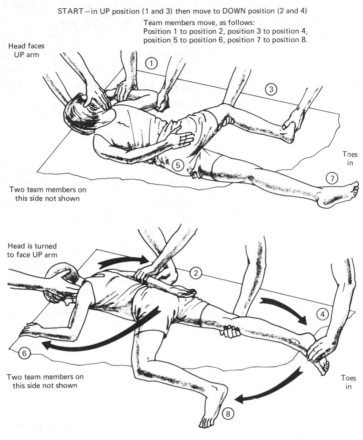

START—in UP position (1 and 3) then move to DOWN position (2 and 4)

Team members move, as follows:
Position 1 to position 2, position 3 to position 4,
position 5 to position 6, position 7 to position 8.

Head faces
UP arm

Two team members on
this side not shown

Toes
in

Head is turned
to face UP arm

Two team members on
this side not shown

Toes
in

Perform _____ Sessions per day for _____ Minutes per session.

Reprinted from P. I. Meyers and C. C. Hammill, *Methods for Learning Disorders.*
John Wiley & Sons, Inc.

FIGURE 3.1b

(a) Cross-pattern—three man team. (b) Homolateral
pattern—five-man team.

also reports research that supports the proposition that hand preference
is inherited. Ramaley suggests that left-hand preference is a Mendelian
recessive trait and most of the evidence supports this contention.

There is a closer association among hand and foot preferences than
between hand and eye preferences. It is more likely that an individual
will be either left-footed and left-handed or right-footed and right-
handed than that he will evidence similar eye-hand preference. One-
hand use, thus, is seen in a variety of man's early animal ancestors and

therefore would not seem to be evidence of the height of neurological development in modern man as stated in Delacato's theory.

Current neurological literature suggests that one must go further than merely suggesting that one or the other hemisphere is dominant in the control of behavior in an individual. Rather, in order to be correct, one must state just what functions seem to be controlled by which hemisphere. A child who writes words poorly may have a lesion in his left hemisphere, which is generally in control of ideo-motor behaviors; while at the same time he may be able to draw pictures of forms and objects well, indicating a freedom of problems in his right hemisphere, which controls certain spatio-motor behaviors. Certain speech functions are mediated in the left hemisphere, while others are apparently under the control of the right side of the cortex.

Child development literature suggests extensively that children do not develop in accordance with the theory advanced by Delacato: several visual processes mature rather early, prior to the emergence of accurate motor attributes. Ocular processes involved in visual tracking have been found to mature by two years, and perfect gait patterns are not usually seen in children until their fourth year.

Delacato seems also to ignore social-emotional factors in the application of the method. He suggests that a child be made to crawl, despite his protestations to the contrary, by the forceful presence of a physical education teacher. In contrast, Temple Fay, to whom Delacato attributes his basic rationale, wrote that the child is "not merely a motor expressive robot to be tuned up or activated as we choose . . . motivation is in the hoped for and possible purpose that this returning function might serve . . . the true art of therapy lies not in what is done, but how the patient may receive it."

The techniques inherent in this program have also been questioned on practical grounds. The American Academy of Pediatrics found the methods fatiguing and disruptive of normal family life. Rabinovitch stated that the creeping and crawling techniques are regressive and may bring about emotional disturbance. Whitsell similarly offered a medical opinion, in a comprehensive evaluation of the method, that concludes with the suggestion that the Delacato techniques "have not been validated and are not consistent with accepted neurological principles." Furthermore, Whitsell states that "this method may best be regarded as experimental, potentially harmful, and not to be recommended for general use at this time."

A number of studies that might be termed descriptive rather than scientific have been published by the Philadelphia Institute for the Achievement of Human Potential containing data supporting the worth of the programs. Several reviewers, however, have found the methodologies to be something less than sound. Albert Harris and others have concurred with Glass's term "of dubious value."

Other more scientific tests of the veracity of the methods conducted outside the Institute established for their propagation have produced findings that are not generally supportive. Anderson tried cross-patterning and creeping on kindergarten children and intermediate grade students and found that children within these groups with lower I.Q.'s and with lower initial reading ability did not improve. A carefully controlled study by Robbins similarly found that the Delacato program produced no significant differences in a variety of measures, including the ability to make left-right judgments. Yarborough, using a stereoscopic method intending to lateralize children similar to the Delacato techniques, found no evidence of significant benefit in reading. McCormick, Poetker, and Schnobrich found no significant changes when employing Delacato procedures with first-grade children. These latter investigators disregard a nonsignificant analysis of variance, however, and point out a gain in mean scores to bolster a positive hypothesis. Additional research by Stephens, Cunningham, and Stiger, conducted in 1967, also fails to support the validity of the Delacato methods and theory.

Within recent years the Delacato method has been the target of additional criticism. Seven major medical and health organizations [12] have stated that patterning was "without merit" and chided its supporters for claiming cures without documentation. The opinions of medical and research personnel thus seem almost unanimous in their condemnation of the methods and theories advanced by this method of reading remediation.

Freeman summarized objections to the Delacato method in an article in the 1967 *Journal of the American Medical Association.* In essence, he contends that the practices are contraindicated because they make the parents therapists, and that they may indeed treat the brain itself, assertions that may serve to heighten parental anxiety concerning the child and the reading practices they may have employed. Furthermore, Freeman suggests that many of the theoretical assumptions are untenable, including the hypothesis that rigid patterning will somehow produce successful results manifested in peripheral functions because of the suggestion that the brain itself is being trained.[13]

[12] American Academy for Cerebral Palsy, the American Academy of Physical Medicine, the American Congress of Rehabilitation Medicine, the Canadian Association for Children with Learning Disabilities, the Canadian Association for Retarded Children, the Canadian Rehabilitation Council for the Disabled, and the National Association for Retarded Children.

[13] The reader should consult Freeman's article for a detailed account of his important observations.

The criticisms, however, have not gone unnoticed by the individuals advancing these unusual methodologies. The Institute's formal reply to the "Official Statement" rendered by the medical and health organizations previously referred to, as well as to the criticisms by Freeman, Robins, and Glass, appeared in a series of articles published in *Human Potential* in 1968.

In general, its text refutes one-by-one the points made against the Doman-Delacato method by the American Academy of Cerebral Palsy. The publication suggests that theory building is necessary to advancements in scientific endeavor, and thus, their efforts in formulating theories should not be unduly censured. Furthermore, they assert that while they do not claim that their method is productive in the remediation of *all* children, their methods *have* been demonstrated to be superior to traditional methods of dealing with the problems of brain-damaged youngsters. And finally, they insist that their own research does support the validity of the methodologies and that they are constantly searching for improvements and refinements in the techniques they employ.

Several positive outcomes may have arisen from the publicity given to this method, however. Some severely retarded and brain-damaged children have perhaps made some improvement in mobility owing to the kinesthetic and social stimulation they have received at the hands of adherents of the techniques. Perhaps with improved and more comprehensive types of sensory stimulation of this nature (tactual, auditory, as well as visual and kinesthetic), more improvement may be achieved with children and adults formerly assigned to the back wards of mental hospitals for the profoundly retarded and physically handicapped.

Research carried out by individuals like Dr. Clara Lee Edgar in California and Dr. Ruth Webb in Iowa (referred to in greater detail in Chapter 7) are examples of the work that, in superficial ways, is related to the assumptions and techniques advocated by Delacato.

Summary

Upon examining the practices advocated by the last four theorists reviewed, one may detect more similarities than differences. Both Getman and Kephart advocate a body-image exercise termed "angels-in-the-snow" (in a back-lying position, the child sweeps his arms and legs along the floor in various patterned movements). Although three of them advocate the use of the trampoline, they do so for different reasons. The activities to heighten directionality and writing skills proposed by Kephart, Barsch, and Getman are similar. Both Getman and Delacato emphasize the importance of encouraging the child to creep prior to walking. Further, three stress the importance of the acquisition of specific developmental tasks in proper sequence. Both Getman and Kephart propose that there is a motor base to the intellect. However, they take slightly different paths to explain silent thought. Getman suggests the importance of level three "eye movement patterns," which replace the need for constant exploratory movement, and Kephart suggests that even silent thought is accompanied by postural tensions, thus attempting to provide additional evidence that movement is the basis of intelligence.

Both Getman and Delacato suggest that motor training will improve a wide variety of human attributes: Getman includes speech, hearing, sound teeth, and communicable diseases in his list; Delacato is even more expansive including language disorders, specific reading disability, mental deficiency, ocular problems (strabismus, myopia, etc.), athetosis, Parkinson's disease, aphasia, delayed speech, stuttering, and poor spelling.

Delacato and Kephart both evidence a lack of sophistication concerning current knowledge about neural functioning. Kephart's suggestion that the cerebellum mediates balance, for example, is only about one sixth correct, for several other structures, such as the motor cortex and the occipital areas, take part in this complex behavior. His suggestion that the functioning of a single neuron will result in a large number of neurons "misfiring" (thus interrupting innumerable other functions) is unsupported by any evidence of which I am aware. It is probable that the average normal child has several thousand damaged neurons within his nervous system that are not reflected in any discernible sensory, motor, or intellectual problems. Kephart's labeling of the Kraus-Weber tests as an evaluation of posture and balance (when in truth it is a test of trunk strength and flexibility) leads one also to question his knowledge of motor assessment techniques.

Delacato's writings are similarly poorly grounded in neurology. He suggests at one point, for example, athetosis and Parkinson's disease both have their etiology within the midbrain. His discourses on neural function omit references to important cerebral structures, such as the corpus callosum, the limbic system, the thalamus, and the reticular formation.

Getman oversimplifies the reading process and the manner in which reading problems are caused (i.e., ocular deficiencies). Delacato is also guilty of rather global speculation. He oversimplifies the nature of a number of human attributes including spelling and writing ("both are varying degrees of the same problem") and myopia ("caused by the stress of fatigue of using the eyes at near-point, and reading deficiencies, the result of the lack of complete development of binaural abilities").

All four men seem to pass over some of the subtleties within the developmental processes in children. A number of child development experts, including those who are quoted in some of the theoreticians' texts, would take issue with the neat veridical (Kephart's term) manner in which they suggest infants and children develop. Visual abilities seem to precede motor abilities, and motor abilities fragment into locomotor and manual abilities at a rather early age, unlike the simple picture presented with the theories discussed. Indeed, Kephart's statements seem to reflect incorrect notions of how infants develop because he suggests in one of his films that infantile reflexes "flow from the head to the feet." He continues by stating that these reflexes also evolve into voluntary movement patterns, whereas, in truth, many infantile reflexes terminate prior to the emergence of accurate voluntary movements.

Delacato's concept of infant reflexes also appears to be somewhat distorted. He insists that training in what he terms the tonic-neck reflex is an important first step in the recapitulation of motor experiences. He then proceeds to demonstrate this reflex elicited in a face-down position wherein the arm is flexed toward the side to which the head is turned. However, the tonic-neck reflex is elicited in infants in a face-up position! It is difficult to determine, additionally, why this particular reflex was selected by Delacato for training purposes out of at least thirty from which he might have selected.

Barsch's speculations and orientation are similar to those of Kephart and Getman. However, he expresses himself in language that is more colorful and presents a more global picture of functioning than both of them. Unlike Getman's and Kephart's writings, however, little research has been inspired by his theoretical schema, while at the same time his statements seem to have been based upon clinical speculations and observations, rather than data related directly to the methodologies he espouses.

Despite the theoretical and practical inadequacies of these four writers, I believe that the theories and practices have had some positive effects on educational theory and practice. For example, some of the children exposed to some of their programs may have indeed improved, although not perhaps for the reasons contained within the theories. A neurologically impaired child who is looked at, reacted to, and talked to while he is crawling on the floor for several hours a day may begin responding better because of the social stimulation he is receiving, if the physical punishment inherent in the method is not too oppressive. Children who are kept at visual, visual-motor, or motor tasks for increased periods of time may improve in a variety of learning situations because of a prolongation of their attention spans. The literature on transfer suggests that some components of one task are probably aiding the acquisition of a second task while other components are probably impeding it. The change in the second task (i.e., classroom learning) is probably a result of both the negative and positive qualities of the initial task. Thus, while motor activity itself may not enhance learning in a direct way through movement, there are ancillary components of the motor task (i.e., doing *something* for increased periods of time) that may positively transfer to academic learning. An increasing number of studies suggest that attention span influences learning, and attention span may be improved by various techniques available to the classroom teacher (see Chapter 10).

Similarly, the practices contained in the program of Getman and Kephart indeed should improve the *motor abilities* of children to whom they are applied; motor abilities are important in school as they permit the child to guide his hand accurately when writing and to catch a ball when playing. It is believed that increased attention has been paid to the child with minimal neurological problems found in the normal school populations because of the notoriety accorded these theories. These children, constituting from 5 to 20 percent of most "normal" populations of children, are at a disadvantage. This is obvious to them and to their parents and teachers when they attempt to compete in various ways with their more capable peers.

Further research on these practices contained within these theories should certainly be stressed. In particular, the following problems should be studied:

1. Efforts should be made to delineate the manner in which individual differences in children may be affected by the practices advocated by Getman, Delacato, and Kephart. For example, it is possible that the child from the higher-income home may benefit more from increased exposure to motor activities than the child from the lower socioeconomic areas. The latter may be improved more educationally by exposure to verbal-linguistic tasks and exercises than balance-beam walking. The effects of motor activities leading to learning populations of boys should also be studied. The intellectual functions of children with various levels of arousal, using divergent learning strategies and from different I.Q. groups, should be studied as a function of various kinds of perceptual-motor training.

2. Increased emphasis should be placed on research that attempts to delineate just what components of whose program changes what kinds of children in what ways. If an entire program of the activities advocated by Kephart is applied to a group of children, there is no way, when finished, to determine which of the activities changed what attributes. Thus attempts should be made to isolate the effects of single variables within a given motor task on academic performances of various kinds. For example, it has been suggested that failure of a child to fixate on the printed page may stem from emotional stress. Thus, balance-beam walking or trampoline jumping ("motor stresses") while watching a point on a wall may habituate the child to fixate under stress, an

improvement that may, in turn, positively transfer to the classroom in which he is asked on fixate on a page under academic stresses imposed by his teacher.

3. Attempts should be made to incorporate a number of sensory stimulations into programs for the profoundly retarted and physically handicapped. Tactual, auditory, visual, and kinesthetic stimulation combined in the correct tasks to the correct degree may aid the severely retarded to react more appropriately to the objects, situations, and other stimuli.

BIBLIOGRAPHY

ALLEN, K. E.; HENKE, L. B.; HARRIS, F. R.; BAER, D. M.; and REYNOLDS, N. J. "Control of Hyperactivity by Social Reinforcement of Attending Behavior." *Journal of Educational Psychology* 58 (1967): 231–37.

ANDERSON, RUSSELL W. "Effects of Neuro-Psychological Techniques on Reading Achievement. Ph.D. dissertation: Colorado State College, 1965.

AUSUBEL, DAVID P. "A Critique of Piaget's Theory of the Ontogenesis of Motor Behavior." *Journal of General Psychology* 109 (1966): 119–22.

AYERS, JEAN A. "Patterns of Perceptual-Motor Dysfunction in Children: A Factor Analytic Study." *Perceptual and Motor Skills*, Monograph Supplement 1–V20, 1965.

BARSCH, RAY H. *Achieving Perceptual-Motor Efficiency, A Space-Oriented Approach to Learning*. Seattle: Special Child Publications, 1965.

BAYLEY, NANCY. "Behavioral Correlates of Mental Growth—Birth to Thirty-Six Years." *American Psychologist* 5 (1968): 1–17.

BELMONT, LILLIAN, and BIRCH, H. "Lateral Dominance and Right-Left Awareness in Normal Children." *Child Development* 34 (1963): 257–70.

BLOOM, BENJAMIN S. *Stability and Change in Human Characteristics*. New York: John Wiley & Sons, 1964.

BRENNER, M. W., and GILLMAN, S. "Verbal Intelligence, Visuomotor Ability and School Achievement." *British Journal of Educational Psychology* 35 (1965): 75.

BROWN, ROSCOE. "The Effects of a Perceptual-Motor Education Program on Perceptual-Motor Skills and Reading Readiness." Presented at the Research Section meeting, American Association for Health, Physical Education and Recreation (AAHPER), St. Louis, Mo., April 1, 1968.

CRATTY, BRYANT J. *Active Learning*. Englewood Cliffs, N.J.: Prentice-Hall, Inc., 1971.

———. *Some Educational Implications of Movements*. "Is Movement the Basis of Intellect?" Seattle, Wash.: Special Child Publications, Inc. 1970.

CRATTY, BRYANT J., and MARTIN, M. M. *Perceptual-Motor Efficiency in Children*. Philadelphia, Pa.: Lea and Febiger, 1969.

DELACATO, CARL H. *Treatment and Prevention of Reading Problems*. Springfield, Ill.: Charles C Thomas, Publisher, 1959.

———. *The Diagnosis and Treatment of Speech and Reading Problems.* Springfield, Ill.: Charles C Thomas, Publisher, 1963.

———. *Neurological Organization and Reading,* Springfield, Ill.: Charles C Thomas, Publisher, 1966.

DINGMAN, H. F. "Factor Analysis of Eye Movements with Reading Scores." *Perceptual and Motor Skills* 8 (1958): 37–38.

EAMES, T. H. "The Ocular Conditions of 350 Poor Readers." *Journal of Educational Research* 32 (1938): 10–16.

———. "Comparison of Eye Conditions Among 100 Reading Failures, 500 Ophthalmic Patients and 150 Unselected Children." *American Journal of Ophthamology* 31 (1948): 713–17.

———. "Visual and Related Factors in Reading." *Review of Educational Research* 19 (1949): 107–17.

FAY, TEMPLE. "Basic Considerations Regarding Neuromuscular and Reflex Therapy." *Spastics Quarterly* Vol. 3, No. 3, September 1954. Published by the British Council for the Welfare of Spastics, 13 Suffolk St., Haymarket, London, S.W.1.

FISHER, KIRK L. "Effects of a Structured Program of Perceptual-Motor Training on the Development and School Achievement of Educable Mentally Retarded Children." U. S. Department of Education, Bureau of Research Monograph, Pennsylvania State University, 1969.

FLEISHMAN, EDWIN A.; THOMAS, PAUL; and MUNROE, PHILIP. "The Dimensions of Physical Fitness: A Factor Analysis of Speed Flexibility, Balance, and Coordination Tests." Technical Report No. 3. The Office of Naval Research, Department of Psychology, Yale University, September, 1961.

FROSTIG, MARIANNE. *Movement Education: Theory and Practice.* Chicago: Follet Educational Corporation, 1970.

GESELL, ARNOLD, and AMES, L. B. "The Development of Handedness." *Journal of General Psychology* 70 (1947): 155–75.

GETMAN, G. N. *How to Develop Your Child's Intelligence.* A Research Publication, Luverne, Minn.: G. N. Getman, 1952.

GETMAN, G. N., and KANE, ELMER R. *The Physiology of Readiness, An Action Program for the Development of Perception for Children.* Minneapolis: P.A.S.S., Inc., 1964.

GILBERT, LUTHER C. "Genetic Study of Eye Movements in Reading." *Elementary School Journal* 59 (1963): 328–35.

GLASS, GENE V. "A Critique of Experiments on the Role of Neurological Organization in Reading Performance." Monograph, Center for Instructional Research and Curriculum Evaluation, University of Illinois, 1967.

GORELICK, MOLLY C. "The Effectiveness of Visual Form Training in a Prereading Program." *Journal of Educational Research* 58 (1965): 315–18.

GRUBER, E. "Reading Ability: Binocular Coordination and the Ophthalmograph." *Archives of Ophthamology* 67 (1962): 280–88.

HALGREN, M. R. "Opus in See Sharp." *Education* 81 (1961): 369–71.

HARING, NORRIS, G., and STABLES, JEANNE MARIE. "The Effect of Gross Motor Development on Visual Perception and Hand-Eye Coordination." *Journal of the American Physical Therapy Association* 46 (1966): 129–35.

HARRIS, ALBERT J. "Diagnosis and Remedial Instruction in Reading." In *Innovation and Change in Reading,* 67th Yearbook, Part II of the National Society for the Study of Education, Chicago: University of Chicago Press, 1968, 159–99.

HARRIS, N. L., and HARRIS, CHESTER W. "A Factor Analytic Study of Flexibility." Presented at the Research Section meeting of the National Convention of the American Association for Health, Physical Education, and Recreation, St. Louis, Mo., March 30, 1963.

HECAEN, H., and AJURIAGUERRA, J. *Left-Handedness; Manual Superiority and Cerebral Dominance.* New York: Grune & Stratton, Inc., 1964.

HILDRETH, G. "Manual Dominance in Nursery School Children." *Journal of General Psychology* 72 (1948): 29–45.

HONZIK, M. P.; MACFARLANE, J. W.; and ALLEN, L. "The Stability of Mental Test Performance Between Two and Eighteen Years." *Journal of Experimental Education* 17 (1948): 309–24.

HUMPHREY, J. H., and SULLIVAN, D. D. *Teaching Slow Learners Through Active Games.* Springfield, Ill.: Charles C Thomas, Publisher, 1970.

ILLINGWORTH, R. S. *The Development of the Infant and Young Child, Normal and Abnormal.* London: E. & S Livingstone, Ltd., 1967.

INSTITUTE FOR THE ACHIEVEMENT OF HUMAN POTENTIAL. "A Position Paper." Philadelphia, Penna.

JOHNSON, DALE I., and SPIELGERGER, C. D. "The Effects of Relaxation Training and the Passage of Time on Measures of State and Trait Anxiety." *Journal of Chemical Psychology* 24 (1968): 20–23.

KEOGH, B., and SMITH, C. E. "Changes in Copying Ability of Young Children." *Perceptual and Motor Skills* 26 (1967): 773–74.

KEPHART, NEWELL, C. *The Slow Learner in the Classroom.* Columbus, Ohio: Charles E. Merrill Publishing Co., 1960.

———. "Perceptual-Motor Aspects of Learning Disabilities." *Exceptional Children* 31 (1964): 201-206.

KINSBOURNE, M., and WARRINGTON, E. K. "Development Factors in Reading and Writing Backwardness." *British Journal of Psychology* 54 (1963): 145–46.

KIPHARD, E. J. "Unser Kind ist ungeschickt" (*Our Child is Awkward*). Reinhardt, Munchen (Germany), 1966.

KIPHARD, E. J., and HUPPERTZ, H. "Erziehung durch Bewegung" (*Education Through Movement*). Durr. Bed Godesberg (Germany), 1968.

KRIPPNER, STANLEY. "Relationship Between Improvement and Ten Selected Variables." *Perceptual and Motor Skills* 19 (1964): 15–20.

LAPRAY, MARGARET, and ROSS, RAMON. "Auditory and Visual Perceptual Training." In *Vistas in Reading.* Edited by J. Allen Figurel. International Reading Association *Conference Proceedings* 9 (1966): 53–32.

LEBOULCH, JEAN. *L'Education Par Le Mouvement* (*Education Through Movement*). Paris: Les Editions Socials Francaises.

LEDERER, J. "The Reading Clinic in Department of Optometry." University of New South Wales. *Australian Journal of Optometry* 43 (1960): 1–6.

LYLE, J. G., and GOZEN, J. "Visual Recognition, Developmental Lag, and

Strephosymbolia in Reading Retardation." *Journal of Abnormal Psychology* 73 (1968): 25–29.

LYNN, RICHARD. "Individual Differences in Introversion-Extraversion, Reactive Inhibition and Reading Attainment." *Journal of Educational Psychology* 51 (1969): 318–21.

LYONS, C. V., and LYONS, EMILY B. "The Power of Visual Training, As Measured in Factors of Intelligence." *Journal of the American Optometric Association* 35 (1954): 255–62.

MACCOBY, ELEANOR, E.; DOWLEY, EDITH M.; and HAGEN, JOHN W. "Activity Level and Intellectual Functioning in Normal Pre-School Children." *Child Development* 36 (1965): 761–69.

McCORMICK, C.; POETKER, BETTY; SCHNOBRICH, JANICE N.; and FOOTLICK, S. WILLARD. *Improvement in Reading Achievement Through Perceptual-Motor Training.* Chicago: Reading Research Foundation, Inc., July 1967 (mimeographed).

MERRELL, D. J. "Dominance of Eye and Hand." *Human Biology* 29 (1957): 314–28.

MEYERS, P. I., and HAMMILL, D. D. *Methods for Learning Disorders.* New York: John Wiley & Sons, Inc., 1969.

MOSSTON, MUSKA. *Teaching Physical Education.* Columbus, Ohio: Charles E. Merrill Publishing Co., 1966.

NEVILLE, DONALD. "A Comparison of the WISC Patterns of Male Retarded and Non-Retarded Readers." *Journal of Educational Research* 54 (1961): 195–97.

OFFICIAL STATEMENT. "The Doman-Delacato Treatment of Neurologically Handicapped Children." *Archives of Physical Medicine and Rehabilitation* 49 (1968): 183–88.

ORTON, S. T., "Visual Functions in Strephosymbolia." *Archives of Ophthamology* 30 (1943): 707–17.

PARK, G. E., and BURRI, C. J. "The Effect of Eye Abnormalities on Reading Difficulties." *Journal of Educational Psychology* 45 (1943): 420–30.

PEIPER, ALBRECHT. *Cerebral Function in Infancy and Childhood.* New York: Consultants Bureau, 1963.

RABINOVITCH, R. "Neuropsychiatric Factors." Paper read at the annual meeting of the International Reading Association, Detroit, 1965.

RAMALEY, F. "Inheritance of Left-Handedness." *American Naturalist* 47 (1913): 730–38.

ROACH, EUGENE G. "Evaluation of an Experimental Program of Perceptual-Motor Training with Slow Readers." In *Vistas in Reading.* Edited by J. Allen Figurel. International Reading Association, *Conference Proceedings,* 1966, pp. 11, 446–50.

ROBBINS, M. P., and GLASS, G. V. "The Doman-Delacata Rationale: A Critical Analysis." In *Educational Therapy,* Edited by J. Hellmuth. Seattle Special Child Publications, Vol. 2, 1968.

ROSS, DOROTHEA. "Incidental Learning of Number Concepts in Small Group Games." *American Journal of Mental Deficiency* (1970), pp. 718–25.

RUTHERFORD, WILLIAM L. "Perceptual-Motor Training and Readiness." In

Reading and Inquiry. Edited by J. Allen Figurel. International Reading Association, *Conference Proceedings* 10 (1965): 194–96.

SCHAFFER, AMY, and GOULD, J. D. "Eye Movement Patterns as a Function of Previous Tachistoscope Practice." *Perceptual and Motor Skills* 19 (1964): 701–702.

SINCLAIR, C. "Ear Dominance in Pre-School Children." *Perceptual and Motor Skills* 26 (1968): 510.

SMITH, OLIN W. "Developmental Studies of Spatial Judgments by Children and Adults." *Perceptual and Motor Skills* 22, Monograph Supplement I (1966): 3–73.

STEPHENS, W. E.; CUNNINGHAM, E. S.; and STIGLER, B. J. "Reading Readiness and Eye-Hand Preference Patterns in First Grade Children." *Exceptional Children* 33 (1967): 481–88.

STRAUSS, A. A., and LEHTINEN, L. E. *Psychopathology and the Education of the Brain Injured Child, Vol. I: Fundamentals and Treatment.* New York: Grune & Stratton, Inc., 1947.

STRAUSS, A. A., and KEPHART, N. C. *Psychopathology and Education of the Brain Injured Child, Vol. II: Progress in Theory and Clinic.* New York: Grune & Stratton, Inc., 1955.

TAYLOR, STANFORD E. "Eye Movements in Reading: Facts and Fallacies." *American Educational Research Journal* 2 (1965): 187–201.

THOMAS, E. W. *Brain-Injured Children.* Springfield, Ill.: Charles C Thomas, Publisher, 1969.

TINKER, M. A. "The Study of Eye Movements in Reading." *Psychological Bulletin* 43 (1946): 93–120.

———. "Perceptual and Oculomotor Efficiency in Reading Materials in Vertical and Horizontal Arrangements." *American Journal of Psychology* 68 (1955): 444–49.

———. "Recent Studies of Eye Movement in Reading." *Psychological Bulletin* 55 (1958): 215–31.

WAGNER, GUY W. "The Maturation of Certain Visual Functions and the Relationship Between These Functions and Success in Reading and Arithmetic." *Psychological Monograph* 48 (1937): 108–46.

WHILDEN, P. O. "Comparison of Two Methods of Teaching Beginning Basketball." *Research Quarterly* 27 (1956): 235–42.

WHITSELL, LEON, J. "Delacato's 'Neurological Organization': A Medical Appraisal." *California School Health* 3 (1967): 1–13.

WISE, JAMES H. "Performance of Neurologically Impaired Children Copying Geometric Stick Designs with Sticks." *Perceptual and Motor Skills* 26 (1968): 763–72.

YARBOROUGH, BETTY H. *A Study of the Effectiveness of the Leavell Language-Development Service in Improving the Silent Reading Ability and Other Language Skills of Persons with Mixed Dominance.* Ph.D. dissertation: University of Virginia, 1964.

ZUSNE, L., and MICHELS, K. "Nonrepresentational Shapes and Eye Movements." *Perceptual and Motor Skills* 18 (1964): 11–12.

4

Developmental Perspectives

The Emergence and Integration of Intellectual and Motor Behaviors in Infancy and Childhood

In a previous chapter, intelligence and physical activity were discussed within a historical context. This chapter considers the developmental dimensions of these same components of human ability. Several problem areas will be dealt with: (1) the interrelationships between mental and motor abilities within a developmental continuum from birth through adolescence; (2) the manner in which early indices of psychomotor capacity reflect selected indices of adolescent and adult intelligence collected later in life; (3) an exploration of selected theories incorporating concepts dealing with perceptual-motor functioning and intellectual capacities.

Developmental Theories Combining Sensory—Motor and Intellectual Functioning

PIAGET

Jean Piaget began to theorize about the unfolding of the human intellect in the 1920s, at a time when other scholars were engaged in the construction of tests that often lacked a valid rationale. The translation of his works into English in the 1950s not only stimulated additional thought about intelligence, but also encouraged some psychologists to begin to construct tests reflecting his penetrating insight. Others have begun to apply relatively valid scientific measures to some of the behaviors and schema that Piaget described. Piaget envisions the development of human intelligence as reflecting simultaneous processes of *adaptation* to the environment, which involves equilibrium between the organism and his world through various mental operations. He considers adaptation to be composed of two complementary processes termed *assimilation* and *accommodation*. The process of *accommodation* suggests that inherently humans tend to modify their behavior (or physiological functioning) in response to demands placed upon them by their environment. *Assimilation* refers to the tendency to incorporate elements of the environment directly into the organism in various ways. Thus, in a physiological sense, the processes of digestion involve the transformation of food into a form the body can use, while in the psychological sense, confrontation with various objects and/or events result in their assimilation into a behavioral framework. In addition to the basic concept of adaptation, Piaget also gives prominence to the concept of *organization*. This latter term means the tendency for all species to systematize their behaviors into coherent and meaningful systems of increasing complexity as maturation occurs.[1] Piaget does not place great emphasis upon individual differences in behavior, and this may be one of the several weaknesses of his theories. At the same time, the early data he collected was primarily composed of exceedingly detailed observations obtained from his own three daughters, Lucienne, Laurent, and Jacqueline.

Piaget was one of the first to view the infant as something other than a passive receptor of stimuli only able to react. This Swiss child development expert correctly predicted the emergence of research findings that suggest that infants engage in a great deal of perceptual and cognitive activity shortly after birth, although in rudimentary forms. Piaget, suggesting that the infant is equipped only with a "behavioral armament" of reflexes at birth, believes that learned behaviors or *schema* begin to appear shortly thereafter. For example, while the infant is born with the reflex tendency to suck any object touching his mouth, the tendency to bring the hand to the mouth is not inherent, but constitutes one of the earliest schema to appear in the behavioral repertoire. Similarly, Piaget conceives of the early appearance of a "looking schema,"

---

[1] Although, according to Piaget, these systems may be either psychological or biological in nature, in his main writings about the unfolding of intelligence, the primary emphasis is upon psychological systems.

which he characterizes as active searching rather than passive scanning of the environment.

Piaget correctly formulated a rather complex and flexible theory to explain the development of human intelligence. Perceiving the step-by-step unfolding of *schema* and the reasonably orderly appearance of psychological structures depending upon acquired behaviors, he emphasizes frequently that (a) it is difficult to attach exact chronological ages to the appearance of specific behaviors, and (b) more than one schema within a single behavioral sequence will be observable in the same infant at the same time in his life. He emphasizes the suggestion that the appearance of various schema *must* necessarily appear in the order he describes; indeed it appears impossible for a more sophisticated schema to become evident prior to the emergence of more primitive ones.

Piaget divides intellectual development into four major parts: the sensory-motor period from birth to two years of age; the pre-operational period from two to seven years of age; the concrete operational period from seven to eleven years of age; and the period characterized by the emergence of formal operations from eleven years of age and older. This discussion will concentrate upon the behavioral characteristics of the sensory-motor period, as well as behaviors at the termination of this period signaling the transition from basic sensory-motor operations to higher level intellectual schema.

The Sensory-Motor Period.   According to Piaget, the infant, equipped with reflexes of survival value, begins to exhibit complex behaviors within a limited range even during the first days of life. For example, sucking reactions are seen in relation to numerous objects, in addition to those affording nourishment. Although viewed as a naturalist by some critics, Piaget emphasizes that the infant's reactions are molded by both the possession of innate behavioral tendencies and by environmental events even during this initial part of the sensory-motor period. Thus, Piaget contends that the infant's behavior during this early stage is marked by the tendency to generalize, expand, and exhibit a limited range of behaviors.

The second sub-stage in the sensory-motor period, emerging about one month after birth, is characterized by simple habits centered around the infant's own body. Piaget has termed these "primary circular reactions" triggered by chance behaviors on the part of the infant, which in turn, lead to advantageous or interesting results that encourage their re-performance. Thumb sucking would fall into this behavioral category. Even in this early period, the schema may tend to become more organized and complex as, for example, when the thumb is brought to the mouth with increasing accuracy and apparently under volitional control.

This second sub-period within the sensory-motor stage is also marked by what have been called "primitive anticipations." That is, the infant may evidence sucking reactions when arranged in various ways in his mother's arms, thus suggesting that the kinesthetic information received from bodily sensations becomes associated with the feeding act. This is further evidence of the process of accommodation.

Piaget also describes motivational processes, and he suggests the importance of a curiosity in the formation of an increasingly complex behavioral schema. A second important motivational concept alluded to is the tendency to imitate. Thus, in these early months, the infant may reflect in similar, though primitive representations, the mother's smile and simple gestures and vocalizations by adults.

Piaget suggests that even during these early stages, rudimentary appearances of cognition are evidenced in primitive reactions reflecting concepts about reality. Basic dimensions of the infant's conception of reality, space, time, and causality emerge, concepts that will be expanded during later months and years. For example, Piaget finds that the infant's initial understandings of objects and their movement and function in the world are based upon obvious coherences: that sounds emerge from a mouth; that objects, when noisy, can be looked at if the head is turned, etc. These early concepts, however, are rather primitively manifested, and it is not until later that the infant evidences one of the important transitions between sensory-motor and conceptual development—termed "object permanence" by Piaget.

Next to appear in the sensory-motor period, between the fourth and tenth month, are what Piaget calls "secondary circular reactions." These more complex schema are behaviors that are in reaction to and in relationship with various *external* events in the environment, as contrasted to the more primitive circular reactions that primarily involve behavior in relation to the child's own body. Toys hanging over the crib are struck, first accidentally, and then purposively. Moreover, during this period the child begins to evidence behaviors that Piaget terms "signifiers," that is, the child may not choose to exhibit the total response needed to contact an object but may only exhibit a partial movement of the arm or leg that could carry out the complete act. Piaget suggests that this is one of the first signs that the infant is becoming ready to replace thought for action, for in later periods of the child's life these "signifiers" may disappear entirely, being replaced by "mental manipulations of objects."

In this third stage in the sensory-motor period, the child continues to elaborate on his concepts of reality and of the permanency of objects. For example, during the previous stage, an infant would not search for a vanished object that was desired, while in this stage the infant will visually anticipate future positions of objects. At the same time, he can obtain an object through a reaching response even though the response might be interrupted and momentarily terminated or the object may be partially hidden from view.

Stage four is marked by the coordination and elaboration of secondary schema and occurs just prior to the first birthday in normal children. Imitation becomes more precise. During this stage, object permanence concepts become more sophisticated with the infant not only searching for objects that are temporarily out of view, but initiating new and unique motor behaviors when instigating and carrying out these searchings. This is evidence that the infant is able to perceive mental images of objects and can attach permanence to objects without the necessity to contact them in direct ways or to see them.

The sensory-motor period's fifth stage, from twelve to eighteen months, is marked by the appearance of what Piaget names "tertiary circular reactions." New and unique motor behaviors are initiated in response to the infant's apparent desire for novelty and the need to satisfy his curiosity. Behavior thus becomes less conservative and is aided by the emerging ability to explore the world via locomotion. The infant may attempt old behaviors in relation to new objects. When he finds that old behaviors do not work or that the new objects also possess new qualities, he will then be willing to modify and expand response tendencies. The infant during this stage can not only imitate in increasingly complex ways, but will discover new means of attaining goals and of changing and manipulating his environment.

The sixth stage (eighteen months to two years) is characterized as the time in which the beginnings of thought are increasingly manifested. These beginning conceptualizations show themselves in several ways:

1. The infant may engage in imitative behaviors without the presence of a model. That is, he will apparently begin to react in response to mental representations of the vocalizations and/or imagined movements of others, rather than to react only to their direct presence, as was necessary during the previous stages.

2. The concept of the permance of objects is fully elaborated during this stage. Objects may be found when they have undergone invisible displacements within the child's space field. (For example, when a ball rolls under a table, the child will search for it in a logical position to which he will deduce it has rolled, rather than simply search for it at the point at which it disappeared, as in the past.)

Thus, this final transitory stage stands between the sensory-motor period and the second period, which is marked by the emergence of increasingly complex symbolism and thought. By this time, the child is apparently able to formulate mental constructs representing either behaviors or images of objects not physically present.

Movement and Cognition.   Most interesting is the suggestion by Piaget that direct and observable movement may undergo several developmental transitions in relation to activity:

1. Initially, what might be termed "accidental movement responses" trigger voluntary activity.

2. During the next stage, movements may be incomplete or total. An incomplete act, "signifier," may merely suggest a total act such as a partial arm movement toward an object hanging over the crib, whereas the complete movement would involve actually striking the object. The "signifier" may be a partial response to *do* something or a partial "avoidance" response.

3. Still later, the child may begin to evidence what might be termed "covert rehearsal" of motor acts as conceptual or imaginary movements replace overt ones. Thus, during these latter stages, a child will become able to engage in mental trial-and-error behavior without direct obvious action.

Summary and Implications.   It appears that Piaget's constructed theory about mental development (with the sensory-motor behaviors merely a means through which mental operations initially manifest themselves) emphasizes the *quality* of the movements the child manifests and the undergirding reasons and thought accompanying the motor activity rather than the motor activity itself. At the same time, he suggests that a wide range of behaviors have their genesis in direct and overt action; his emphasis throughout is on what the child *does,* and in this realm he suggests that the initial meanings and usages of language stem from director motor acts as the child interacts with his environment.

It seems that more effective programs of movement education than are presently available could be constructed if those imitating them would refer more to Piaget's concepts and sub-theories.

As with any theory that attempts to deal with so large an expanse of information and complex behaviors, Piaget's concepts may not be applicable to all children in all situations. For example, it is difficult to explain the obvious adequate intellectual functioning of some physically handicapped children by reference to the importance Piaget attaches to the sensory-motor phase of development. It is apparent that the development of the intellect among certain atypical children may occur along diverse routes, dissimilar to those taken by Piaget's three daughters.

With reference to Piaget's concepts, workers with the severely physically handicapped are beginning to construct scales with which to assess the mental functioning of these unfortunate children. They are starting attempts to evaluate the *quality* of a child's actions in tasks surrounding the concept of object-performance, to cite one example. In this manner, they are beginning to differentiate at rather early ages between groups of children with cerebral palsy, who may also evidence varying degrees of mental incompetence, from those who are similarly physically handicapped but who may exhibit adequate or above average mental functioning.

Piaget's writings contain many lessons for teachers of all subjects and those who work in several modalities including movement. He places great emphasis on the fact that children, especially young ones, learn best from concrete activities that are often best carried out with movement responses and in game situations. Educators who are sophisticated enough to interpret Piaget's ideas and translate them into educational strategies should develop programs that are highly effective.

Moreover, important implications for educators can be found in the emphasis upon motivational principles, which include the seeking of novelty and the searching for complexity on the part of children. Additionally, the apparent inherent search for equilibrium that is engaged in by children, and which Piaget views as a critical component in the educational process, gives credence to the concepts of Bruner and of Mosston: both suggest that the creation of some kind of intellectual stress within the day's lesson resulting in dissonance leads to the formation of more sophisticated and increasingly complex mental schema or structures when resolved.

A FOUR CHANNEL MODEL FOR THE STUDY OF HUMAN MATURATION

Another conceptual model has been proposed that also attempts to explain the emergence of various types of behaviors in the maturing infant, and at the same time contains axioms that allude to the interrelationships between various components of the child's personality. In essence it says that abilities within four primary sub-areas emerge, at least in crude form, during the early days of an infant's life. The performance of these abilities is primarily reflective of motor, verbal, perceptual, and intellectual functioning. Further, it is hypothesized that abilities within the four channels, or one or more of the channels themselves, may evidence varying degrees of what has been termed "blunting" or "stimulation" due to the presence of facilitating or retarding environmental or inherent variables.

Like Piaget, the model assumes that the emergence of various abilities may be due either to the triggering of inherent tendencies by physiological-neurological mechanisms, or to the presence of various environmental supports. Examples of apparently inherent tendencies are the appearance of the smile on the faces of children blind since birth and the adequate locomotor functioning of Indian infants after being confined to their mother's back during the early months of life. Evidence of the validity of the supposition that environmental conditions may mold abilities is the observation that reading requires exposure to the printed page, and in bike-riding, the bicycle must be present and available to the child.

This model emphasizes the importance of the central cognitive channel of abilities, pointing out that, if this particular channel is blunted, the proliferation of abilities is likely to terminate at late childhood, instead of continuing into the adolescent years. Moreover, it is also hypothesized that apparent overuse of abilities on one channel, such as motor activity, may tend to blunt the emergence of abilities within another channel or channels.

Two primary tenets are advanced to explain the complex interrelationships between abilities on the same channel, as well as the integration of abilities found on separate channels (i.e., the motor and intellectual "branches"). It is assumed that as a child matures, functional connections, or "bonds," are formed between various abilities. At the same time and slightly later in life, some functional bonds may appear to dissolve.

Some examples that may be cited for the formation of bonds between formerly unrelated abilities include the following:

1. As a child matures he begins to form bonds between the visual shape of objects and the kinesthetic (motor) impressions as he handles them, together with bonds to the verbal and cognitive channels as he begins to name the objects and to attach meaning to their existence.

2. Reading may be characterized as the formation of bonds between word shapes, visually perceived, and the verbal-cognitive symbol they represent.

3. Walking, in the infant, suggests that bonds are being formed between the visual impression of his moving feet and the alternating movement needed in this motor act.

Examples of the tendency to dissolve bonds later in life which may not continue to be functionally very useful, include the following:

1. As children gain in reading proficiency, they tend to exhibit less mouth and lip movements when reading; thus, the dissolution of bonds to the movement of the lips from the visual-impression of the word might be hypothesized.

2. As writing and walking proficiency are gained, the child need not visually inspect his hand at all times when writing and can walk

without a similar kind of bond formed between vision and movement. Adults can write their names with their eyes closed, while proficient athletes need not watch a moving ball at all times in order to intercept it.

Bonds also may be formed between two attributes to compose a complex functional "piece" of behavior and then later combined with a third or fourth. Two behaviors may be wedded during several periods of a child's life: for example, he may track a ball at about the sixth month of age while other abilities are "bonded in" later (such as locomotor activity and hand activities as the child becomes able to "play the outfield" and correctly intercept a ball hit by an opponent).

These functional ties (bonds) may also be placed within a second classification system. Some, those normally emerging in children, might be termed "natural bonds." The bonds between the motor qualities and the visual, perceptual, and cognitive qualities needed for a child to express himself in written language are examples of these. At the same time, a second type of bond might be classified as "synthetic in nature. These are bonds that educators might employ when aiding a child to circumvent some learning difficulty. Learning to spell by hopping into squares containing numbers pairs a motor ability (hopping) in an unusual (synthetic) way with the conceptual and perceptual abilities needed to spell or to recognize letters and word shapes.

Functional connections (bonds) between movement and intellectual functions are constantly being formed and dissolved throughout the lifetime of individuals. For example, initial learning of a motor skill usually requires an inordinate amount of verbal and cognitive rehearsal. After the skill is mastered, the bonds between the motor attributes on the verbal and/or cognitive channels become less distinct or may dissolve entirely.

For teachers this model has various implications, some of which are enumerated below:

1. To deal effectively with a given portion of the child's personality, one must be familiar with the type of emergent abilities that are typical at various ages.

2. Additionally, teachers should be aware of the various functional connections between the facet of behavior they are interested in modifying and other components of behavior within other channels.

3. When working with children with learning problems or other dysfunctions, one should be sensitive to perceptual, motor and/or language abilities that may not be emerging at proper times, and at the same time, bonds between attributes that may not be forming properly.

4. Furthermore, teachers might become aware of the manner in which

they might aid a child to dissolve bonds that no longer contribute to efficient functioning.

5. The various unusual learning strategies employing movement experiences, intended to enhance academic abilities including reading, mathematics, language, and the gaining of science concepts, might be viewed, within the framework offered by the model, as "synthetic bonds formed by the teacher to circumvent various kinds of blunting seen in groups of attributes on the part of children with learning difficulties.

This model, like that of Piaget, is a reasonably flexible though complex one. Unlike Piaget's, however, it does not deal with the "whys of emergent behaviors, it merely chronicles the appearance of various abilities.

Some of the tenets within this conceptual framework are similar to the ideas in the writings of Illingworth.

The book by Koronski, *Integrative Activity of the Brain*, contains concepts gained from a study of neuroanatomy that are also similar to those contained in the model described.

While further research is needed to verify some of the tenets outlined, factorial analyses by Clausen, Meyers, Dingman, and others have contributed to the formation of the basic concepts outlined. The subtle interactions between cognitive and motor behaviors might well be depicted on this model in the form of numerous bonds that are constantly in the processes of forming and dissolving as new motor tasks are discovered, thought about while initial practice is engaged in, and then automatized to the point where little attention need be given the task by the performer.

With reference to the model being considered, however, it may also be possible to describe in more exact terms individual differences in normal youngsters, as well as the manner in which various handicapped children may mature. For example, the concept of "blunted" attributes describes a child with some physical and/or mental handicap.

With Piaget's ideas, it is not easy to deal from a theoretical standpoint with the success of a child with cerebral palsy, or one born without arms and legs, in intellectual tests administered later in life.

Statistical Comparisons

A more operational approach might be taken in addition to the two theoretical perspectives in considering the relationships between emergent motor and intellectual abilities. This information stems from several longitudinal studies that contrasted selected measures of perceptual-motor ability and intellectual abilities collected in infancy and childhood with similar measures obtained from the same subjects in adolescence and adulthood.[2]

Despite the different conditions under which these studies were carried out, as well as the disparity of measures employed, the mental growth curves derived from each resemble each other to a marked degree. Particularly within the first two years, there seems to be an accelerated growth of mental capacity, with the curve of improvement flattening out by the ages of 11–15 years.

Bloom, who analyzed correlational data from Bayley and others, suggests that in terms of intelligence measured at age seventeen, at least 20 percent is developed by age one, about 50 percent by age four, about 80 percent by age eight, and 92 percent by age thirteen. These percentages are depicted in Figure 4.1.

The prediction of intelligence measures collected in late childhood and adolescence from single scores earlier in life is often a tenuous undertaking. As Maurer, Hofstaetter, and Cronbach pointed out, the tests used in the later years are heavily saturated with cognitive skills and verbal abilities, whereas the earlier ones often reflect psychomotor abilities. Thus, when single measures are compared, it is unlikely that significant correlations between intelligence test scores before the eighth year will be seen when compared with those later in life.

There are two logical and statistical strategies that may be employed, however, to heighten the relationships between early and later measures of intelligence. One is to suppress statistically components of the earlier scores reflecting psychomotor qualities and then to compare the remaining scores with those collected later. The correlations obtained have reached as high as .4 and .5 when scores reflecting cognitive abilities collected from two- and three-year-olds are contrasted with those scores also reflecting cognitive function from the same children at eleven and seventeen years of age. However, if point-to-point correlations are computed between scores collected at two and three and scores collected later without refining the measures to reflect similar intellectual qualities, the correlations have been found to be essentially non-existent.

[2] These include the Harvard Growth Study reported by Anderson in 1939; the University of Chicago Study by Freeman and Flory in 1937; the California Guidance Study by Honzik and her colleagues published in 1938; the Berkeley Growth Study reported by Bayley in 1949 and 1968; the Brush Foundation Study by Ebert and Simmons; and the study by the Fels Institute staff, *From Birth to Maturity* by Kagan and Moss, published in book form in 1962.

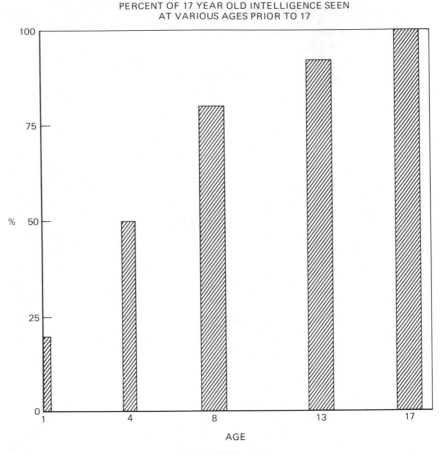

PERCENT OF 17 YEAR OLD INTELLIGENCE SEEN
AT VARIOUS AGES PRIOR TO 17

FIGURE 4.1

Percent of 17-year-old intelligence seen at various ages prior to 17.

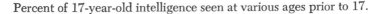

A second manner in which early indices of intellectual ability will be found to predict reasonably well scores collected later is in utilizing more than one score from each age grouping. Bayley essentially carried out this operation by combining the results of testings given to infants and children at ages six months, one year, one and one-half years, and two years, with results collected at seventeen and eighteen years of age, and again moderate correlations were obtained ranging up to .55.

Hofstaetter, who also analyzed Bayley's statistics in a 1954 study, using factor analytic techniques, found that three groupings of tests could be discerned. Up to the age of twenty months, for example, the main tests contributing to the evaluation of a child's intelligence were those that seemed to reflect what Hofstaetter termed "sensory-motor alertness," while from forty months upward, tests loaded with this factor contributed "practically nothing" to the variance of mental-age scores.

The second factor that seemed to emerge was important in tests purportedly contributed to by a quality that Hofstaetter names "persistence," or the tendency to act in accordance with an established set rather than being influenced by interfering situations and stimuli. This factor emerged at about the twentieth month and continued to be reasonably important until about the fifty or sixth year. Thus, this second factor implies a somewhat rigid type of behavior, while the first factor suggests a sensory-motor flexibility.

The final factor that emerged, as Figure 4.2, and continued to remain important until late childhood, was suggested by Hofstaetter as reflecting the ability to manipulate symbols and to engage in planning and in abstract behaviors. He suggests that this corresponds, to some degree, with Spearman's "G" (a general quality).

The emergence of these factors in the tests given by Bayley is seen in Figure 4.2.

In a more recent investigation, Bayley affords more insight into the qualities in infants that seem to predict, to at least a moderate degree, the quality of intelligence seen later in life. Extending her previous study until her subjects were thirty-six years of age, she found that most predictive of intelligence in her adult male subjects were early measures denoting the quality and duration of visual attention they evidenced. While in the scores she analyzed from females, Bayley found that early qualitative vocal behaviors were most predictive of later intellectual competency.

Other qualities emerging in a factor analysis of the scores collected monthly from the fifty-four subjects during the first fifteen months of their lives included: manual dexterities, object relations, social responsiveness, and visual following. None of these final four qualities evaluated in infancy seemed predictive of later adult intelligence.

It thus appears that only with careful analysis of the qualities underlying tests taken in infancy and adulthood, can one adequately predict, with even moderate degrees of accuracy, the nature of intelligence in adolescence and adulthood by inspecting measures collected earlier. Not until the age of eight, unless "purified," is it usual to find intelligence tests containing items similar to those found in adult measures of intellectual capacity. If earlier measures are used for comparative purposes, they must be carefully analyzed for the "intellectual content" their per-

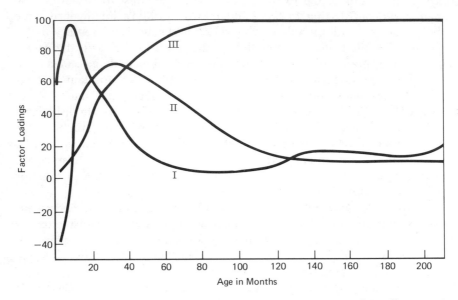

Reprinted from P. R. Hofstaetter, "The Changing Composition of Intelligence: A Study in T-Technique," *Journal of Genetic Psychology.*

FIGURE 4.2

formance reflects. Otherwise, they may be found, in a gross manner, to be evaluating qualities different from those tested in adulthood.

Summary

There are many subtle and complex interactions between motor and intellectual behaviors in infancy. For example, Piaget seems to point out that, while intelligence may only be evaluated by inspecting movement responses, it is the quality of these responses and the intent they reflect that are most important in the assessment of the unfolding intelligence. While trace responses seem to procede complete responses (during the first year of life, cognitive efforts are seemingly assessable through inspection of observable behavior) by the second year of life, infants begin to evidence the tendency to engage in a great amount of imagery, mental manipulation, and non-observable trial-and-error behaviors that are difficult for the observer to assess. Thus, Piaget seems to suggest that movement first phases in and then phases out of the child's intellectual life, unless, of course, the primary focus of the behavior remains to engage in some kind of complex motor skill.

The four-channel model also suggests the existence of numerous bonds between motor and intellectual behaviors forming near birth and then, at times, phasing out as the individual needs no longer to pay conscious attention to the increasingly familiar movements needed to carry out life's necessary functions. At the same time, this model accommodates to unusual teaching strategies (some of which are covered in other chapters) in which movement tasks are employed to enhance academic functions and language development.

Finally, the data suggests that only if similar measures are contrasted can one hope to predict scores in intelligence tests collected early in life, from those obtained later; or, if early measures purporting to evaluate the intellect are combined, again moderately significant correlations may be obtained. In general, it is usual to find that dissimilar measures of intelligence containing a preponderance of psychomotor items are given to infants and children, as compared to those measures that confront older children, adolescents, and adults. In the latter case, the majority of the sub-tests characteristically evaluate some kind of verbal-symbolic ability.

BIBLIOGRAPHY

ANDERSON, L. D. "The Predictive Value of Infant Tests in Relation to Intelligence At Five Years." *Child Development* 10 (1939): 203–12.

BAYLEY, N. "Consistency and Variability in the Growth of Intelligence from Birth to Eighteen Years." *Journal of Educational Psychology* 75 (1949): 165–96.

———. "On the Growth of Intelligence," *American Psychologist* 10 (1955): 805–18.

———. "Data on the Growth of Intelligence Between Sixteen and Tweny-One Years as Measured by the Wechsler Bellevue Scale." *Journal of General Psychology* 90 (1957): 3–15.

———. "Behavioral Correlates of Mental Growth—Birth to Thirty-Six Years." *American Psychologist* 23 (1968): 1–17.

BLOOM, BENJAMIN S. *Stability and Change in Human Characteristics*. New York: John Wiley & Sons, Inc., 1964.

CATTEL, P. "Constant Changes in the Stanford-Binet I.Q." *Journal of Educational Psychology* 22 (1931): 544–50.

CLAUSEN, JOHANNES. *Ability Structure and Subgroups in Mental Retardation*. Washington: Spartan Books, 1966.

CONNOLLY, K. J., ED. *Mechanisms of Motor Skill Development*. London: Academic Press, 1970.

CRATTY, BRYANT J. "Model for the Study of Human Maturation." In *Perceptual and Motor Development in Infants and Children*. New York: The Macmillan Company, 1970.

CRONBACK, L. J. *Essentials of Psychological Testing*. New York: Harper & Row, Publishers, 1960.

EBERT, E., and SIMMONS, K. "The Brush Foundation Study of Child Growth and Development, I: Psychometric Tests." *Monograph on Social Research and Child Development* 8 (1943): 1–113.

FREEMAN, F. N. and FLORY, C. D. "Growth in Intellectual Ability as Measured by Repeated Tests." *Monograph on Social Research and Child Development* 2 (1937).

HOFSTAETTER, P. R. "The Changing Composition of 'Intelligence': A Study in T-Technique." *Journal of Genetic Psychology* 85 (1954): 159–64.

HONZIK, M. P.; MACFARLANE, J. W.; and ALLEN, L. "The Stability of Mental Test Performance Between Two and Eighteen Years." *Journal of Experimental Education* 17 (1948): 309–24.

ILLINGWORTH, R. S. *The Development of the Infant and Young Child*, 3d ed. Edinburgh and London: E. & S. Livingstone, Ltd., 1967.

KAGAN, J., and Moss, H. A. *Birth to Maturity: A Study in Psychological Development*. New York: John Wiley & Sons, 1962.

KONORSKI, JERZY. *Integrative Activity of the Brain—An Interdisciplinary Approach*. Chicago: University of Chicago Press, 1967.

MAURER, K. M. *Intellectual Status at Maturity as a Criterion for Selecting Items in Pre-School Tests*. Minneapolis: University of Minnesota Press, 1946.

MEYERS, C. E., and DINGMAN, HARVEY F. "The Structure of Abilities at the Preschool Ages: Hypothesized Domains." *Psychological Bulletin* 57 (1960): 514–32.

PIAGET, JEAN. *The Language and Thought of the Child*. Translated by M. Gabain. London: Routledge & Kegan Paul Ltd., 1926.

———. *The Origins of Intelligence in Children*. Translated by M. Cook. New York: International Universities Press, Inc., 1952.

II

INDIVIDUAL DIFFERENCES

5

Intelligence and
The Superior Athlete

Introduction

For well over one hundred years, numerous articles have appeared
in many countries to explain the psychological dimensions of athletic
performance. While the early efforts in this general area were more
descriptive than scientific, more recent writings have been based
upon reasonably well-conducted studies. This type of research has
flourished particularly in countries whose athletic aspirations are associated with their political goals.[1]

Shortly after the Russian Revolution, for example, several research
laboratories were established in that country in which the study of
the psychology of physical activity was a central focus of these efforts.
A similar interest is seen not only in contemporary Soviet research
reports, but also in investigations in the Eastern European countries,
which are largely under the influence of Russia.

Throughout the world, however, various efforts have been made
to explain the psychological factors influencing superior athletic performance. Since the turn of the century in Germany, for example,

[1] Much of this literature has been reviewed in the text by Vanek and
Cratty, *Psychology of the Superior Athlete*, New York: The MacMillan Company, 1969, in Chapter 1, "A Brief History of Sports Psychology," pp. 7–38.

articles on the intellectual and personality dimensions of sports performance have appeared in various forms.

These scholarly efforts began to coalesce on an international
scale in the 1960s. Sports psychology, and particularly that emphasizing
superior athletic performance, was given added impetus in 1964 with the
founding of the International Society for Psychology in Sport, with the
first meeting chaired by Professor Ferruccio Antonelli, a Roman psychiatrist. At this writing, the International Society is composed of approximately thirty-five national societies and totals about fifteen hundred
members in most of the countries of the world.

Although the research topics of interest to these behavioral scientists
are numerous and include the broad spectrum of interests found in large
universities' departments of psychology, some of the research reports
have dealt with the manner in which measures of intelligence interact
with certain types of sports performance.[2] At the same time, the ideas
one is able to obtain from these studies and the inferences that the
findings point to are more suggestive than substantial. The studies are
often based upon clinical observations rather than "hard data," while the
data that have been collected have not always been accorded acceptable
statistical treatment.

The work, however, is often highly creative. The social scientists
in Eastern Europe, in particular, have displayed remarkable ingenuity
in the approaches they have taken. Their ideas are deserving of further
exploration, while some of their conclusions have formed helpful guidelines for individuals who consider themselves superior athletes, or for
tutors of advanced athletic performers.

In general, this work falls into several reasonably discrete classifications:

1. The relationships between I.Q. and the sports in which individuals
participate. Often, these data are found in studies that also contain
information concerning personality trait structures of athletes in specific
sports.

2. The manner in which tactical training in a sport reflects in improved
performance.

3. The manner in which general information extended to performers

[2] Papers concerning the social psychology of sports teams, the manner in
which clinical methods have aided superior athletes, the relationships of
various physiological measures to emotional state and athletic performance,
and basic topics in motor learning have appeared in the Society's proceedings.
A second International Congress was held in 1968 in Washington, D.C. A copy
of the proceedings may be obtained from the Athletic Institute, Chicago, Illinois; Gerald Kenyon, editor.

about the physiological, psychological, and social parameters of physical activity may elicit superior effort.

4. The ways in which specific intellectual components of various sports, when trained for, may influence subsequent performance. The studies exploring practice in serial memory as influential of slalom skiing are examples of investigations within this category.

5. The ways in which intellectual traits contribute to accurate self-assessment and "self-management" via relaxation training and similar techniques.

The research and speculations concerning the personality and intellectual traits possibly needed by athletes under varying degrees of stress and in selected sports form the beginnings of a fascinating area of applied psychology.[3] Moreover, the studies of the relationships between various perceptual traits and physiological measures indicative of arousal and readiness to perform not only constitute a helpful source of information about athletes themselves, but in a broader context contain helpful cues concerning the nature of functioning under the stresses of life, work, love, and war.

Perhaps with further research and the subsequent applications of the findings, coaches interested in eliciting superior athletic performance may not only be aided in their efforts, but may indeed begin truly to expand the intellectual horizons of the young men and women in their charge. With additional work, the terms "athletic intelligence," "sports sense," and similar phrases may begin to assume more exact meanings than may be attached to them now.

Intelligence in What Sportsmen?

Research emanating from Eastern Europe and the United States generally substantiates the manner in which social stratification in some ways influences an individual in selecting a sport in which to participate. It has been found, for example, that most superior athletes in Olympic competition in Eastern Europe possess at least average intelligence, and often their I.Q. scores are well above average. But a clear division exists between the intelligence quotient of sportsmen practicing activities to which they had been exposed in college and the intelligence test scores of men practicing sports usually not associated with a college.

Thus, it has been found that athletes in the team sports, such as

[3] America's first Ph.D. program in Sports Psychology is being instituted at UCLA at the time of this writing, combining efforts of staff members in the Departments of Psychology, Athletics, and Physical Education.

basketball, ice hockey, and the like, will score higher on standardized measures of I.Q. than others participating in activities requiring more force and power than team strategy (i.e., shot putting and boxing). This finding should not be misinterpreted, however, for what is apparent is that individuals who have had the opportunity to attend college (though perhaps the good luck of being a part of the culture which is more highly privileged), are those not only more likely to score high in the tests of I.Q. containing verbal-vocabulary sections that correspond to the qualities needed for entrance to, and are enhanced in, a college, but are the same people who have the opportunity to hone their team sports proficiencies in these same institutions.

In the United States, as in certain parts of Europe, the individual who may be less fortunate from a social and economic standpoint, is more likely to have to "fight his way up" and to extend his personal effort in individual sports, often those requiring frequent and painful bodily contact.

Case studies of athletes in various European countries indicate that those with more academic backgrounds and with higher scores on I.Q. tests, as would be expected, are better equipped to engage in self-assessments of the psychological and physiological data collected about themselves than are their less well-educated teammates. Those less well-endowed intellectually seem also to have a more difficult time engaging in self-administered relaxation and activation training prior to competition. After competition, understanding the reasons for success or failure seems similarly more difficult for those athletes posting lower I.Q. scores.

Further study on this topic might well result in the formulation of a typology of sports activities with respect to the quality and kind of intellectual traits necessary for their successful execution. This type of classification has already been formulated with reference to differences in the general psychological stresses apparently imposed (and hypothetically required of competitors) in various athletic events. Furthermore, recent factorial studies of personality trait scores of athletes are beginning to confirm the validity of the typology of "sports stresses" that has appeared.[4]

---

[4] This classification of sports with regard to the psychological stresses they impose and, by inference which is reflective of the traits required by successful competitors, includes sports requiring strategy and interaction with others, those involving imminent physical harm, those in which all-out effort dissipates stress, those in which stress builds up as competition progresses (i.e., archery and shooting), and those in which there is a strong aesthetic element (e.g., gymnastics, figure skating, etc.). See Chapter 2, "A Typology of Athletic Activities Based Upon Their Psychological Demands," in Vanek and Cratty, Psychology and the Superior Athlete, p. 39–45.

Intellectual Pre-Training Strategies

Athletes left to their own devices often engage in various behaviors prior to competition. While some of these strategies are difficult for the observer to discern and are more ritualistic than pragmatic, other kinds of pre-competition mental activities have come under the scrutiny of sports psychologists in Eastern Europe during the past decades.

ACTIVATION AND RELAXATION

There has been a great deal of emphasis in Russian and Czech literature upon what might be termed "relaxation training" prior to competition. This training, using various muscle relaxation strategies accompanied by verbal cues, has been used not only to lessen the arousal-activation levels of athletes who may be "too high" for optimum effort in tasks requiring both accurate as well as forceful movements, but also to raise an athlete's level of activation. This latter goal is accomplished first by "bringing down" an athlete, asking him alternately to relax and then tighten his muscles to varying degrees. This is usually interpolated by deep breathing and sometimes by imagining that the limbs are becoming warm. The athlete is then verbally exhorted to "get high," "do his best," or whatever verbal instruction and encouragement will work to activate him. It has been found that by these methods one can apparently activate an athlete to higher levels than would be accomplished if he were "brought up" from a base line level, but at the same time these levels of activation, reflected in measures of blood pressure, respiration rate, and palmar conductivity, persist for as long as forty-eight hours.

These techniques that at times can become reasonably complicated, are often administered by a clinical psychologist working with the teams; at other times it is to the advantage of the athlete to administer these techniques to himself.[5] It has been found that only the more intellectually able individual is able to accomplish this. Moreover, as some of the techniques involve immediate visual feedback of the changes in physiological measures (e.g., inspecting graphs of heart rate and respiration at the time the training is being given), it takes a reasonable amount of academic background to interpret correctly the fluctuating needles.

[5] One of the most capable women athletes in the world in the late 1960s informed the team psychologist that she could engage in this type of pre-task training herself and indeed had been doing so for a period of time.

INTELLECTUAL PRE-PLANNING

It is common knowledge that divers and gymnasts frequently think through their exercises or dives prior to performing them. This kind of mental practice effect is covered in another chapter (8) and yet has implications for the present discussion. While it is difficult to determine just what an athlete is thinking during these periods of reflection, collecting introspective reports from athletes has prompted one researcher to suggest that this first thinking through occurs via visual imagery, while following the event, the tendency is to rehearse verbally the action and the possible problems that occurred.

Interesting research has been carried out, using a world-class high jumper as a subject, in which it was the intent to clock the duration of time the athlete engaged in some kind of pre-jump thought. Collected prior to numerous jumps, these times were then compared with the actual efforts achieved. In general, it was found that there seemed to be an optimum amount of time spent in this kind of reflective activity which, if not reached or exceeded, resulted in less than optimum effort.

In another study, a number of triple jumpers were encouraged for several months to spend numerous periods a week thinking through the mechanics of the relatively complicated event in which they participated. They were asked to think through and to verbalize about the actual leg and arm movements in the correct order when carrying out the jump. A control group with similar abilities was not exposed to this mental practice.

Although the jumping efforts of the mental practice group was superior to that of the controls, similar to some other studies of this nature, the data did not seem to be treated with any measure of distribution of scores considered. Only raw averages were compared.

The general research on motor learning supports the efficiency of what has been termed "verbal pre-training," carried out prior to the execution of complex motor skills. Further research within this general area should produce findings that are helpful to athletes and to their tutors, particularly if the proper controls are employed, acceptable statistical methods are used, and a sufficient number of subjects are involved.

ISOLATION

The planning and execution of a comprehensive program of physical training necessary for successful performance in most athletic events is usually in the hands of an athletic instructor or coach. It might be hypothesized that to some degree the efficiency of the training plan derived is dependent upon the academic background and intellectual capabilities of the mentor. Superior athletes, just as in the case of unexperienced school boys, rely to varying degrees upon the coach's judgment when preparing for competition.

It is often the case, however, that an athlete, particularly one approaching world-class performances, must separate himself physically from his familiar surroundings and from the coaching and training strategies of those to whom he has become accustomed. He must, for example, move to an Olympic preparation area and come under the jurisdiction of an unfamiliar coach and coaching techniques only weeks before he must face the world's best.

The available clinical observations seem to make it imperative for athletes facing this kind of isolation not only to become aware of the nature of the methods which seem to work best with them, but at the same time to receive practice in "working themselves out" several months before they must be on their own. The athlete, it has been speculated, should practice or "model" this kind of isolation from his coach and plan his own workouts prior to the time he must actually leave his familiar training surroundings. It is, of course, apparent that the intellectual grasp such an athlete has of himself and of appropriate training strategies should, to a large degree, influence his success in maintaining and improving his condition within the unfamiliar environment prior to and during high level competition.

Although this topic has not been accorded systematic exploration via published research, it would seem that it is an important intellectual dimension of superior athletic performance, one that should be accorded attention by behavioral scientists.

SHORT- AND LONG-TERM MEMORY

There have been studies exploring another interesting facet of athletics with implications for the quality of intellectual "equipment" an athlete brings to his event. Several kinds of sporting events require the ability to memorize quickly the terrain or other characteristics of the situations that are unique to each competition. This is true, for example, in the case of slalom skiing. Each course is different; moreover, a given course may change to a significant degree by extended use during the same competition.

In this situation a skier must quickly memorize not only the order of the gates, but their placement and characteristics as he ascends past them on his way to his first run. Before subsequent efforts, he must again make an assessment of possible changes in track conditions that might have transpired because of his own and his competitors' efforts.

This research is not extensive, but in general, has taken two main directions. In one case, an attempt has been made to aid short-term serial memory by actually exposing skiers to memory exercises in which they were required to repeat lists of nonsense syllables and the like. It is probable, however, that serial memory abilities in adults are highly specific to the material memorized and, thus, memory for numbers or nonsense syllables is not likely to correlate with nor to improve one's memory of the nature of a slalom course.

Other research has exposed skiers to various slalom courses and then asked them to repeat verbally the placement of the gates and other characteristics of the course. In these same studies, skiers have been asked to draw the courses after being permitted a quick inspection trip. In general, this course of action seems more successful: not only have better drawings apparently been rendered by the more proficient skiers, but there seem to be some training effects elicited by this method.

It is apparent that other sporting events require varying amounts of long-term and short-term memorization. But the research on other aspects of sports, with regard to memory, is largely lacking. Such questions as whether remembering the characteristics of one's opponents will contribute to winning might well be explored in further studies.

PACE AND TIME-SENSE

Sports psychologists in the Eastern European countries, as well as those in Germany and the Netherlands, have long been intrigued with various perceptual factors as they may relate to superior athletic performance. They have explored, for example, the elusive "ball sense" and have devised studies in which the blindfolded identification of balls (via the hands and feet) has been required of subjects.

Another perceptual quality has also been accorded a great deal of investigation. It is a common observation that runners and swimmers possess, to varying degrees, a sense of time or pace that enables them to swim or run more "intelligent races." Whether such a quality is primarily perceptual or intellectual is debatable. Some would argue that this kind of judgment is derived primarily from unconscious indices of bodily stress perceived by the individual as he extends himself to varying degrees; others would opt for the fact that knowledge of space and of elapsed time is more cognitive than perceptual. In any case, the studies of this ability have produced some of the more fascinating findings in this entire area.

It has been found that, with practice, athletes can acquire a remarkable sense of pace and are often able to tell within tenths of a second just how fast they have run a quarter-mile or even a half-mile. The quality, in other words, seems highly trainable and superior in better athletes with long experience.

Moreover, the research also indicates that judgments about one's elapsed time in a given race begins to become blunted when undue stress is imposed on the individual either prior to or during the competition itself. This kind of perceptual "fuzziness" is, of course, frequently documented in studies in which visual-perceptual distortions are recorded under various stressful conditions. Studies of this nature, exploring the sense of pace in athletes, are largely absent in Western scientific literature.

TACTICS

It is obvious that, to varying degrees, sports require some ability to constantly modify tactics, movements, and strategies. This quality is needed in individual sports: running, swimming, boxing, and the like, as well as in team sports. It is often difficult, particularly for experienced athletes, to separate the influence of physical ability from that of experience in tactics when evaluating over-all performance.

This topic has interested many sport psychologists in Europe during the past fifty years. Although at first their speculations appeared more in the form of narrative essays than in scientific papers, their later efforts were marked by attempts to objectify what might be termed the "tactical requirements of various sports" as well as the qualities needed in individual athletes to cope successfully with the necessarily complex decisions.

Attempts are continually being made to evaluate tactical abilities of individual athletes. Great care is taken to follow the athlete through a sports season, carefully recording the degree to which his responses on a soccer field, for example, are appropriate ones. The score derived is often compared with the coaches' ratings of the athlete's proficiency and success.

In an effort to objectify further this quality, another interesting strategy was employed. In several sports, sets of pictures of actual situations that might be encountered in a game were photographed and put on slides. A given slide might depict, in the case of soccer, a group of athletes from both teams running to reach a ball that is also in view. A similar picture (slide) might be taken of an ice hockey game showing the manner in which the defense is aligning itself within the static time dimension shown. Several uses were then made of these slides. In some cases, series were shown to an athlete and he was asked, as quickly and accurately as he could, to report three or four things: (1) What was happening at the time the picture was taken? (2) What happened just before the picture was taken; where was the ball coming from and what were the players doing? (3) What would probably happen just after the picture was taken; where was the ball or puck going? Who would obtain it?, etc. (4) Finally, what would he do in interacting in the situation? What would he do to prevent a goal, for example, or what would his reactions be as a member of either team.

The quality as well as the speed of the athlete's response to these pictures was recorded, and together with information obtained from coaches, it was used as one index of athletic proficiency. It was sometimes found, for example, that the quality of the responses from the athlete and the coach's assessment of his tactical abilities corresponded highly, while at other times this was not true.

The second primary way in which this particular type of "game" was employed was to train athletes to become better tacticians in their particular sport. It was felt that not only would tactical ability be improved by actually playing the game, but that these abilities might be improved by exposing athletes to the rather stable situations provided by the pictures. The pictures were usually presented rather quickly via a tachistoscope.

Learning of this approach to evaluating tactical ability, sports psychologists in the United States are currently working out problems related to administration and scoring of similar tests designed around athletics common to this country. At this point, the problem in scoring and recording the data, as well as in producing the pictures themselves, are rather formidable. Behavioral scientists plan to compare scores on this type of test obtained from successful versus unsuccessful sports performers.

Summary

As the reader must be aware, the research on this topic is still in its infancy, and much of that which has been carried out displays more energy and creativity than expertise. Therefore, the opportunities to make a contribution to this complex topic are limitless.

The subject may be approached from a sociological, theoretical, or pragmatic standpoint (i.e., what intellectual qualities are important in successful execution of what sports, and/or what abilities may be developed through various sports?). In general, the available data indicate that standardized tests evaluating adult I.Q. are of little help in as-

Reprinted from Miroslav Vanek and Bryant J. Cratty, *Psychology and the Superior Athlete,* New York: Macmillan, 1970.

FIGURE 5.1

Athletes' tactical abilities are often evaluated in experiments in which pictures of sports interactions are quickly flashed as shown. After the picture is no longer present, the athlete must determine what players were present, where the ball was, what the athletes were doing, what they probably will do next, what they probably did just prior to the picture, and what he would do in the situation. It is usually found that better tacticians in the field are also those who do best in this type of experiment. These techniques have also been used to train tactical abilities in team-sport athletes. Picture series for soccer, ice hockey, and basketball have been employed in this manner.

sessing athletic potential within all ranges of competition and ability. At the same time, it would seem that factor analyses, in which various measures of long and short-term memory are inserted, together with various components of the more valid personality scales, may result in helpful information being made available to the coach and to his capable charges.

BIBLIOGRAPHY

ANTONELLI, F., ED. *Proceedings,* First International Congress of Sport Psychology. Rome, 1965.

CRATTY, BRYANT J. *Movement Behavior and Motor Learning.* 2d ed Philadelphia: Lea and Febiger, 1967.

GAGAJEVA, G. M. "Takticeskije Myslenie v Sporte" "Tactical Thinking in Sports Activity." Teor. Praktika Fix. Kult., 6, 1951.

HRASE, J. "Vyuziti Aktivni Slovni Metody pri Nacviku Trojskoku" ("The Use of the Active World Method in Training the Triple Jump"). *Studie z Pedagogiky a Psychologie (Studies in Pedagogy and Psychology),* Prague, 1958, 169–84.

JEGUPOY, L. F. "Zapominanije Slalomnoj Trassy" ("Recording of a Slalom Track"). *Voprosy Psichologii Sporta (Questions of Sports Psychology).* Edited by A. C. Puni, Moscow, 1955.

KANE, K. E. "The Discrimination of Sports Types by Means of the I.P.F." Paper read at the British Psychological Society Conference, March, 1966.

KROLL, WALTER, and CRENSHAW, WILLIAM. "Multivariate Personality Profile Analysis of Four Athletic Groups." Paper read at the Second International Congress of Sports Psychology, Washington, D.C., 1968.

MACAK, M. "Relaxacne-Aktivacni, Autoregulacni Zasah. Metoda Nacviku a Psychologicka Charakterestika" ("The Relaxation-Activation, Self-Regulative Action. The Method of Training and the Psychological Characteristic"). *Csl. Psychologie (Czechoslovakian Psychology),* 3, 1964.

MUELLER, S. "Nervositat Vorstartzustand bei Boxern" ("Nervousness Prestart Tensions in Boxers"). *Theorie und Praxis der Korperkultur* 10, Leipzig (1961): 8.

OGILVIE, BRUCE E. "Psychological Consistencies Within the Personality of High Level Competitors." *Journal of the American Medical Association,* Special Olympic Year Edition, September-October 1968.

PUNI, A. C. "Ueber die Aktive Rolle der Vorstellungen bei der Aneignung von Bewegungsfertigkeiten" ("Concerning the Active Role of Ideas in Motor Learning"). *Teorija i Praktika Fiskultury,* Moscow 9, 1947.

RAFALOVITSCH, A. G. "Znacenije Samostojatelnovo Opredelenija i Spravnitelnoj Ocenki Vremeni v Razvitii 'Cuštva Vremeni' u Begunov" ("The Meaning of Self-estimation of Time on the Development of the "Time Sense in Runners"). *Voprosy Psichologii Sporta (Questions of Sports Psychology),* Moscow, 1955.

STRANSKY, A. "Typy Slovnich Instrukci a Vyznam Jejich Sledovani pro Nacvik a Regulaci Specialnich Pohybovych Dovednosti" ("The Importance of Research in Different Types of Verbal Instructions for the Training of

Special Motor Skills.") *Csl. Psychologie* (*Czechoslovakian Psychology*) 10 (1966): 4.

SVOBODA, B. "Takticke Mysleni Hracu v Kosikove" ("Tactical Thinking of Basketball Players"). *Teorie a Praxe Telesne Vychovy*, Prague, 1, 1965.

VANEK, MIROSLAV. "L'Entrainement Modele" ("Model Training"). *Proceedings*, First International Congress of Sports Psychology. Edited by F. Antonelli. Rome, 1965.

VANEK, MIROSLAV, and HOSEK, V. "Tachistoskopicke Vysetreni Hracu Jako Ukazatel Kvality Rozhodovani" ("Tachistoscopic Investigations of Players as Indicators of the Quality of Their Judgment"). Paper read at the meeting of Sports Psychologists in Harachov, Czechoslovakia, 1967.

VANEK, MIROSLAV, and CRATTY, BRYANT J. *Psychology and the Superior Athlete*. New York: The Macmillan Co., 1970.

6

Retarded Children
in Action

the effects of
physical activity programs upon
measures of intelligence and
academic abilities

Historical Perspective

During the dark ages, The Christian ethic rejected the use of vigorous bodily activities as somehow ungodly. It was not until the threads of more enlightened philosophies (nurtured by such foresighted humanists as Jean Jacques Rousseau in the late 1700s) began to weave themselves into helpful educational fabrics that an environment was created that enabled educators to suggest that apparently hopeless children and youth might be helped to change. *Pereira* in Spain, a contemporary of Rousseau, working through the other senses, was able to aid deaf-mutes to communicate.

From this setting came Itard, trained as a physician of the deaf. Familiar with the work of Pereira, he learned of a "wild boy" found wandering in the province of Aveyron in France, who apparently maintained himself like an animal. Although Pinel, the senior psychiatrist at the Bicetre in Paris, had diagnosed Victor as an incurable idiot, Itard set to work for a period of five years (1800-1805), attempting to educate the unfortunate youth primarily by exposing him to the social stimulation that he apparently had been missing.

Although Itard acknowledged defeat, the limited and unexpected success he *had* achieved attracted the attention not only of the Pope, but also of one of his students, Edouard Seguin, a physician, educator, and neurologist. Seguin not only began to classify retarded children into several categories (those with superficial or profound idiocy) but also began to expose them to the various sensory training methods that Itard and Pestalozzi had been using at the time. Seguin came to the State Institution in Massachusetts in the 1840s, and by exposing American educators to his system of "teacher techniques" involving primarily exercises in sensory-discrimination, played a large role in stimulating the establishment of schools for the retarded. Several of the techniques outlined by Seguin are found in contemporary tests of intelligence and in programs of education for the retarded.

Seguin was influenced not only by Itard, but also by Froebel and Pestalozzi. In turn, Seguin's ideas were noted and further refined by the gifted Roman physician, Maria Montessori, who shortly after the turn of the century established "orthoprennic schools" in Italy, separating retarded children from mentally ill adults with whom they had been formerly housed. Montessori brought not only energy, but keen insights and a system to the education of the retarded. Her charm and genius for communication both orally and via her writings prompted the establishment of schools that today have proliferated and may be found in most of the world's civilized countries.

The principles outlined by Montessori, as well as the creative materials she developed, are currently an important part of programs for the retarded and many environments established for the education of the normal child. She formulated several laws, which have since been found valid. For example, her "laws of sensitive periods in development" have their present-day counterparts in the studies of early visual-perceptual attentiveness and imprinting in infants and children; while her suggestion that the organism is directed irresistibly toward well-defined activity is reflected in studies of how novelty and complexity of stimuli elicit attentive and manipulative behavior in young children.

Her successes with the young retarded children with whom she worked were often remarkable; some learned to read and write so well that they were able to take their places in schools with normal children. And although it remained for Alfred Binet and others to establish exact measuring tools for the evaluation of the intellect (Chapter 2), her principles and techniques are important underpinnings of programs for normal as well as for retarded children.

During these same decades there was a parallel interest within the scientific community that provided bases for attempting to improve abilities of retarded children in various ways. This interest was in the much discussed problem of how much an individual's mental abilities were formed by the culture and how much were due to heredity.

While Galton and others, who were the first spokesmen on this topic, often opted for the heredity side of the argument, others, using the then new tool of statistical correlation, provided data that suggested that at least a part of an individual's mental abilities were dependent upon the child's rearing and his cultural experiences. While correlation coefficients between father-son intelligence measures were usually found to be positive, they were never perfect, and the findings from co-twin control studies usually revealed the modifiability of abilities in the "trained" sibling. Perry, for example, found that about 28 percent of children emerging from marriages of parents whose I.Q.'s ranged from 70-85 performed intellectually at least at normal levels, well above that of their parents.

Despite the apparent modifiability of retardate mental abilities through training, there was little systematic study of this problem using scientifically valid measures. The studies that were conceived were usually beset with methodological problems related to sampling, as well as findings that were difficult to interpret due to the omnipresent "emotional impact" of the experimenter himself upon the abilities exhibited by the impressionable subjects.

At the same time, the work which was carried out in the early 1900s did not include the instigation of program content in which motor activity was a primary variable possibly contributory to the changes elicited. Although Maria Montessori suggests in some of her writings that large muscle activity could be a helpful learning channel, similar in impact to the visual, tactual, and auditory she so successfully explored, she did not go beyond several suggestions for line-walking tasks to improve the balance of young children.

In 1958, however, there were two studies which, together and separately, provided the impetus for renewed interest not only in the manner in which educational procedures might improve retardate abilities, but specifically in how vigorous activities of the larger muscle groups might contribute in positive ways to the betterment of less capable children and youth. The subjects in one of these studies were educationally retarded boys in England, while the other participants were laboratory rats.

Cooper and Zubek, in the latter part of the 1950s, raised both bright and dull rats under three different conditions: (a) an "enriched environment" consisting of swings, bells, tunnels to slide in, ramps, and the like; (b) a normal environment consisting of the natural habitat for laboratory rats; and (c) a restricted environment, with a case containing only food and water. Their findings were highly promising and suggested that an enriched environment providing for an abundance of motor behaviors, exploratory activities, and the like is particularly helpful in improving the abilities of dull rats (a 27 percent improvement in maze performances was recorded in the less capable group), while a restricted early environment had a negative effect upon the bright rats, increasing their errors by 44 percent. They extrapolated their findings "to the human core" and suggested that the manipulation of intelligence may be primarily a matter of economics and of providing proper sequences and conditions.

The second 1958 study was carried out by an English educator, James Oliver, and involved boys judged educationally subnormal. Here again, the data produced gave heart to those who might have been supportive of an environmentalistic approach to the manipulation of human destiny. Dr. Oliver's results are reviewed in detail in a later section of this chapter; however, in general, he found that a program of traditional physical education activities, including fitness tasks and the like, resulted in significant changes in the intellectual measures of the participating subjects.

This kind of experimentation and speculation continued through the 1960s and into the 1970s. The programs of gross bodily activities to which retarded children have been exposed have varied in structure, intensity, and content. Some have been rather rigid and highly structured, specifying exactly what movement should be made, in what order, and when by the children exposed to them. Others have permitted more decision making on the part of the subjects, have encouraged exploratory behaviors, and in other ways have included a great deal of intellectual as well as physical participation.

Although only a small number of studies have explored intellectual and/or academic change as a result of exposure to various programs of physical activity, those that have been carried out have included subjects at all points along the intellectual measuring scale. Drs. Edgar and Webb, for example, have focused their attention upon the severely and profoundly retarded child, while Widdop, Kershner, and others have studied the trainable retardate (about 40-50 I.Q.). The majority of the studies, however, have employed subjects, usually boys, who fall within the "educable" category (I.Q. about 70). Additionally some investigators have included a variety of measures in their studies, including those seeking to evaluate various academic competencies, including mathematics and the like, together with measures of social adjustment and emotional stability. Others have focused primarily upon verbal and non-verbal measures of intelligence.

There seems to be a considerable discrepancy between the large number of theoretical statements proclaiming the virtues of movement programs for retarded and educationally handicapped youngsters and the comparatively smaller number of studies that have appeared whose findings either support or refute these expansive proclamations of success. At the same time, the available data does begin to outline at least three types of guidelines for interested educators, clinicians, and researchers:

1. Many of the studies contain helpful and clear explanations of activities that should result in the improvement of various academic and cognitive abilities. Thus, there are some substantial and clear practical guidelines available to educators.[1]

2. It is clear that valid findings can emerge from future studies of this nature only if the effects of experimenter contact with the subjects is properly controlled. Retarded children are particularly susceptible to extra attention given to them by an experimenter or his assistants and will usually perform better on any task or test subsequently administered to them. Thus, there are obvious guidelines for future researchers within the protocols of the studies now available.

3. Relatively simple sensory-motor experiences, sequentially arranged and administered for rather prolonged periods of time, will usually provide more help for the profoundly and severely retarded youngster than for the intellectually more capable retardate.[2] Needless to say, the procedures, usually arduous to apply and expensive to carry out, must be accompanied by a positive philosophical commitment by those extending the fiscal and physical efforts.

With these types of guidelines in mind, I will attempt to review some of the available evidence that links intellectual and academic change to exposure to vigorous muscular activities of various kinds. The implications of these studies for more sophisticated programs of future research will become obvious to scholars reviewing the source material in detail, while the opportunities for improved service, which the program content suggests, are similarly limitless.

The Profoundly and Severely Retarded Child

In the United States, communities are beginning more and more to accept and accommodate the retarded child who evidences an obvious ability to benefit from some kinds of education. The educables (around 70 I.Q.) are being accepted into the family, and school systems are

---

[1] Some of these tasks will be outlined in detail in chapters 11 & 12, dealing with reading, mathematics, and similar academic abilities.

[2] We have recently designed a study in which profoundly and severely retarded children will receive ten months of sensory-motor experiences, administered from *six-eight hours a day!*

becoming increasingly accommodating, instituting classes for their benefit often within schools for the average child. To an increased degree,
classes for trainables are similarly being instituted in the 1970s. In previous decades, while it was often the responsibility of the parents to
establish, finance, and staff programs for these children, to an increased
degree public education has instituted programs on their behalf. This
condition seems to encourage more parents to keep these children within
the family constellation, rather than permit them to reside in an institu-
tional setting. The result of this enlightened community and parental
acceptance of retarded children in the upper I.Q. ranges, however, has
resulted, in some parts of the country, in a greater percent of severely
and profoundly retarded children being relegated to residential care.[3]

These more severely involved children require care around the
clock. They seldom evidence bowel control, for example, nor can they
usually feed themselves, both conditions that make their maintenance
extremely expensive and difficult. Fortunately, there are individuals
within these institutions during recent years who not only possess the
academic backgrounds to begin to cope with these children and to insti-
gate improvement, but also have been able to obtain funds to test out
the programs they have conceived.

These programs have relatively modest goals: to make the children
more self-sufficient, to enable them to adapt more readily to simple
demands made upon them, to improve their self-concept, and to permit
them generally to lead a happier life.

In general, the programs designed to meet these objectives have
several things in common:

1. They are composed of a variety of sensory and motor experiences,
including vivid visual ones (shining flashlights in order to elicit basic
attentive responses); tactual administrations of various kinds (rubbing
the limbs with towels to heighten bodily awareness); auditory (ringing
bells to elicit head turning responses to the source of sound); and
movement experiences (attempts to manipulate the body in basic
reflexive and adaptive patterns similar to basic voluntary movements
seen early in infancy). Many of the latter activities involve assistive
activity on the part of a therapist.

2. The programs involve rather prolonged periods of educational
therapy, usually at least one-and-one half to two hours a day. Often, the
time and expense is so great that the "teams" of educators consist of
individuals who are mentally deficient themselves (educable retardates)
who work under the direction of psychologists.

[3] In one institution in California, over 50 percent of the children have
I.Q.'s under 35, while 35 percent have been evaluated as having I.Q.'s under
19!

3. The programs differ in the specific types of activities to which the children are exposed, but in general most have reasonably rational sequences incorporated into them. They are also characterized by tasks that involve a great deal of change in the child's visual field, but a relatively small amount of physical effort. For example, the "Stomach Board" is frequently employed (a board with roller skate wheels), which permits a child to lie on his stomach and with a slight extension of a hand or leg to move himself quickly along the floor.

4. In order to evaluate the programs' success, those administering them have been forced to devise evaluative instruments containing rather basic and simple response patterns. Although Dr. Edgar has employed the Gesell Schedules evaluating motor-adaptive, language, and personal-social behaviors, Dr. Webb has devised a check list that is named the AMMP Index, which attempts to assesses the child's awareness, movement, manipulation of environment, posture, and locomotion.

In general, effort has been made to determine whether the children's responses are somehow improving qualitatively, rather than simply quantitatively. Thus, Piaget's concepts have been woven into some of the assessment devices developed for the evaluation of possible improvement in this type of child.

The rather comprehensive programs to which these children are being exposed seem generally to be eliciting the desired changes. I have witnessed marked improvement in children who formerly exhibited only rather vegetative responses and observed they could walk to the dining room, feed themselves, were beginning to exhibit language understandings, rudimentary speech, and even were able to sight read several words including their own names and those of their classmates!

Moreover, the data from the rather few studies confirm the efficiency of the programs of movement and sensory experiences to which these rather severely impaired children have been exposed.[4] Significant changes in Webb's AMMP scale have resulted by her use of techniques that include: exposing children to various vivid sensory experiences to heighten levels of awareness; rolling, rocking, swinging, and bouncing movements to improve kinesthetic perception; various manipulative activites to improve environmental adaptation; and sequences of locomotor activities to achieve posture and adequate gait. The scale has proved to be a reliable measure with the most marked improvement in the movement portion. A number of children exhibited both approach and avoid-

---

[4] One does not ever encounter children labeled as "severely or profoundly" retarded who are free from movement problems or who possess the ability to speak with any clarity at all.

ance reactions for the first time after training periods lasting from five to ten months, while thirty-one out of thirty-two subjects improved in measures of locomotion and posture.

The research in this area by Dr. Edgar has produced similarly encouraging findings. Using the previously described Developmental Schedules devised by Gesell, Edgar found that significantly more improvement was realized by her experimental groups as contrasted to the controls. For example, after eight months of training, the eleven experimental subjects had improved by about 100 percent in the language sub-scale, while the controls had improved only about 30 percent. Similar dramatic gains were seen on the adaptive scales and on the personal social scale (improvement again of 100 percent), as well as on the adaptive scale of the evaluative measure used.

Edgar concluded that some of the techniques aided the children in discriminating between their own body parts and parts of their environment, in increasing attention span, as they were forced to attend for increasing amounts of time upon motor tasks (i.e., while walking a balance beam), while at the same time various intellectual components in their motor adaptive behaviors seemed to emerge, including the important concept of "object permanency" alluded to by Piaget.[5]

The clinical and experimental work in this area of research and service is obviously still in its infancy. Further gains in improving the efficiency of these children will take place with a refinement of testing instruments, a more detailed and structured application of training and educational methods, and a more enlightened interest on the part of public and private funding agencies reflected in increased financial support.[6]

The Trainable

The trainable, by definition, is usually considered a child who cannot benefit from traditional academic training, but who can be taught to engage in acceptable social self-care skills and can otherwise deal with

[5] The children would be seen to remove screens in order to reach objects of whose existence they evidenced an imaginal awareness even though they could not directly see them.

[6] If from a humanistic standpoint, one cannot justify the great expenditure of time and monies on these children, it is possible to justify funds expended by computing savings in staff time. This is usually elicited when the round-the-clock care necessary to maintain these children is reduced significantly as the children become able to meet their own needs for nourishment, recreation, and elimination after exposure to intensive sensory-motor training programs of the type described.

recreational and simple vocational tasks. His I.Q. is usually between 40 and 55, depending upon the definition of the term employed by the state in which he resides. While much of the time he is in residence in a state or privately supported home for retarded children, there is an increased tendency to retain him within a family setting and to educate him in a day school for retarded children.

A large percent of the children classified as trainable evidence the characteristics of Down's Syndrome (Mongoloid), and thus possess a number of genetically determined problems involving sensory, motor, endocrine, and neural functioning. The motor abilities of the trainable are, as a group, found to be from two to four years behind those of so-called normal children. Within a population of trainables, however, it is not unusual to find a wide variety of movement capabilities.

Most of the early research to determine the effects of physical activity upon academic and intellectual functioning utilized the more capable and perhaps more available educable retardate. At least two studies portend further productive work in this area. One of these employed the rather structured techniques advocated by Delacato, while the second compared the cognitive-movement approach of Mosston to a less intellectually laden "perceptual-motor approach."

In 1967, John Kershner exposed twenty trainables to an intensive program of patterning, creeping, crawling, and similar activities written about by clinicians within the Institutes for Human Potential in Philadelphia. His findings included positive and significant changes in the I.Q. scores elicited from the experimental group, as well as improvement in scores evaluating creeping ability. The third finding was labeled "puzzling" by more than one reviewer, insofar as his control group registered more positive changes in a comprehensive battery of perceptual-motor items. To explain this third finding, Kershner seemed to engage in some post-hoc hypothesis formation, as he suggested that it was due to the validity of some of Kephart's statements, rather than attempting to link it to the conceptual framework by Delacato that he professed to be researching originally.

In 1969, a Canadian researcher, James Widdop, and his colleagues at McGill University produced a study whose intent was to compare the effects of two different programs of movement experiences upon the intellectual, social, and emotional behaviors of 102 boys and girls labeled trainable (one of the few studies of this type employing girls). The ages ranged from six to fifteen years, while their I.Q.s ranged from 31 to 49.

The make-up of the programs demonstrates the contrast of methodologies that can be introduced into educational methods in which movement plays a part. For example, the program labeled "Perceptual-Motor

Training" emphasized hand-eye coordination and various perceptual items involving awareness of spatial relationships, body position in space, and similar qualities. Taking cues from both Kephart and Barsch, Widdop included activities intended to heighten eye movement control, laterality, visualization (retain sensory input), body image (shape, extent, and positions of the body in various situations), and motor planning (the ability to decide upon a course of action and then carry it out with correct timing and spatial dimensions).

The second program was termed "Educational Gymnastics" and emphasized decision making and problem solving. Specifically, this second program contained sixteen movement "themes" suggested by Laban, as well as problem-solving behaviors outlined by Mosston. The latter included problem solving, seeking alternatives, exploring alternatives, and selecting appropriate responses on the part of the participating children.

Both groups were found to evidence improvement on all of the measures obtained, with most progress evidenced by the younger children. In both the younger and older groups the most improvement in boys seemed due to the educational gymnastics approach, while the girls improved most within the perceptual-motor program. The most marked changes were seen in measures of social maturity (the Vineland Scale and the Cowell Scale,) as well as in the Peabody Picture Vocabulary Test.

Recommendations emerging from this study revolved around optimum time for this type of training (twenty minutes daily), as well as the suggestion that trainables should be first exposed to a rather basic perceptual-motor approach and then progress to an educational gymnastic emphasis in which more conceptual processes are inserted. This progression should terminate, Widdop suggests, with help in playing recreational games so as to prepare children to participate in communication-recreational activities.

The superficial nature of the data in this area is obvious from the aforementioned review. For example, there are no studies, of which I am aware, specifically exploring changes that may be elicited in either movement or cognitive processes by trainables evidencing Down's Syndrome. Studies do indicate that they are significantly impaired as a group in a variety of perceptual-motor measures. Widdop's suggestions for an integration of basic motor activities with those incorporating decision making by the children, are probably sound ones. With further work more exact educational guidelines should become available in order to maximize the effects of programs incorporating vigorous bodily movement upon the social, emotional, academic, and intellectual measures obtained from trainable retardates.

The Educable

The educable retardate is often difficult to distinguish from a normal child. Both in appearance and in social skills he or she can frequently mask intellectual deficiencies when in superficial contact with other children and with adults. Their deficiencies often reveal themselves in games in which the rules are more complex and in social situations that may prove stressful and demanding intellectually.

Generally, their I.Q. range is from about 60 to 79, and their classrooms are often placed within schools for normal youngsters so that they may participate as much as possible in the athletic and social life of their chronological peers. Like some trainables, they can often engage in simple vocational tasks and can often work quite well if the demands of the job are not too great. Some find their way to "sheltered workshops" containing young adults with similar intellectual abilities, while others can function in less demanding jobs within the "unsheltered" portions of the community.

Although the educable is on the whole more physically capable than the trainable, his proximity to normal children when engaged in play may lead him to perceive feelings of inferiority more often than the less capable trainable. Moreover, the level of fitness and physical proficiency the educable may evidence is influenced not only by whether or not any concomitant neurological problem is evidenced that might interfere with motor coordination, but also by the availability of programs of physical activity. For example, several years ago it was found that about 45 percent of all retarded children were given no physical education programs. Of the others, the amount of time each spent in physical education during a single week was directly related to the motor abilities exhibited by both boys and girls.

The educable has been the subject in most of the research programs exploring intellectual change accompanying physical activity. The 1958 studies by Oliver, for example, employed educables. In these studies with nineteen experimental subjects, Oliver replaced all academic subjects, with the exception of arithmetic and English, for a period of ten weeks, with a program of physical education, remedial exercises, and recreative team sports. The control group received its regular allotment of physical education two times a week, plus the usual after-school games.

Several tests of I.Q. were administered, including the Goodenough Draw-a-Man Test, Porteus Maze Test, and the Terman-Merrill. Tests of motor educability, athletic ability, and physical fitness were similarly used in a pre- and post-test situation. Significant gains were seen in the experimental group in every test except that of motor educability and Raven's test of mental age. On the other hand, the control group showed no significant gains in any of the test items.

Oliver cited a number of reasons for the improvement, including the improvement of confidence because of increased athletic achievement, with the subsequent "happier atmosphere" which was engendered. The effects of increased interest and attention were also cited as important factors in molding the scores obtained when testing the experimental group at the completion of the study.

This study by Oliver created widespread interest, and happily some of this interest was channeled into further research in which more of the possibly affective variables were better controlled. For example, in 1965 Corder reported a study of a group to whom special attention was accorded, but that had no special physical education program (an "officials" group). Twenty-four boys of subnormal intelligence were placed in three groups and given a program of progressive resistance exercises lasting five weeks, one hour per day. Significant differences between the training group and the control group were obtained on the full scale of the WISC (Wechsler Intelligence Scale for Children), as well as in the verbal scale of the WISC. However, there were no significant differences in the scores when the efforts of the experimental group were compared to those of the group receiving special attention but no exercises.

The findings of this study, together with those of the study by Solomon and Prangle, indicated that with the proper controls a simple and basic program of traditional exercises and physical education activities, whose content is determined by a teacher, will have no effect upon I.Q. measures, although the expected change will occur in various measures of physical ability.

Reflecting a more sophisticated approach to the study of interactions between measures of intelligence and programs of physical activity are two recent studies by Ross and by Rarick and his student, Broadhead. The latter took place in suburbs outside Houston, Texas, and its intent was to compare the effects of an individualized art program and a program of physical activity upon the change in various measures of motor, emotional, social, and intellectual competence on the part of 275 children labeled educable retardates. The programs lasted for twenty teaching weeks, with thirty-five minutes a day devoted either to the physical education program or to the individualized art program.

In general, it was found that both the art and physical education program elicited significant changes in modifying the emotional, motor, and intellectual behavior of the retarded youngsters than was true among the children having only their regular instructional programs. Changes in motor performance, as would be expected, were more marked in the physical education group, while emotional changes were more positive in the group exposed to an art program. Most successful was the physical education program that was oriented toward the individual and his needs rather than toward simply meeting group objectives! The most marked changes were seen in the older children and in the boys rather than the girls.

The individualized physical activity program consisted of a number of well-conceived problems to solve; for example, an emphasis was placed upon a variety of activities using apparatus of various kinds, as well as techniques intended to help the children intellectually analyze basic bodily movements independent of any apparatus. Various types of jumping and landings were explored by the children, while when using apparatus, for example, a variety of ways in which to use a rope was explored. In general, the appendix of this report contains a rich source of activities upon which teachers of the retarded might draw when instituting programs intended to involve children intellectually in both art programs and programs of more vigorous physical activity.

In 1970 Dorothea Ross also published research indicating how intellectual content directed toward social learning and toward acquiring number concepts within a program of small group games might elicit positive changes in the abilities of educable mentally retarded children. Twenty EMRs participated in a nine-month game program in which there was intentional learning in game skills and in basic number concepts. There were highly significant changes in basic number concepts obtained in the experimental group, significant changes in the ability to respond consistently to verbal directions as well as to evidence appropriate social behaviors with peers on the part of the participating children. Ross, in this and in previous studies, used modeling techniques in order to initiate and reinforce the behaviors she desired. This consists of having instructors "act out" transgressions of the children in games after they occur, in order to present a model for acceptable behaviors and at the same time to reduce punishment and censure felt by the children themselves.

The experimental subjects scored significantly higher than did the controls in a comprehensive test of number concepts, including the use of original numbers to five, recognizing small groups, enumerating eight objects via counting and the like. Higher scores were also achieved by the experimentals in a quantitative vocabulary test. Ross proposes a model that has been postulated in less elaborate form by previous investigators researching similar change in retarded children using a games approach. The model looks like this:

initial sequences→ expectancy of failure→
performance failure changed to one of success→
expectancy of success→ performance success.

(The arrows should be read "leads to.") This reversal of a failure syndrome in retarded children through success in play has been alluded to by most of the previous investigators whose work has been cited.

Summary and Overview

Although the evidence is scarce, and at times the studies lack polish, adequate controls, and the proper descriptions of the subjects, the accumulated evidence does indicate that significant intellectual and academic changes may be elicited in groups of retarded youngsters through exposure to properly planned programs of physical activity. Moreover, the available evidence indicates that on the lower intellectual levels such programs might well contain relatively structured and basic sensory-motor tasks, while, when working with older trainables and educables, the efficiency of the motor program improves upon the insertion of intellectual components and/or of techniques that, in direct ways, promote the acquisition of academic abilities and concepts.

Further research might well concentrate upon specific groups of retardates, those retarded because of apparent cultural-environmental factors versus those whose retardation can be traced to genetic causes, children with Downs Syndrome versus those trainables who do not evidence the "ten signs of the stigmata." Moreover, it seems highly important to design research so that the effects of individual program components can be properly assessed upon the academic, social, emotional, and/or academic tests given before and after the movement program.

BIBLIOGRAPHY

BARSCH, RAY H. *Achieving Perceptual-Motor Efficiency; A Space-Oriented Approach to Learning*. Seattle: Special Child Publications, 1967.

COOPER, R. M., and ZUBECK, J. P. "Effects of Enrichment and Restricted Early Environment on the Learning Ability of Bright and Dull Rats." *Canadian Journal of Psychology* 12 (1959): 164.

CORDER, W. D. "Effects of Physical Education on the Intellectual Physical and Social Development of Educable Mentally Retarded Boys." Unpublished special project. Nashville, Tenn.: George Peabody College, 1965.

CRATTY, BRYANT J. *Motor Activity and the Education of Retardates.* Philadelphia, Pa.: Lea and Febiger, 1969.

——. *The Perceptual-Motor Attributes of Mentally Retarded Children and Youth.* Los Angeles County, Calif.: Mental Retardation Services Board, 1966.

EDGAR, CLARA LEE; BALL, THOMAS S.; McINTYRE, ROBERT B.; and SHOTWELL, ANNA M. "Effects of Sensory-Motor Training on Adaptive Behavior." *American Journal of Mental Deficiency,* Vol. 73, No. 5, March, 1969.

GALTON, FRANCIS. *Hereditary Genius,* 2d ed. London, Macmillan & Co., Ltd., 1892.

KEPHART, N. C. "Perceptual Motor Aspects of Learning Disabilities." *Exceptional Child* 31 (December 1964): 201–206.

——. *The Slow Learner in the Classroom.* Columbus, Ohio: Charles E. Merrill Publishing Co., 1960.

KERSHNER, JOHN R. "An Investigation of the Doman-Delacato Theory of Neuropsychology as It Applies to Trainable Mentally Retarded Children in Public Schools." Monograph, Bureau of Research and Development, Department of Public Instruction, Pennsylvania, May 1967.

LABAN, R. *Modern Educational Dance.* London: Macdonald & Evans, Ltd. 1945.

LOWE, BENJAMIN J. "The Effects of Physical Conditioning on the Cognitive Functioning of Educationally Sub-normal Boys." Birmingham, England: Department of Psychology, 1966.

MONTESSORI, MARIA. *Dr. Montessori's Own Handbook.* New York: Frederick A. Stokes, 1914.

MOSSTON, M. *Teaching Physical Education.* Columbus, Ohio: Charles E. Merrill Publishing Co., 1966.

OLIVER, J. N. "The Effects of Physical Conditioning on the Sociometric Status of Educationally Sub-Normal Boys." *Physical Education* 156 (1960): 38–46.

——. "The Effects of Physical Conditioning Exercises and Activities on the Mental Characteristics of Educationally Sub-Normal Boys." *British Journal of Educational Psychology* 28 (1958): 155.

PERRY, N. *Teaching the Mentally Retarded Child.* New York: Columbia University Press, 1960.

RARICK, G. LAWRENCE, and BROADHEAD, GEOFFREY D. *The Effects of Individualized versus Group Oriented Physical Education Programs on Selected Parameters of the Development of Educable Mentally Retarded and Minimally Brain Injured Children.* Sponsored by the United States Office of Education and Joseph P. Kennedy Jr. Foundation, 1968.

ROSS, DOROTHEA. *The Use of Games to Facilitate the Learning of Basic Number Concepts in Pre-School Educable Mentally Retarded Children.* Final Report, December 1967, Project No. 6–2263, U.S. Office of Education.

——. "Incidental Learning of Number Concepts in Small Group Games." *American Journal of Mental Deficiency,* pp. 718–25, 1970.

SOLOMON, A., and PRANGLE, R. "Demonstrations of Physical Fitness Improvement in the EMR." *Exceptional Child* 33 (November 1967): 177–81.

WEBBE, RUTH C. "Sensory-Motor Training of the Profoundedly Retarded." *American Journal of Mental Deficiency* 74, No. 2, September 1969.

WIDDOP, J. H.; BARTON, P.; CLEARY, B.; PROYER, V. A.; and WALL, A. E. *The Effects of Two Programmes of Physical Education Upon the Behavioural and Psychological Traits of Trainable Retarded Children.* A study financed by the Quebec Institute of Research in Education, Contract No. 68-AS-11-04-02. Montreal, Canada: McGill University, 1969.

7

Children With Learning Difficulties

Introduction

Perhaps no other trend has been more prominent in education during the past five to six years than the one that resulted in the identification of children with learning difficulties and the exploration of strategies through which they might be aided. These children have always been in the schools of the United States, but often attention was focused upon their more obvious problems and disruptions (i.e., they were "bad" boys), while at other times, children with more profound learning and mental difficulties had forced these youths into the background.

Interest in these children began in the years following World War II with the publication of texts by Strauss and his colleagues. During the late 1940s and 50s clinicians, such as Marianne Frostig and others began to devise curricula for their remediation, while by the 1970s the literature dealing with this type of child became voluminous.

These children with learning difficulties are not mentally retarded, but rather will often score at around the average or above average in portions of intelligence scales. They characteristically have high or at least average verbal I.Q.s derived from the verbal and vocabulary items on such tests, but often score well below average on tests of perceptual-motor functioning on the same evaluative batteries.

Within a group of children evidencing learning difficulties, however, there are several often ill-defined subdivisions. Some of these children cannot achieve well in school because of a lack of congruence between the culture represented by the school and the culture in which they were born. Others are beset by emotional problems of varying degrees of severity that tend to "blunt" their classroom efforts. Still others might be identified as evidencing subtle or obvious signs of nervous system impairment reflected in disturbances of sensory and motor functions when accorded a neurological examination. Often a child evidences more than one of these difficulties. For example, the discoordinate child labeled as neurologically impaired may (indeed, usually) show distinct signs of emotional disturbance.

The strategies that have been formulated to assist this type of child are varied and range from diverse kinds of training programs to enhance visual-perceptual attributes that are often deficit; training in auditory-perceptual functions that are similarly often impaired; to the usually more helpful eclectic approach in which a variety of strategies are employed at the same time, following a comprehensive evaluation of the child's emotional, social, perceptual (visual and auditory), motor, academic, and intellectual functioning.

During the past twenty years certain clinicians [1] have focused their main efforts in remediation upon the motor functions of children with learning difficulties. The speed and enthusiasm with which some of the remedial activities involving movement experiences were taken up by teachers and sundry "educationalists" was truly remarkable. One observer suggested that it was evident that "little can be done to stop an idea whose time has come." And predictably, both scientist and charlatan have participated in this "movement movement," contributing often helpful ways to remediate the coordination problems of clumsy children, but at other times offering rather flimsy straws at which parents and teachers might grasp with less than the promised miracles occurring.

While it is true that many children with academic learning difficulties also evidence coordination problems, it is similarly apparent that at least as many children who are not achieving well in classrooms are free from coordination problems. It is also true that a substantial proportion of children born without limbs, or evidencing rather obvious motor impairment (cerebral palsy), may indeed score well on standardized academic tests.

[1] Several of whom are reviewed in Chapter 3.

However, there have been several helpful outcomes of this interest in movement as a possible remedial tool in the correction of more global learning difficulties:

1. Clumsy children have been exposed to helpful kinds of remedial techniques.

2. Teachers have begun to observe and to become concerned about the more obvious problems evidenced by children, including lack of coordination at play, with the resultant social ostracism, and ineptitude when attempting to transcribe thoughts to paper. To an increased degree, the more progressive elementary schools in all parts of the country are instituting special programs of activities intended to help the child with coordination problems.

3. A third outcome of contemporary interest in perceptual-motor [2] functioning of children has been a proliferation of studies designed to explore some of the possible relationships between movement, academic learning, and intelligence.

While more than a few of these studies have been formulated by the scientifically naïve, the data emerging from some point to helpful ways in which motor experiences might contribute in positive ways to the education of normal children and to the welfare of children with learning problems of various kinds. Some of this literature will be examined in the pages that follow.

Correlational Studies

Overall, even with children evidencing learning difficulties as subjects, only low and usually positive correlations will be obtained when contrasting scores from motor ability tests to scores from tests of perceptual, academic, and intellectual functioning. Correlations rarely exceed .3 or .4, which indicates a "common variance" (the r^2) of from

---

[2] The term "perceptual-motor" has been employed in at least two ways by various writers. The more scientifically oriented writers use the term to suggest that most of the time, when a voluntary motor act is initiated and sustained, certain sensory processes are vital to its proper execution. A less precise interpretation of the term involves placing a two-headed arrow on the hyphen (perceptual↔motor) and further suggesting that movement activities will positively affect a variety of visual-perceptual abilities. The latter use of the term has been examined in greater detail in Cratty's *Perceptual and Motor Development in Infants and Children.* (Macmillan, 1970), but in summary is rather naïve, unscientific, and unsupported by the majority of the experimental evidence available.

9 percent to 16 percent. Thus, when correlations of this size are obtained, from 91 percent to 84 percent of the qualities measured are separate and specific to the motor test and to the intellectual and academic test. Correlations of this magnitude are found in the numerous studies by Ismail and his colleagues.[3] Furthermore, in this same search, slight but significant correlations were found between such diverse human qualities as height and arithmetic reasoning (+.34), which can only be explained by reference to the chance correlations that are likely to emerge when over forty items are correlated with each other (1600 correlations).

At the same time, when viewed categorically, it is sometimes found that groups of children with learning difficulties will evidence motor abilities that are less than those expected of children of the same age functioning well in classrooms. In a study I carried out in 1966, for example, it was found that children tested in the Los Angeles City schools and labeled as educationally handicapped posted average scores on three of six perceptual-motor tests, which were below scores obtained from educable retardates, and considerably below norms of normal children. This test data appears in Figure 7.1. The tests in which the EH children were deficit included one of the verbal recognition of body parts, involving left-right orientation, one of static balance, and one of agility involving movement in a vertical plane (i.e., "how fast can you get up?" from a back lying position). Indeed, minimal neurological impairment, which is sometimes found in groups of children with learning difficulties, is usually manifested in balance problems, thus accounting for this kind of finding.

One must be careful, however, to determine just why one might obtain low correlations between various tests of mental and motor ability. Often, it would seem that an inordinate number of intellectual "elements" are contained within various complex motor performance items. For example, it is frequently found that children with learning difficulties cannot verbally identify their body parts in reasonably complex ways (i.e., "touch your left shoulder with your right hand"), but rather than evidence a body-image deficit, inability to perform the above task correctly might, in truth, be caused by problems in short-term auditory memory or in auditory sequencing. Again, using the above example, to carry out the command properly, the child must remember and correctly translate into movement at least six or seven distinct conceptual acts (i.e., "First take my hand, my right hand, move it to my left; second,

[3] In most of the studies carried out by Ismail, the ages of his subjects were not partialled out, and also absent are the reliability coefficients of the various tests employed.

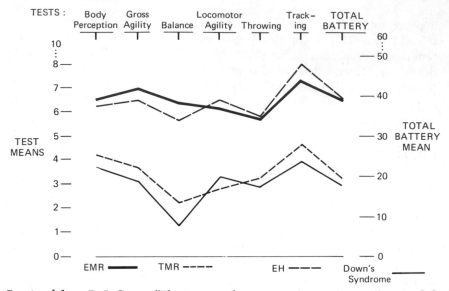

Reprinted from B. J. Cratty, "The Perceptual-Motor Attributes of Mentally Retarded Children and Youth." Monograph sponsored by the Mental Retardation Services Board of Los Angeles in cooperation with the Dept. of Physical Education, U.C.L.A., the Los Angeles County Dept. of Parks and Recreation, and the Special Education Branch of the Los Angeles City Schools, 1966.

FIGURE 7.1

Inter-group comparison of mean scores in six test categories.

touch my left shoulder," etc.). In tests comparing mental performance with physical performance in retarded children, one is likely to obtain higher correlations when the motor task is reasonably complex ("squat, thrust your legs to the rear, return to a squat, and stand"), than if it is a simple test of explosive power (i.e., "see how high above your standing reach can you reach while jumping").

Ismail frequently obtained small but statistically significant correlations (.3 and .4) between tests labeled "arm-coordination" and tests of intelligence when using children with learning disorders as subjects. Upon careful examination of the type of coordination tasks employed, however, it is apparent that serial memory plays an important part in their execution similar to the serial memory items that make up a portion of most intelligence tests administered to children. ("Place both hands to the front, then out to the sides, up in the air, down to the sides, etc.," in correct order).

Despite the frequent finding that groups of children with learning difficulties evidence average scores that are below the norms, this is not always found to be true in motor ability tests. In a study we carried out in 1968, for example, we sought to obtain a control group whose performances could be compared to children with whom we worked in a clinical setting and who had been identified as minimally neurologically handicapped by examining pediatric neurologists. For these controls, we tested children, in a large progressive suburb of Los Angeles, who had been placed in classes for the educationally handicapped. They were at least two years behind their peers academically and evidenced normal or above normal I.Q.'s. Somewhat to our surprise, however, these children, numbering twenty-eight, did not evidence mean scores that were below the norms on a comprehensive battery of motor tests.

These children did, however, have problems when playing. They could not relate well socially on the school yard and would usually return to their classroom too overaroused to work well under the more confining classroom environment. This research was followed up by the writing of a syllabus containing low-organizational games and relaxation training activities for the use of their teachers. At the same time, placing all of them on balance beams to aid in their general perceptual organization would have been less than appropriate insofar as their balance abilities were well within the normal ranges.

In one of the most comprehensive evaluations of normal children's perceptual-motor (psychomotor) and academic abilities, Cawley and his colleagues, in a series of studies, contribute quite a bit to our understanding of these relationships. Their conclusions include the observation that "there is no indication that psychomotor ability traits and reading characteristics are substantially related."

Moreover, as a result of the application of factor analytic techniques, four separate and independent factors were identified when the scores from reading tests, various tests of visual-perceptual efficiency, and psychomotor tests were compared. These factors included one composed of scores from tests that might be characterized as consisting of reading and language characteristics (word recognition, vowel sounds, etc.); a second containing scores involving associational qualities in reading; a third (independent of the first two) containing scores reflecting various perceptual characteristics of developing children. In a study reported in 1970, we also found that scores from tests of gross motor control (balance agility, etc.), "loaded" in a factor separate from one containing scores from tests describing pre-reading competencies (i.e., letter recognition, pattern recognition, spelling, and the like).

The available research indicates that while it is not unusual to find coordination problems among groups of children labeled academically deficient, more often, it is difficult to predict academic ability by exposing children to tests of motor competency. At the same time, a child or youth with a normal I.Q. evidencing academic problems may be free from perceptual-motor problems.

Some researchers have attempted to illuminate the possible remedial effects of programs of perceptual-motor education upon the academic abilities of children with learning problems. The results of these studies together with their implications are contained in the section that follows.

Causal Studies

The common finding that coordination problems are prevalent in groups of children evidencing other learning difficulties has prompted more than one clinician to advance programs of remediation containing a preponderance of movement tasks. More encouraging has been the number of researchers who have been encouraged to carry out studies checking on the meaning of motor-mental relationships within these groups. Although some of the studies seem guided more by emotion than by acceptable scientific principles, there have been several respectable attempts to explore the complexities of motor-mental relationships in groups of children having learning difficulties.[4]

Some of these studies were briefly reviewed in Chapter 3. The paragraphs that follow discuss a select group of representative recent investigations. More thorough reviews of this literature are contained in the text by Myers and Hammill and in Cratty's *Perceptual and Motor Development in Infants and Children*.

In 1966, Robbins' study was one of the first well-controlled investigations of the Delacato method. Using 126 subjects in three groups, the children (in the experimental group) from second-grade classes on Chicago's South Side were exposed to a three-month program that emphasized cross-pattern creeping, walking, avoidance of music, and other

---

[4] It is a commonly stated platitude, in courses dealing with educational research and methodology, that an unfortunate fifty-year lag occurs between the discovery of new methods and techniques by researchers and the adoption of these practices into the schools. However, in the case of the efficiency of perceptual-motor training, at least a five- to ten-year lag should have been permitted to transpire between the presentation of the claims for the various programs and the adoption of the methodologies in schools and in homes. A time period such as this might have been devoted to evaluating the veracity of the claims before exposing children to the methodologies advanced. At this writing, however, this time period has elapsed, and thus it is possible to evaluate the efficiency of the various programs. To some degree this evaluation was covered in Chapter 3.

"sidedness" and cross-patterning activities. Although the children were not chosen because they evidenced specific learning difficulties, it would be expected, if the Delacato theory is a valid one, that significant improvements would be seen in the children's ability to engage in various academic tasks, including reading and arithmetic, and in various perceptual-motor activities (creeping and the like).

Robbins' findings did not support any of the sub-hypotheses he formulated. No improvement was seen in reading, in arithmetic, and in the motor measures obtained on the part of the experimental subjects when compared to the controls. Although several facets of Robbins' study have been criticized (i.e., the short time to which the children were exposed to the creeping and crawling activities, the lack of learning, and motor deficits in the subject population, etc.), the investigation was one of the first whose findings cast doubts upon the efficiency of basic patterning and locomotor activities in the improvement of academic abilities, as suggested by Delacato.

A second more recent study carried out by Kirk Fisher produced findings that might also prove discouraging to advocates of the perceptual-motor theory advanced by Kephart. Fisher employed as subjects fifty-four children with learning difficulties who also evidenced deficits in perceptual-motor abilities (as evaluated by the Purdue Perceptual-Motor Survey). The Wechsler Intelligence Scale for Children was administered prior to and following a twice-a-week program of perceptual-motor training that lasted for four and one-half months. Two other comparable groups of children acted as controls; one was given special attention in the form of exposure to recreational games, while the other was accorded only regular classroom activities.

Unlike many studies of this problem, Fisher's investigation was well-conceived, proper controls were employed, and a favorable student-teacher ratio was used during the training (2:1). Again, there was no evidence that this type of short-term training in motor abilities significantly affected the intellectual functioning or school achievement of the children involved. Even when the sub-scores derived from performance items on the WISC were inspected for improvement, no significant differences were recorded. At the same time, there were no significant differences on the Perceptual-Motor Survey itself following training, a rather surprising finding since the Kephart-type training items follow rather closely the test items of the Survey. Although significant correlations were recorded between the scores on the Perceptual-Motor Survey and the Stanford Achievement Test, they were on the order of +.3 and +.4.

Other studies hypothesizing change in intellectual abilities, following exposure to structured perceptual-motor programs, have resulted in similar negative findings. Still others have been so poorly designed that no valid conclusions may be reached upon inspection of their findings.[5]

More promising however, have been findings from a series of studies by McCormick and his colleagues at George Williams College in Illinois. The first three groups of first grade children were exposed to what was termed "perceptual-motor" training which lasted for seven weeks, administered twice a week for forty-five minute sessions. The experimental group was significantly superior to the controls in tests of reading and intelligence; a group, inserted to control for the Hawthorne effect, showed gains intermediate to the controls and experimentals and were not significantly different from the experimentals in the critical scores inspected.

A second study employed sixty-four children, twenty-four of whom were identified as having average intelligence but were reading below grade level. (The Metropolitan Reading Test was used.) The perceptual-motor trained group of low achieving readers made significant gains beyond those of the control group, although no group controlling for special attention was inserted into this study.

A third study employed "underprivileged" white and black children as subjects. After three months of training, the experimental group exhibited significant gains in reading comprehension, while the controls did not. Again, however, no control was employed for "attention effects" between the experimenters and the children, even though in the first studies of this series, McCormick, et al. found the Hawthorne effect to be of considerable importance in influencing the findings.

A detailed inspection of the training procedures employed by McCormick and his colleagues, however, affords clues as to why the training procedures might have positively influenced the reading scores. For example, at one point the investigators state that they exposed the children to one-half hour of practice in reading comprehension. Other activities included sequences of movements to remember, gradually increasing in number and complexity, thus resembling the serial memory tasks in I.Q. tests. Practice in auditory discrimination employing movement tasks was also used in the training, as were activities stressing "motor planning," such as prior "thinking through" of complex movement sequences. It is, thus, not surprising that this kind of relatively complex perceptual-motor training (including the described cognitive tasks, auditory dis-

---

[5] In a study by Ismail and Gruber, for example, the investigators permitted teachers of the children to discard as subjects those children whose I.Q. test scores did not truly reflect the children's intelligence as seen by the teachers; this suggested that the I.Q. tests were invalid as evaluative instruments.

crimination, memory tasks, and sight reading drill) would elicit change in a wide range of academic and intelligence test scores in three studies.

A program we have carried out in the central city of Los Angeles during the past three years contains similarly complex cognitive elements, although the media through which the instructors work is "movement oriented." In pilot studies carried out in 1967, it was found that highly significant changes were elicited in children with low potential (but at least average I.Q.s), by exposing them to tasks involving pattern recognition, serial memory, letter recognition, auditory-visual translations of letters and letter combinations, and spelling involving phonics methods.

Follow-up studies carried out during the school years 1969-70 and 1970-71 similarly produced positive findings. These latter studies were better controlled than the first pilot effort and contained groups that attempted control for the aforementioned Hawthorne effect (the effect of extra time and attention given to children with learning difficulties). In all these latter studies the vast majority of the children posted scores on I.Q. tests (Peabody Picture Vocabulary and the SRA Non-Verbal Test) that were well within the average range. At the same time, these children were evidencing obvious learning problems as assessed by their classroom teachers when given standardized tests of achievement and reading potential such as The Metropolitan Reading Readiness Test.

Summary

It appears that when children with learning difficulties are exposed to structured programs of perceptual-motor training in which there is a lack of "cognitive and/or academic elements," little change is to be expected on tests of intelligence and academic abilities including reading. On the other hand, when the programs of motor activities contain a number of tasks that challenge such children intellectually and encourage them in lead-up activities to various academic tasks or to exercise basic qualities long found to be necessary to effective reading (i.e., auditory discrimination, visual pattern recognition, visual, auditory short-term and long-term memory, and the like), significant improvement in various academic competencies is likely to be forthcoming. It is hoped that further research will provide prescriptive programs of perceptual-cognitive-motor education more exactly matched to the deficits pre-tested in the children acting as subjects, rather than simply exposing an ill-defined group of children to some program of perceptual-motor education that the investigator (a priori) deems helpful and important. Moreover, the available research describes programs whose content is so varied and complex that determining just what program content influences what changes in children is a more than difficult undertaking.

Although it is not uncommon to find, among children with learning difficulties, an unusual number who evidence motor problems, slight positive correlations are often found between academic tests and those purporting to evaluate perceptual-motor functioning. The causal studies perhaps spawned by these correlations and observations vary markedly in quality and in the degree to which the program contains various academic and/or intellectual elements. Moreover, when factorial analyses have been carried out using subjects in early childhood, perceptual-motor items and academic test scores usually "load" in separate factors.

BIBLIOGRAPHY

CAWLEY, JOHN F.; GOODSTEIN, HENRY A.; and BURROW, WILL. *Reading and Psychomotor Disability Among Mentally Retarded and Average Children.* Storrs, Conn.: The University of Connecticut, 1968.

CAWLEY, JOHN F.; BURROW, WILL; and GOODSTEIN, HENRY A. *An Appraisal of Head Start Participants: Expanded Considerations on Learning Disabilities among Disadvantaged Children.* Storrs, Conn.: The University of Connecticut, 1968.

CRATTY, BRYANT J. *Perceptual and Motor Development in Infants and Children.* New York: The Macmillan Co., 1970.

———. *The Perceptual-Motor Attributes of Mentally Retarded Children and Youth.* Los Angeles: Mental Retardation Services Board, 1966.

CRATTY, BRYANT J. and MARTIN, M. M. *The Effects of a Program of Learning Games Upon Selected Academic Abilities in Children with Learning Difficulties.* Washington, D.C.: U.S. Office of Education, Bureau of Handicapped Children, 1970.

CRATTY, BRYANT J.; IKEDA, NAMIKO; MARTIN, M. M.; JENNETT, CLAIR; and MORRIS, MARGARET. *Movement Activities, Motor Ability and the Education of Children.* Springfield, Ill.: Charles C. Thomas, Publisher, 1970.

DELACATO, CARL. *The Diagnosis and Treatment of Speech and Reading Problems.* Springfield, Ill.: Charles C. Thomas, Publisher, 1963.

FISHER, KIRK L. *Effects of a Structure Program of Perceptual Motor Training on the Development and School Achievement of Educable Mentally Retarded Children.* Washington, D.C.: Bureau of Research, Office of Education, Department of Health, Education, and Welfare, 1969.

FROSTIG, MARIANNE, and HORNE, D. *Teacher's Guide, The Frostig Program for the Development of Visual Perception.* Chicago: Follett Educational Corp., 1964.

GETMAN, G.; KANE, ELMER; HALGREN, MARVIN; and McKEE, GORDON. *Developing Learning Readiness.* Teacher's Manual. New York: McGraw-Hill Book Co., 1966.

ISMAIL, A. H., and GRUBER, J. J. *Motor Aptitude and Intellectual Performance.* Columbus, Ohio: Charles E. Merrill Books, Inc., 1967.

KEPHART, NEWELL C. *The Slow Learner in the Classroom.* Columbus, Ohio: Charles E. Merrill Books, Inc., 1960.

McCARTHY, JAMES and McCARTHY, JOAN. *Learning Disabilities.* Boston: Allyn and Bacon, Inc., 1969.

McCORMICK, CLARENCE; SCHNOBRICH, JANICE; and FOOTLIK, S. WILLARD. *Perceptual-Motor Training and Cognitive Achievement.* Downers Grove, Ill.: George Williams College, 1967.

McCORMICK, CLARENCE C.; POETKER, BETTY; SCHNOBRICH, JANICE; and FOOTLIK, S. WILLARD, "Improvement in Reading Achievement through Perceptual-Motor Training." Manuscript submitted to *Research Quarterly,* AAHPER, 1966.

McCORMICK, CLARENCE; SCHNOBRICH, JANICE N.; and FOOTLIK, S. WILLARD. "The Effect of Perceptual-Motor Training on Reading Achievement." submitted for publication, in press, *Academic Therapy Quarterly,* 1967.

MYERS, PATRICIA, and HAMMILL, DONALD, *Methods for Learning Disorders.* New York: John Wiley & Sons, 1969.

ROBBINS, MELVYN, "A Study of the Validity of Delacato's Theory of Neurological Organization." *Exceptional Children* 32 (1966): 517–23.

STRAUSS, A. A., and LEHTINEN, L. E. *Psychopathology and Education of the Brain Injured Child.* New York: Grune and Stratton, Inc. 1947.

III

EXERCISE, ATTENTION, AND MOTOR SKILL

8

Mental Components of Motor Skill Learning

The major emphasis of this book is upon intellectual and academic functions and how they are manifested in various degrees of muscular involvement. In this chapter, however, the other side of the coin is examined. Data and theories are explored that help to illuminate the mental components ingrained in skilled motor performance and learning.

There are very few types of overt observable behavior that are not guided, at least during the initial stages of learning, by some kind of conscious thought. Only the rapid and reflex-like withdrawal of the hand from a hot stove and similar movements lasting for a second or less are relatively free from processes that would be termed mental. Most of the time, however, conscious thought either precedes or accompanies action. Scholars have shown varying degrees of interest in what is termed "mental practice," or conceptualization, upon subsequent performance and learning of physical skills. The content and data emerging from this research also are reviewed.

Historical Background

Research in mental practice and in mentalistic processes accompanying measurable behavior has enjoyed varying degrees of respectability within the scientific community during the past 120 years. The beginnings of the study of psychology, when articles were philosophical in their orientation, were marked by voluminous essays in which there was much concern about the thoughts, imagery, and similarly difficult-to-measure mental processes that appear to underlie various kinds of behavior and task performance. Although some of these might appear to the present day behavioral scientists to be unscientific, a thorough consideration of their content can often provide helpful "leads" to important problems that statistical procedures and technology may help to illuminate.

The early history of experimental psychology, both in the New and Old World, is marked by a continual ideological struggle by individuals who tended to break away from this type of introspective psychology and who presented ideas that were based upon rather exact laboratory experiments of measurable observable behavior.

This objectivism in psychology introduced by Wundt in Leipzig in the late 1800s and championed by Watson and others in America around the turn of the century, while bringing respectability to psychology in the total community of scientific scholars, tended to suppress interest in, and studies about, human mental processes for a number of years. However, in the writings of Freud and others of the psychoanalytic school in the 1920s and 1930s one is able to discern a penetrating interest in some of the more subtle, and difficult-to-measure, aspects of human behavior.

By 1930, a few scholars who started as rather strict behaviorists began to turn again to mentalistic explanations of behavior, rather than to rely solely upon the turnings of rats in mazes and the ability of humans to repeat lists of nonsense syllables. Tolman, for example, began to collect evidence that even rodents seemed to form mental-conceptual maps of the maze patterns, while the concern of Kofka and Kohler, the German Gestalt psychologists, illuminating such processes as "insight" and the "eureka effect," which purportedly accompany the solving of problems they set before primates, also attracted the interest of psychologists and educators. Tolman and Honzik also found that even when the various chains of kinesthetic responses used by rats as they traversed mazes were disturbed in subsequent trials (by flooding the mazes, forcing them to swim, or by altering their gait patterns through surgery), their learning seemed to improve and to continue.

The keenly observant and creative Gestalt psychologists also observed that some covert trial-and-error practice was apparently taking place within the minds of their subjects, as the apes they studied would with frequency solve various multistage problems that were placed before them.

There are many aspects to the study of the mental-cognitive operations apparently occurring when considering and executing complete motor skills. Among these dimensions are the following:

1. One may consider *when* the institution of certain instructions by another individual may facilitate skill learning within a program comprising several practice trials.

2. The nature of the instructions to rehearse a skill mentally may be considered as related to skill improvement and retention. Individuals have been instructed to imagine themselves performing the skill, to verbalize the sequences in the skill (say it over in their minds), or to imagine themselves observing another individual performing the skill.

3. Some studies have explored the influence of various personality and intellectual traits of the learners as a function of the opportunities given them to practice a skill mentally.

4. Skills of various degrees of complexity have been studied as possibly influential of instructions to engage in their mental rehearsal, conceptualization, or mental practice.

5. Several of the researchers have studied the effects of physical practice versus simply permitting subjects to observe the performance of a motor task. No attempt may be made to structure the thinking of the observing subjects, and indeed their "minds" may not in truth be occupied with the task they are watching. The results of these studies, however, are quite interesting and are reviewed in these pages.

6. The frequency of opportunities and/or instructions to practice a skill mentally have also been studied as productive of varying degrees of task improvement.

7. Most helpful have been the findings from several researchers' studies that explore the possible influences of varying combinations of actual physical practice with mental practice upon the ultimate skill levels attained.

8. A few researchers have also been interested in the influence of instructions to rehearse a skill mentally upon the retention of skill after a period of no-practice has elapsed.

9. Sporadic interest has been apparent over the past forty years in the relationships between mental processes (thinking) and slight muscular responses in the larger muscle groups. The studies of Jacobson in the 1930s have their counterpart in research by Ulrich and others in the 1960s and 1970s.

Most important, when interpreting the data from such studies, is to remember that one can only study the influence of some kinds of *instructions* to perform, modification of performance strategy, mental rehearsal, and the like upon actual performance measures. Obtaining *direct measures*, via physiological (usually electroencephalic) measures of the mental processes involved, when learning various intellectual and/or physical skills, have been less than successful.

Theories Explaining Mental Practice Effects

There have been a number of attempts to explain, within a theoretical framework, the reasons for the usually positive findings in studies exploring the effects of mental practice upon motor skill. Some of these explanations revolve around the possible presence of finite muscular responses that purportedly accompany conceptualization of an action. This explanation, of course, is most acceptable to stimulus-response learning theorists of the Skinnerian school.

Others have proposed theories that contain references to mediating verbal responses that usually insert themselves between most stimulus arrays (or perceptual conditions) and complex motor responses. The latter explanation is likely to be advanced and given credence by those scholars adhering to the Gestaltic or cognitive theory of learning. Clark's verbal-loop hypothesis also falls within this conceptual framework.

NEUROMUSCULAR THEORY

Since the 1930s, research, particularly that by Jacobson and Shaw, has revealed that imagining a movement will likely produce recordable electric action potentials emanating from the muscle groups that would be called up if the movement were to be actually carried out. This same phenomenon has been reported in more recent studies by Ulrich and by Oxendine. In general, this phenomenon has also been confirmed in the subjective reports of those engaged in mental practice studies who have stated, for example, that "during the second trial I felt the clear phenomenon of fatigue in my hand."

Several investigators, in addition to Jacobson and Oxendine, have reported that movements of the eye muscles accompany mental rehearsal of motor skills and that in most cases the nature of the movements are similar to those expected if the individual were actually to perform the task. This tendency to elicit muscular responses during mental work has been termed "the carpenter effect." This phenomenon has been defined as the tendency of any perception or imagination of a motion to produce muscular impulses in the subject which correspond to the overtly-produced motion itself.

However, it is debatable whether the precision of the muscular responses occurring in mental practice studies are similar in precision to the movements if actually carried out. For example, Oxendine reported that, "During mental practices the total body was tense." He also reported that some of his subjects rolled their heads and engaged in similar activities when being asked to imagine themselves engaged in practice on a pursuit rotor. In this latter investigation the soccer kick and jump shot in basketball were employed, both of which are rather exact movements calling for well-regulated sequenced movements.

In what amounts to a pilot study, Ulrich recorded the amount of electric potential emanating from the hands of eighteen retarded subjects while mentally practicing a finger dexterity test. He then separated the group into thirds, according to the amount of muscular tension they evidenced (high, medium, low). The most improvement in the task was recorded by the group evidencing a moderate amount of tension (95 percent improvement as compared to 50 percent and 56 percent of the high and low tension groups respectively). Ulrich concluded that too much tension reflected disorganized and inefficient organization of muscular impulses accompanying thought, while the low group was probably not activated enough. On the other hand, the moderately activated group, evidenced in the muscular tension measures obtained on an electromyograph, were most productive insofar as the muscular responses accompanying their thoughts more closely matched the actual demands of the task.

It is believed that before such a simple neuromuscular way of explaining positive effects of mental practice becomes a tenable model, further research is needed in which not only the general presence of rather diffuse muscular tension is measured, but also the subtle changes of tension in various muscle groups in temporal sequences must be recorded during mental practice sessions.

As seen in Chapter 10, most mental activity is accompanied by general rises in muscular tension, rises that may simply be a reflection of rather global activation-arousal, rather than of the mental practice of a specific motor skill.

Ulrich obtained highly significant physiological changes evidenced in upward shifts in respiration and heart rates, changes in groups of subjects who have been asked to rehearse mentally a relatively passive task involving finger dexterity. These data have not been thoroughly studied in conjunction with mental practice. But at the same time, Ulrich's findings lend validity to theories purporting to explain mental practice effects based upon fluctuations of various physiological indices denoting activation and arousal.

IDEATIONAL ELEMENTS THEORY

It has been observed that one of the paramount differences between animals and men seems to be the ability of the latter to attach symbols to motor tasks, which usually results in apparently better memory. Most motor skill practice, particularly during the early phases, is accompanied by what might be termed "verbal mediation," self-directed sub-vocal verbal rehearsal of the skill attempted. Glanzer and Clark have suggested that most perceptual information is translated into word series, which are retained until time for some kind of reproduction or interpretation. Acceptance of this principle leads to several other speculations that relate to the mental practice or observation effects upon motor skill acquisition.

For example, as Glanzer and Clark found if, when subjects were asked to translate perceptual arrays into verbal descriptions, they produced positive retention of the figures to be reproduced later, in the same way the practice of a precise verbal description of a "perceptual array" composed of movement sensations would also be likely to result in more accurate later reproduction of the skill to be acquired. Since the 1920s, Lambert and Ewert, as well as Warden, found that verbalization of styles of maze tasks resulted in more proficient performance than when subjects were asked to rely upon remembering muscular responses (the kinesthetic method). Warden concluded that there is a substitution of pre-formed unit responses (composed of muscular-word units?) that prepared a helpful base for motor skill learning composed of a verbal pattern.

AN OVERVIEW

In summary, however, it is believed difficult to place one's total confidence in either an ideational-mediation model or a neuro-motor model when explaining mental practice or observational practice effects upon the acquisition of complex motor responses. In several studies, for example, it was found that when tasks were more complex, there seemed to be more tendency of the subjects to rely upon verbal self-descriptions and less tendency to exhibit muscular tensions. Moreover, within the same task, subjects were observed not to evidence highly individual differences, but to modify the nature of the various behaviors they manifested during mental rehearsal as practice sessions progressed. Just as perceptual-conceptual elements seem to begin to "drop out" (with relationship to their importance) as one practices a complex motor skill, so do general and specific muscular tensions as one mentally rehearses reasonably complex movement. Only when the imagined movement is a simple, direct, and forceful weight-lifting task will strong muscle responses continue to be manifested during the period of time subjects are requested to engage in mental rehearsal.

One thus could advance a model that involves what might be termed "verbal-motor practice," and suggest that the involvement of either facet of the personality, even during mental rehearsal periods, changes as a function of practice and as a function of task familiarity and complexity in relationship to the learner's capacities and maturational level.

WHEN TO CONCEPTUALIZE

There have been several helpful studies relative to temporal aspects of mental rehearsal and the offering of instructions during and prior to the learning and performance of a motor skill.

In one of the most sustained programs of study of perceptual-motor skills, Fleishman produced findings that point to several practical guidelines within this general area. For example, factor analytic studies of the degrees to which various factors apparently contribute to the acquisition of several complex skills indicate that, during initial trials, various conceptual and perceptual factors are most important and contribute most to skill improvement. On the other hand, during the latter stages of learning, such motor competencies as reaction time and measures of kinesthesis correlated highest with the performance of complex criterion tasks used.

Follow-ups based upon these findings studied the insertion of instructions appropriate to the stage of learning in which the performer found himself. Thus, during the initial stages of learning, performers were carefully guided through the mechanical principles of the task and permitted to learn about the various spatial relationships of the movements they were to engage in.

During the latter stages of learning, instructions concerning various movement qualities were inserted, just before, as previous research indicated, these kinds of abilities were to become important in skill improvement. The findings of this research program constitute some of the most helpful information emerging from the entire study of human movement capacities. For, with appropriate instructions, and hypothetically with the appropriate concomitant mental activity elicited by these instructions, marked improvement was seen and skill levels were reached that were significantly higher than was attained by various control groups.

Contemporary studies within this same program by Fleishman and his colleagues indicate that if one is to separate individuals into two groups—those evidencing high levels of basic motor abilities and those evidencing high levels of spatial-perceptual-cognitive awareness and ability—exposing both groups to complex motor tasks will result in learning curves that have obviously different shapes.

As can be seen in Figures 8.2 and 8.3, those possessing high conceptual-spatial abilities evidence quick early improvement but tend to

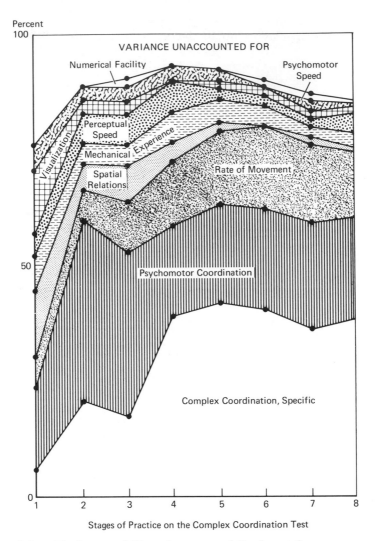

Reprinted from Fleishman and Hempel, courtesy of *Psychometrika*

Figure 8.1

Percentage of variance (shaded area) represented by each factor at
different stages of practice on the Complex Coordination Test.

plateau when the latter stages of a task are reached, in which their
particular competencies do not play a major role.

In contrast, those possessing relatively high levels of the motor attri-

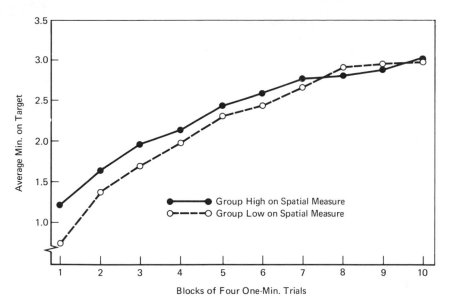

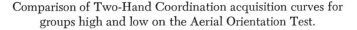

From E. A. Fleishman and Simon Rich, "Role of Kinesthetic and Spatial-Visual Abilities in Perceptual-Motor Learning," *Journal of Experimental Psychology*, Vol. 66, No. 1., 1963, Fig. 1, p. 9. Copyright 1963 by the American Psychological Association and reproduced by permission.

FIGURE 8.2

Comparison of Two-Hand Coordination acquisition curves for groups high and low on the Aerial Orientation Test.

butes needed during the latter stages of task performance evidence performance curves that are positively accelerated as practice progresses.

Data of this type also point out what may be the optimum time to conceptualize without physical practice when attempting to acquire a motor task. Recent data point to the possibility that mental practice is not only most effective during the beginning stages of skill learning, but during the early stage may be equal in effectiveness to actual physical practice of the skill! In summary, therefore, these findings suggest that mental practice will aid in skill acquisition during the practice stage where mental-conceptual-perceptual components correlate highest with the performance level of the skill under study.

SKILLS MOST IMPROVED BY MENTAL PRACTICE

The literature substantiates what would be a common-sense supposition, that is, that more complex skills, particularly those involving some kind of throwing-aiming hand-eye coordination, are most improvable through conceptual or mental practice. Skills that are relatively simple, not involving several stages to be integrated together, on the

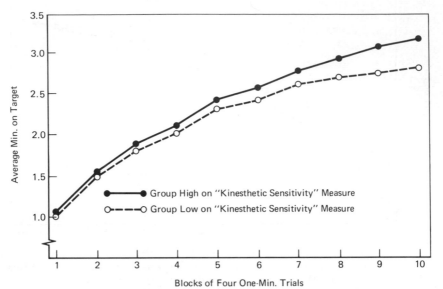

Blocks of Four One-Min. Trials

From E. A. Fleishman and Simon Rich, "Role of Kinesthetic and Spatial-Visual Abilities in Perceptual-Motor Learning," *Journal of Experimental Psychology*, Vol. 66, No. 1., 1963, Fig. 2, p. 9. Copyright 1963 by the American Psychological Association and reproduced by permission.

FIGURE 8.3

Comparison of Two-Hand Coordination acquisition curves for groups
high and low on the Kinesthetic Sensitivity measure.

other hand, show little or no improvement with mental practice, but instead require actual physical output.

The principle obviously arising from this finding suggests that mental practice will aid the learning of a specific skill to the degree to which mental factors are important in that skill's performance.

INDIVIDUAL DIFFERENCES IN MENTAL PRACTICE EFFECTS

For the past three hundred years scholars have been aware of individual differences in human abilities. While the first differences explored were such simplistic attributes as reaction time and the like, more recently relatively subtle differences in imagery have been explored. Some of the strategies that have been employed to study mental practice effects have included looking at how individual differences in the way people perceive and organize information influence how people covertly acquire skill.

Some types of abilities and characteristics do not apparently influence the benefits of mental practice. The preponderance of evidence indicates that scores derived from standardized I.Q. tests are in no way predictive of practice effects, while the study by Perry produced data that indicated that no sex differences seemed to exist in the improvement of motor ability scores as a function of mental practice on five different tasks.

Other investigators have found, however, that individuals higher in general measures of motor ability and in "games ability" generally derive more benefit from mental practice than do less physically able individuals. However, it is difficult to determine whether those high in motor ability are also those more highly motivated to improve within the experimental situations, or whether real differences in the various groups studied did exist.

VISUAL AND KINESTHETIC PERCEPTUAL MEASURES AND MENTAL REHEARSAL BENEFITS

Moderate correlations have been obtained (.63) between percent improvement due to mental practice and various measures of visual memory. For example, in a study by Whiteley, it was found that those subjects who could remember where on a quadrant various subjects had been placed were generally those who benefited more from mental practice of a physical skill.

However, no significant correlations were obtained between improvement in a motor skill mentally rehearsed and measures obtained from the Gottschadlt test of figure-ground perception. Measures of spatial relations obtained by Wilson also failed to correlate with mental practice gains, while similar non-significant correlations were obtained by Start, who compared measures of kinesthesis with improvement scores obtained when exposing subjects to a gymnastic skill.

In general, the data suggest that standard measures of kinesthesis, visual memory, figure-ground perception, and the like are not likely to be highly predictive of improvement in motor skill due to mental practice. However, the research is sparse, and more sophisticated studies might reveal individual differences in perceptual abilities predictive of the manner in which at least a portion of the population may benefit from engaging in mental practice of motor skills.

OBSERVATION, MENTAL PRACTICE, AND PHYSICAL PRACTICE COMPARISONS

Various tacks may be taken when offering some encouragement to engage individuals mentally in the learning of motor skills. An experimenter may, for example, present a highly structured list of directions as evidenced by the following:

> I want you to imagine yourself back in the gymnasium, standing behind the throwing line and facing your target. When you feel you have done this as well as you are able, try to mentally rehearse the routine of throwing the ball at the target. Besides trying to see yourself also try to feel yourself going through the routine. Try to see and feel yourself picking up the ball in your hand, taking the ball behind you as you transfer your body weight backwards onto your rear foot in preparation for the throw. Try then to imagine the second part of the action, in which having selected your point of aim on the target, you complete the throw with a forward twisting movement of the body and a forward movement of the arm and hand. Watch the ball during its flight; remember the target has been dusted with chalk and the place where the ball strikes will remain clearly marked after the ball has rebounded from the target. Give this mark careful attention and in your next throw try to make any adjustments in your action and the selection of your point of aim, which you feel will result in a more accurate throw. I shall stop you in 15 minutes time. Now quietly concentrate.

On the other hand, the experimenter may permit the subjects an amount of time for physical as well as mental practice of the skill, as Oxendine and Egstrom have done. Still other experimenters worked with a third group of subjects who were permitted to observe the performance of a skill they were later to reproduce, but at the same time were tendered no formal structured instructions as to how they might imaginably practice the skill.

In general, when improvement of groups is compared, in which one is accorded the opportunity to observe, a second engages in mental practice, and a third is given physical practice, the observation group evidences less improvement than the other two. For example, in a study reported by Ulrich, it was found that the observation group improved 47.4 percent, the "mental training" group achieved a 63.2 percent improvement, while the physical practice group improved 96.6 percent. Most improvement in a task involving finger dexterity was achieved by a group given alternate physical and mental practice, while Ulrich reports that the controls given no practice in the task improved only 20.3 percent on the second testing.

Diagrammed, this comparative improvement is shown in Figure 8.4. Ulrich reports similar results in an experiment in which typing was used as a task.

The findings of the various studies, while often contradictive, have begun to paint a reasonably reliable picture of what one might expect under various types of the mental practice, instructions, and conditions described above.

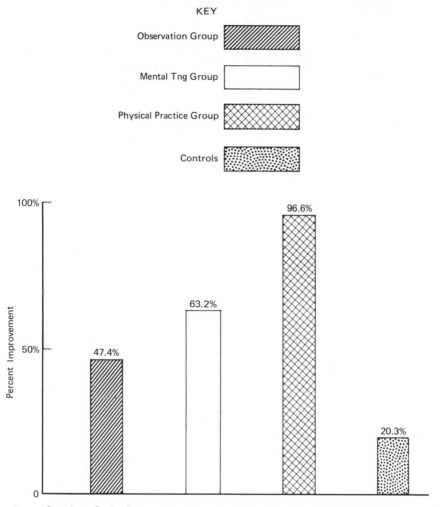

From data by Ulrich, "Some Experiments on the Function of Mental Training on the Acquisition of Motor Skills." *Ergonomics,* Vol. 4, No. 10 (1967) 411–19.

FIGURE 8.4

OPTIMUM TIME FOR MENTAL PRACTICE

There seems to be an optimum time that, if devoted to rehearsing a skill mentally, is likely to produce the most improvement, and that, if exceeded or if not reached, will not produce as marked benefits. Twining, for example, found that about five minutes was as long as one could expect his subjects to concentrate upon the task he asked them to rehearse mentally. Difficult to control in these studies, of course, is what enters the subject's thoughts when he is not instructed to rehearse mentally, and thus estimates about how long he really engages in conceptualization about the skill are probably inaccurate.

Some researchers (Perry for example) asked their subjects to think about things other than the skill involved, while Cratty and Densmore asked their control groups either to engage in a knot-tying task or to count backwards from 100 in a 1962 study to control for mental practice effects during rest. Perry and Morrisett, in separate efforts to control for side-practice effects, confined their studies to periods under two hours.

ALTERNATING PHYSICAL WITH MENTAL PRACTICE

A number of researchers have compared the improvement of groups who have mentally practiced a task with those who have engaged in varying amounts of physical plus mental practice. In general, their findings indicate that some combination is better than engaging only in mental practice. Egstrom's findings indicate that the groups alternating physical and mental practice performed about equally as well as those engaging entirely in physical practice in a task involving hitting a ball toward a target with their non-preferred hand.

At the same time, it seems that familiarity with the task had an important influence upon the percent of physical versus mental practice that may result in optimum improvement. Among novice basketball players, for example, Clark found that physical practice was almost twice as beneficial as mental practice, while with more skilled groups mental practice proved almost equal to physical practice.

RETENTION AFTER MENTAL PRACTICE

Relatively few studies have been carried out to determine the influence of mental practice upon the retention of motor skill. Oxendine found that retention on the part of the various groups in his study did not differ significantly, and Sackett, using a finger maze, obtained the same results. Rubin-Rabson, studying piano playing ability, found that a group who employed physical practice initially and then a mental practice session followed by physical practice, retained best, after a week had passed, than other groups who had either all physical practice, or who first practiced mentally and then physically.

Ulrich also reports an interesting finding in a study that employed a finger dexterity test, and in which a six-month rest period was inserted between initial practice and later testing for retention. The two groups who not only retained best but even evidenced slight improvement were one that was given all mental practice and a second in which mental practice was alternated with physical practice. The other two groups, having had previous physical practice only, and "training" solely through the opportunity to observe the dexterity task, showed significant decrements! Due to the scarcity of data, little can be done at this point relative to a valid interpretation of these findings, however.

Bilateral Transfer

Further evidence of the effects of central thought processes upon skill acquisition is found in the vast number of studies of bilateral transfer of skill. In general, it is found that practice with one hand will improve skill in the other, while Cook and others have even carried out studies that have looked at foot-to-hand and hand-to-foot transfer, usually finding that the most positive transfer is from limbs that are closely adjacent (hand-hand, foot-foot, right foot to right hand, etc.).

The same theories have been advanced to explain this phenomenon as have been described when attempting to illuminate the role of mental practice upon skill acquisition. Some have suggested that trace responses occurring in the non-practicing limb really constitute a kind of muscular practice that readily facilitates skill in the second limb when it is called into use. Others argue for the importance of central processes as influencing the transfer usually measured.

In one of the most convincing studies in this area, findings have been obtained that argue for the marked importance of central-cognitive processes in skill acquisition and in bilateral transfer studies. Eberhard utilized one that engaged in physical practice of a one-handed task, while the second merely observed the execution of the task, being performed by others. He found as much improvement in the first of the groups who had practiced physically as was evidenced in the attempts at the one-handed skill by the group who had engaged in prior observation!

Summary and Overview

During the past thirty years, from twenty-five to thirty studies have explored the effects of mental rehearsal, conceptualization, symbolic rehearsal, and similarly labeled exercises upon the acquisition of skill. An even greater number of investigations have dealt with bilateral transfer effects. In general, their findings lead toward the conclusion that some degree of mental practice combined with physical practice is beneficial to the learning of motor skills.

At the same time, the methodologies employed in these studies often leave much to be desired. Rarely is any attempt made to control the duration of the time the subjects really think about the task, and often the direction given to the subjects purportedly to elicit their concentration upon the task requirements is imprecise or confusing.

The available precise electronic equipment of the 1970s has seemingly not yet been pressed into service to extract and evaluate the exact nature of the neuromotor activity, which may take place during attempts to engage in mental rehearsal. The exact nature of the perceptual processes, also amenable to evaluation using assessment devices presently available, are similarly not adequately evaluated or controlled in the studies whose findings have been published.

Although several studies have produced findings that indicate that mental practice had little or no effect upon the improvement of physical skill and strength, the majority of the research efforts have had positive outcomes. The researchers have found that from twice as much improvement to about ten times as much improvement is seen in groups asked to rehearse mentally (based upon percentage of gain) as compared to no practice groups. However, the data emerging from the majority of the studies indicate that physical practice is from slightly better than mental practice to several times more effective in the case of studies where sheer physical output (endurance or force) is the main requirement in the task.

Thus, the great bulk of the data indicates that speaking of a *motor skill* is misleading and inaccurate. Rather, there are a variety of human skills, having varying degrees of intellectual involvement. Further research should result in more accurate typologies than are presently available, in which to classify human skill with respect to the mental abilities required for their successful execution and acquisition.

BIBLIOGRAPHY

BUEGEL, H. "The Effects of Introducing Ideational Elements in Perceptual-Motor Learning." *Journal of Experimental Psychology* 27 (1940): 111–124.

COOK, T. W. "Studies in Cross-Education: Kinesthetic Learning of an Irregular Pattern." *Journal of Experimental Psychology* 17 (1934): 745–51.

CORBIN, C. "Effects of Mental Practice on Skill Development after Controlled Practice." *AAHPER Research Quarterly* 38 (1967): 5. 34–38.

CRATTY, BRYANT J., and DENSMORE, A. "Activity During Rest and Learning a Gross Movement Task." *Perceptual and Motor Skills* 17 (1963): 250.

EBERHARD, ULRICH, "Transfer of Training Related to Finger Dexterity." *Perceptual and Motor Skills* 17 (1963): 274.

EGSTROM, C. H. "Effects of Emphasis on Conceptualizing Techniques During Early Learning of a Gross Motor Skill." *Research Quarterly* 35 (1964): 472–81.

FLEISHMAN, EDWIN, and HEMPEL, W. "Changes in Factor Structure of a Complex Psychomotor Test as a Function of Practice." *Psychometrika* 19 (1954): 3.

FLEISHMAN, EDWIN, and HEMPEL, W. "The Relation Between Abilities and Improvement with Practice in a Visual Discrimination Reaction Task." *Journal of Experimental Psychology* 49 (1955): 5.

FLEISHMAN, EDWIN, and RICH, SIMON. "Role of Kinesthetic and Spatial-Visual Abilities in Perceptual-Motor Learning." *Journal of Experimental Psychology* 66 (1963): 6–11.

GLANZER, M., and CLARK, W. "Accuracy of Perceptual Recall: An Analysis of Organization." *Journal of Verbal Learning and Verbal Behavior* 1: 289–99.

HARBY, S. F. "Comparison of Mental and Physical Practice in the Learning of a Physical Skill." *U.S.N. Special Division of Central Technology Report* SDC 269-7-25, 1952.

JACOBSON, E. "Electrophysiology of Mental Activities." *American Journal of Psychology* 44 (1932): 677–94.

KELSEY, I. B. "Effects of Mental Practice and Physical Practice upon Muscular Endurance." *Research Quarterly* 32 (1961): 47–54.

KOHLER, W. *The Mentality of Apes.* Transcribed by E. Winter. New York: Harcourt, Brace Jovanovich, 1925.

LAMBERT, J., and EWERT, P. "The Effect of Verbal Instructions upon Stylus Maze Learning." *Journal of General Psychology* 6 (1932): 377–99.

OXENDINE, JOSEPH B. "The Effect of Mental and Physical Practice on the Learning of Gross Motor Skills." Unpublished Monograph, Temple University, Philadelphia, Pa.: Sponsored by U.S. Office of Education, 1967.

RICHARDSON, A. "Mental Practice: a Review and Discussion." Part I. *Research Quarterly* 38 (1967): 95–107.

RILEY, E., and START, K. B. "The Effect of the Spacing of Mental and Physical Practices on the Acquisition of a Physical Skill." *Australian Journal of Physical Education* 20 (1960): 13–16.

RUBIN-RABSON, G. "Mental and Keyboard Overlearning in Memorizing Piano Music." *Journal of Musicology* 3 (1941): 33–40.

SACKETT, R. S. "The Influences of Symbolic Rehearsal upon the Retention of a Maze Habit." *Journal of General Psychology* 10 (1934): 376–95.

———. "The Relationship between Amount of Symbolic Rehearsal and Retention of a Maze Habit." *Journal of General Psychology* 13 (1935): 113–28.

SHAW, W. A. "The Relation of Muscular Action Potentials to Imaginal Weight Lifting." *Archives of Psychology* 35 (1940): 1–50.

START, K. B. "Relationship Between Intelligence and the Effect of Mental Practice on the Performance of a Motor Skill." *Research Quarterly* 30 (1960): 444–49.

———. "The Influence of Subjectively Assessed 'Games Ability' on Gain in Motor Performance after Mental Practice." *Journal of General Psychology* 67 (1962): 159–73.

———. "Intelligence and Improvement in a Gross Motor Skill After Mental

Practice." *British Journal of Educational Psychology* 34 (1964): 85–90.

―――. *Mental Practice.* Unpublished master's dissertation, University of Western Australia, 1963.

―――. "Kinesthesia and Mental Practice." *Research Quarterly* 35 (1964): 316–20.

START, K. B., and RICHARDSON, A. "Imagery and Mental Practice." *British Journal of Educational Psychology* 34 (1964): 280–84.

STEEL, W. I. "The Effect of Mental Practice on the Acquisition of a Motor Skill." *Journal of Physical Education* 44 (1952): 101–108.

TOLMAN, E. C. "Theories of Learning." In *Comparative Psychology.* Edited by E. A. Moss. Englewood Cliffs, N.J.: Prentice-Hall, Inc., 1934.

TWINING, W. "Mental Practice and Physical Practice in Learning a Motor Skill." *AAHPER Research Quarterly* 20 (1949): 432–435.

ULRICH, E. "Some Experiments on the Function of Mental Training in the Acquisition of Motor Skills." *Ergonomics* 10 (1967): 411–19.

VANDELL, R. A.; DAVIS, R. A.; and CLUGSTON, H. A. "The Function of Mental Practice in the Acquisition of Motor Skills." *Journal of General Psychology* 29 (1943): 243–50).

WARDEN, C. "The Relative Economy of Various Modes of Attack on the Mastering of the Stylus Maze." *Journal of Psychology* 7 (1924): 243–75.

WATERLAND, J. C. "The Effect of Mental Practice Combined with Kinesthetic Perception when the Practice Precedes each Overt Performance of a Motor Skill." Unpublished Masters thesis, University of Wisconsin, 1956.

WHITELEY, G. *The Effect of Mental Rehearsal on the Acquisition of Motor Skill.* Unpublished diploma in education dissertation, University of Manchester, 1962.

WILSON, M. F. "The Relative Effect of Mental Practice and Physical Practice in Learning the Tennis Forehand and Backhand Drives." Ph.D. dissertation, State University of Iowa, 1960.

9

Exercise and Fitness
in Academia

Introduction

For the past fifty years various scholars have studied interrelationships
between physical fitness, muscular tension, muscular fatigue, and
measures of intelligence. At times, their searchings have led them to
discover the ways in which modifying activation levels (as measured
by changes in muscular tension) changes intellectual responses. The
relationships between fitness measures and intelligence test scores
also have been computed. Still other researchers have explored the
manner in which various measures of academic performance and
intelligence are influenced by muscular fatigue, elicited in both fit
and unfit subjects.

Both practice and theoretical implications are apparent upon
careful study of the findings of these investigations. For example, a
school administrator may derive some benefit from data relative to
planning an ideal school day, containing periods and activities
tending both to raise and lower levels of arousal and activation. Social
scientists interested in theories relating activation to other parameters
of human behavior might similarly derive experimental as well as
conceptual guidelines upon consideration of the data.

The findings from these studies make it clear that any measure of intelligence or academic performance is a function not only of basic intellectual capacities, but also of the intensity of effort the individual may, or can, apply to the tests placed before him. Evidences of either heightening attention to tests of academic capabilities, or of over-shooting some level of activation and thus blunting intellectual performance are also found in the studies.

At this writing, the research on these topics is indeed sparse. The studies that have contributed to the content of this chapter have been printed in widely scattered sources in Japan, Sweden, Norway, and the United States. Further difficulty is encountered when reviewing the material insofar as the design of some of the studies lacks polish, and at the same time there has been little sustained effort on the part of scholars to explore the complexity of variables that conceivably might influence their findings. Thus, it is hoped that reviewing this material may prompt some readers to embark upon programs of research that might further help to illuminate some of the darker corners of this interesting, but relatively unexplored, cave of knowledge.

The chapter's contents have been divided into two parts, one dealing with the influence of exercise on academic achievement and measures of intelligence, and a second with information concerning fitness-intellectual relationships in school children.

Exercise and Academic Performance

In several writings, exercise has paired with academic performance in at least two major ways: (1) academic performance has been studied *while* the subjects are exercising, and (2) academic competencies have been measured *immediately following* exercise bouts. Several variables have been manipulated by the researchers carrying out these investigations, including the intensity of the exercise loads imposed, the nature of the academic measures obtained, and the fitness levels of the subjects. Hopefully in the future scholars interested in the relationships between participation in exercise and academic performance will, in more exact ways, vary the exercise demands, control the time after terminating exercise and before beginning academic work more carefully, and more exactly specify the fitness levels of the subjects participating.

Despite the shortcomings of the available studies, there are some principles that seem to be emerging from the evidence they contain. For example, it appears that moderate exercise engaged in by fit subjects is likely to be reflected in moderate improvement in academic abilities demonstrated immediately following. Gutin found that conditioned subjects improved slightly in an addition task following five minutes of exercise in a step-up task. Further work by Gutin, using more intensive exercise (running until exhaustion on a treadmill), produced the expected finding that a significant negative effect was elicited in a test of long addition.

Japanese researchers have also been interested in this same interaction between exercise and mental work performed immediately afterward. Matsuda and his colleagues, for example, obtained results similar to those of Gutin. Following light exercise on a bicycle ergometer, Matsuda's subjects' improvement was seen in the learning of a complex discrimination task in both its early and later stages. Kashiwabara and his co-workers, as well as Hayashi and his staff found that there was a curvilinear relationship between amount of prior physical work and later competence in addition tasks. Kashiwabara utilized athletes as well as school children in his studies, whereas Hayashi employed students participating in physical education classes. Aotani also found that decreases in the ability to engage in multiplication and division were recorded after physical activity was carried out on a bicycle ergometer.

It is difficult to compare the often contradictory findings of these studies because of the diverse types of subjects employed, exercise loads imposed, and academic tests administered. In any case, these and other scholars have proposed two different theories to explain the findings obtained:

1. Producing an optimum level of relaxation-arousal through exercise will likely elicit the best performance in mental tasks. This optimum, of course, rests upon the fitness level of the subjects "exercise-stressed," as well as upon their prior and habitual states of activation and the activation levels needed in the performance of the academic work. Thus, within the model described, one would expect the following to be true (and to some extent this has been vertified in the studies reviewed):
a. Fit individuals exposed to moderate exercise will improve performance in tests of mental ability.
b. Unfit individuals will, if over-stressed in exhaustive exercise, evidence decrements in ability to carry out mental operations.
c. Both the unfit and fit are likely to perform tests of academic and intellectual ability equally well, all things being equal and held constant (as they seldom are!).

2. A second physiologically based model has also been advanced by Gutin. Citing the literature in physiological psychology, he explains that the marked decrements in mental work following exhaustive activity may be caused by a shortage of oxygen to the central nervous system (cortex), an anoxia which may conceivably cause decrements both in "mental work" and in performance of complex motor skills.

While these studies explored the manner in which academic performance may rise or fall *after* engaging in physical activity, in studies in Sweden, academic work was presented *at the same time* as varying amounts of physical exertion. The findings again suggest that the previously discussed optimum-arousal model may be a viable one with which to explain the phenomena under consideration. For example, Kronby found that the best performance in mathematics tasks was achieved when subjects were running on a treadmill at about 45 percent maximum effort. The problems were presented to the running subjects via earphones.

Taken together, the findings from these investigations are more suggestive than conclusive. In any case, the data emanating from them provide an interesting starting point from which future investigators may launch more structured and well-controlled efforts.

Fitness and Intelligence in School Children

Two investigations by Railo and his colleagues in Norway contain provocative findings. In one, the intent was to ascertain the differences in sustained academic performance on the part of two groups of school children identified as evidencing high and low levels of fitness. The second study dealt with relationships between age and academic ability and with trends in fitness on the part of children high and low in academic ability.

In essence, the first study suggested that a quality that might be termed "academic endurance" could be significantly different in two groups of children, one labeled high fitness, and the other classified as less fit. The "academic endurance" task presented in these 200 children was truly a formidable one. For the first two hours they were exposed to an I.Q. test, then, following a ten-minute break they were put to hard study. Finally, after a second unsupervised ten-minute break, the experimenter placed before the children a second test of intelligence, comparable but different in content to the first.

Contrary to the expected hypothesis, the children with high fitness levels exhibited significantly lower test scores during the second testing period than were exhibited by the low-fitness groups, despite the fact that the groups were comparable during the first testing session. This same type of finding was found in the boys' and girls' scores treated separately. Railo attempted to explain these findings by reference to several hypotheses:

> 1: The high fitness children also possessed high needs for activity and when frustrated in the confining test-study-test situation, applied themselves poorly the second time they were faced with an intelligence test.

2. When fitness levels are extremely high, the negative effects of the above described frustration might be overcome. Indeed, this was the case in a group of extremely high fitness children.

3. The absence of the sensory-stimulation experienced by the two groups of children, both of which were denied any physical education that day, was more disturbing to the high fitness group than to the low fitness group.

In a previous study by Railo, it was found that a moderate correlation was recorded between physical endurance and a measure of mental endurance, when other variables including socio-economic level, sex, and age were held constant. On the basis of these studies and the findings from a later one, Railo postulates the existence of two types of "intellectual energy." On one hand, he suggests, is what might be termed "potential intellectual energy," represented by how well the individual *might perform* on a test of intelligence. On the other hand, is "dynamic intellectual energy" or in other terms, the actual performance levels evidenced, influenced by short-term and long-term fatigue, momentary motivational level, attitudes about the tests, and similar transitory factors. The dramatic shifts in scores on the part of the two groups of children are illustrated in Figure 9.1.

In a comprehensive investigation carried out in 1967, Railo explored changes in fitness levels of intellectually capable and less "bright" children between grades 4 and 7. Additionally, correlations between measures of fitness and school achievement were computed during these same years.

No significant relationships between measures of *school achievement* (based upon classroom grades) and fitness were obtained, but there were significant negative relationships found between measures of *intelligence* and fitness measured by a test of maximum oxygen intake during exercise. Moreover, this relationship was less marked in the older children than in younger ones.

Furthermore, the measures taken from the over 400 children indicated that from grades 4 to 7, the children with lower I.Q.s evidenced significant drops in fitness levels while those with higher I.Q.s evidenced the reverse trend. This trend is illustrated in Figure 9.2.

Several plausible hypotheses were advanced by Railo to explain these findings, including the following:

1. Early in the school years, dull children channel their energies into physical activity to compensate for their lack of intellectual ability.

2. High intelligence implies a greater ability for self-amusement, primarily available in solitary activity such as reading (amusements not available to the intellectually less capable individual).

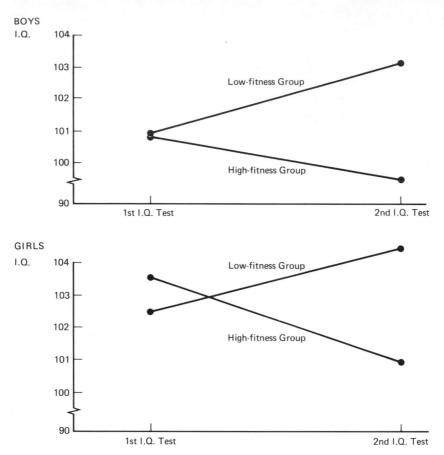

From Willi S. Railo, "Physical and Intellectual Achievement," *Scandinavian Journal of Educational Research,* No. 2, 1969.

FIGURE 9.1

3. With increasing age, bright children become better able to deal with the games of increasing complexity with which they are confronted. More able children, to an increased degree, become attracted more and more to childhood games as they become more of an intellectual challenge by the incorporation of increasingly complex rules and interactions. The games are more complex in late childhood than in early childhood.[1]

Further explanations for the findings included the suggestion that, when physical education is introduced as a regular school subject in the later grades, the dull children are less attracted to it; and that physical

[1] From speech given to North American Society for Psychology in Sport and Physical Activity (Boston, Mass., 1968), by Dr. Brian Sutton-Smith.

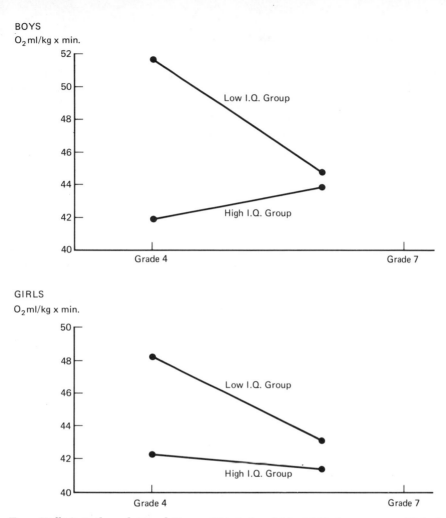

From Willi S. Railo and Sigurd Eggen, Physical and Mental Endurance, unpublished monograph, Norwegian College of Physical Education and Sport, 1967.

FIGURE 9.2

changes during puberty will tend to encourage bright children to participate and become increasingly interested in participating in physical skills.

Railo's findings are helpful in the formulation of additional hypotheses: relative to the concept of dynamic versus potential "intellectual energy," it is apparent that fluctuations in I.Q. test scores may be due to factors other than those inherent in the individual, or to emotional climate, attention span, and those which have plagued testers of intelligence ranging back to Binet.

It is difficult to determine how much one can generalize from these findings to other populations of children within other cultures of the world. Railo attempted to obtain children from a stratified cross-section of the Norwegian population, and included professional people's off-spring, as well as those of factory workers. Until more definitive studies are carried out, particularly those in which intercultural comparisons are made, Railo's work remains the only research, of which I am aware, that explores this type of interesting yet complex topic.

Summary and Implications

Data from the previous studies might suggest several practical implications. For example, both the Japanese researchers and those in Norway found that individual differences in fitness levels, as well as in personality traits (Hayashi), influenced the quality of intellectual work following exercise as well as the amount of "intellectual energy" children brought to tests of intelligence. Thus, one could hypothesize that certain children in a school might be exposed more frequently to vigorous activity than others.[2] The more passive child may be expected to work longer without undue stress in a classroom, while the more active child may need a more active curriculum in which concepts are acted out in movement, (Chapters 11 and 12), and/or more study breaks for exercise and physical education.

If the desire is to produce optimum mental work in office workers and in school children, there also could be more sophisticated studies to determine just how much virogous activity results in individual arousal-activation adjustments which, in turn, cause the more productive intellectual effort. The studies now available contain findings that are only suggestive rather than comprehensive and helpful.

Most helpful, it is believed, is the dichotomy pointed out by Railo of "potential" versus "dynamic" intellectual energy. Perhaps with further thought and more precise longitudinal research studies, exploring how one may "unleash" *dynamic* intellectual energy so that it approximates a youth's *potential* intellectual output will become feasible.

BIBLIOGRAPHY

AOTANI, T. "The Influence of Physical Activity on the Mental Function." *Research Journal of Physical Education* (Japan), Vol. 11, No. 1, 1966.

[2] As Scarr and others have pointed out, there are significant differences in activity levels in infants from birth, differences perhaps reflected later in propensity for activity and fitness levels.

GUTIN, BERNARD, and DiGENNARO, J. "Effect of One-minute and Five-minute Step-ups on Performance of Simple Addition." *Research Quarterly* 39 (March 1968): 81–85.

———. "Effect of a Treadmill Run to Exhaustion on Performance of Long Addition." *Research Quarterly* 39 (December 1968): 958–64.

HAYASHI, T., and YAMAOKA, S. "Research of the Influence of Physical Activity on Intellectual Work." *Research Journal of Physical Education* (Japan), Vol. 10, No. 1, 1965.

KASHIWABARA K, KOBAYASHI T., and KONDO, M. "The Influence of Physical Activity on the Mental Work." (2), *Research Journal of Physical Education* (Japan), Vol. 10, No. 1, 1966.

KISHI, J.; KASHIWABARA K.; SUZUKI T.; KAWASHIMA T.; and NIWA, T. "The Influence of Skiing on the Mental Work." *Research Journal of Physical Education* (Japan), Vol. 11, No. 1, 1966.

KRONBY, B. "How a Person's Numerical Ability is Changed, During Different Loads of Physical Work on the Ergmetric Bicycle." Report from Pedagogisk Psykologiska Institutionen Vid, GIH, Stockholm, Sweden, October 1968.

MATSUDA, IWAO, and SUGIHARA, T. "An Experimental Research of the Effect of Physical Activity on the Mental and Psychomotor Function." *Research J. of Physical Education* (Japan) 13 (March 1969): 242–50.

RAILO, WILLI S. "Physical Fitness and Intellectual Achievement." *Scandinavian Journal of Educational Research*, No. 2 (1969) 103–20.

RAILO, WILLI S., and EGGEN, S. *Physical and Mental Endurance.* Unpublished monograph, Norwegian College of Physical Education and Sport, 1967.

SCARR, SANDRA, "Genetic Factors in Activity Motivation." *Child Development* 37 (1966): 663–73.

10

Intellectual Activity, Activation, and Self-Control

Introduction

Scholars interested in human behavior have taken two primary routes in their explorations. On one hand, they have studied the directions that behavior takes: the selections people make and the manner in which they direct their efforts, attentions, and perceptions. A second primary way is to focus upon sub-problems related to the *intensity* of behavior or activation.[1] The term activation imples that the body is somehow girding itself for action; and most of the time, one of the indices of activation is the appearance of increased muscular tensions.

Within this area, during the past several years, there has been increased interest in two related lines of study: (1) the relationship between various measures of self-control to intellectual and academic performance and (2) the manner in which adjusting levels of activation may contribute in positive ways to improving self-control, heightening school achievement, and aiding intellectual behavior. This chapter contains information and principles derived from these two parallel lines of inquiry.

During the 1930s and 1940s, studies appeared dealing with problems in which "tension," "activation," "arousal," and similar terms

---

[1] Some psychological concepts are inclusive of both direction and intensity, as exemplified by the often inexact terms *"emotion," "motivation,"* and the like.

were employed. These concepts assume that the individual is an energy-producing "machine," capable of marshaling and mobilizing its efforts in a rather total manner when confronted with various tasks. Research in Russia and in the United States during the 1950s explored basic neurological structures that apparently control general levels of arousal and activation (reticular formation and the hippocampus, etc.). Interest in the activation and methods to "de-activate" children were also apparent from other sources. In the period just after World War II, several clinicians described the behaviors of the neurologically-impaired children and referred to the often-observed hyperactivity seen in these youngsters. During the ensuing years, means have been sought by the medical, educational, and psychological communities, often working together, to reduce somehow the levels of arousal.

Some of the research dealing with activation, attention span, and hyperactivity is of a theoretical nature and deals with the physiological signs, as well as the kinds of environmental conditions likely to accompany changes in activation or arousal.[2] Other research of a statistical and clinical nature has been devoted to the manner in which levels of activation may be modified to optimize learning and performance in school children.

Attention (or attentive behaviors) has been measured in a number of ways, and also types of behaviors have been classified as evidence of attention. For example, investigators may simply clock the amount of time a child is apparently engrossed in his work, as is outlined in the study by Hewett. At the same time a rather extensive list of categories of attentive behaviors that have interested researchers was compiled by Moray. This list includes:

1. Mental concentration

2. The general "set" or preparatory state of the individual engaging in academic work

3. Vigilance: the amount of time an individual will visually or auditorily attend

4. Selective Attention: in which attention is frequently, but appropriately redirected from time to time

5. Searching behaviors: in which attention is directed toward seeking something appropriate to attend to rather than upon a single situation or stimulus.

The material in this chapter encompasses several facets of this problem. Several findings within this general problem are dealt with, con-

---

[2] Activation and arousal are often employed synonymously in the literature and also in this chapter.

taining information relating levels of activation to various kinds of academic performance in children.

The third part of the chapter contains a survey of various strategies employed by educators, school psychologists, and physicians in attempting to reduce hyperactivity and enhance attentive behavior in school youngsters. These methods range from the more operational types of relaxation training to the application of behavioral modification of schedules to enhance attentive behavior. Medication may also reduce or raise levels of activation in children and in youth. And within recent years, this important, but at times controversial approach, has been employed by more and more educators, with the help of physicians.

Activation, Self-Control, and Learning: A Survey of Basic Principles

Scientists from a number of disciplines have contributed to knowledge about the relationship of energy mobilization to perceptual and motor behaviors and to emotional and social well-being. Pavlov, for example, was one of the first to note the importance of what he termed the "What is it?" reflex in animals. Prior to their performing a task, Pavlov observed, animals seemed to exhibit a collection of behaviors denoting attention to a stimulus, including changes in their musculature (heightened tonus or tension), visual regard, and other physiological changes in the viscera and cardio-respiratory systems. Within more recent years, neurophysiologists, physiologists, and psychologists have focused more and more on how peripheral evidences of activation may contribute to learning. Some of the evidence from these sources is surveyed below; for a more penetrating look at this area, the student is referred to the text by Duffy.

DEFINITIONS AND RELATIONSHIPS

In general, activation refers to the degree the body is mobilizing itself for some kind of effort or to meet some kind of perceived threat to its well-being. This mobilization is manifested in several ways, including increase in muscular tensions, increased heart rate, respiration changes, and biochemical and hormonal changes.[3] Thus, using measures of this nature, an individual's levels of activation can be plotted during

---

[3] Physiological changes may be indicative of the termination of bodily activities not necessary for action, as well as the "turning up" of those necessary as the body prepares to meet some threat.

a twenty-four-hour period, or for more prolonged periods of time (from the lower levels encountered during deepest sleep, to higher ones manifesting themselves during awakening hours, to peaks seen during times of emotional stress or when maximum physical effort is exerted).

It is also seen that a given individual will evidence relatively the same pattern of activation within his various organs under times of stress or arousal, which are unique and usually unlike the specific patterns seen in another individual. Thus, there are marked individual differences in muscular tensions, heart rate changes measured, and the plottings of an electroencephalogram. Yet the unique way a person's body prepares itself remains relatively consistent from hour to hour and from day to day, whether that person is facing some physical effort or some emotionally upsetting situation.

There is general agreement among experts that there is an optimum level of activation suitable for the best performance in a given task, and that this level varies from task to task and is higher in some (i.e., playing football) and lower in others (doing mathematics problems). Furthermore, there is also a reasonable consensus among scholars that (a) one of the primary signs of emotional stability and a sound nervous system is the ability to adjust one's activation level to that appropriate to the task being faced and (b) conversely, an unstable nervous system or a disturbed personality is often reflected behaviorally in levels of activation that are not appropriate to the task(s) being faced at a given time. Indeed, there is a curvilinear relationship between arousal-activation and optimum performance (graphed below), indicating that, to a point, raising an individual's levels of energy mobilization will usually facilitate a given performance; but if certain limits specific to a task are exceeded, performance will suffer. There is abundant evidence supporting this premise, from the studies in the 1930s in which it was found that squeezing a hand-grip at one-half one's maximum pressure improved serial learning of nonsense syllables, to more recent evidence collected in Stockholm. In this latter study, it was found that running at about 45 percent maximum speed on a treadmill elicited the best mathematical reasoning on the part of subjects who were exposed to arithmetic problems via earphones while they were engaged in this running (Chapter 13).

Further evidence concerning the subtle interactions between activation, muscular tension, and academic abilities was presented in a study by Edfelt in 1960. It was found that good readers characteristically exhibit less tension in the speech apparatus ("silent speech") than poor readers. It was also found that as the material to be read became more difficult, muscular tensions in the vocal apparatus increased. Earlier studies of deaf-mutes indicate that peripheral muscular tension of speech apparatus

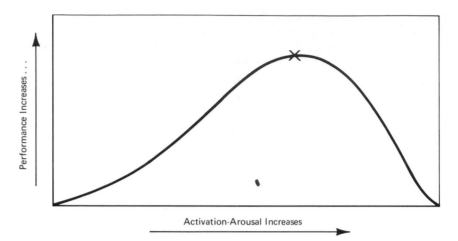

FIGURE 10.1

As arousal-activation increases (horizontal axis) performance improves (vertical axis) to a point, and then begins to be adversely affected as activation continues to increase past the optimum level for that specific task.

is reduced more by the intelligent than by the less intelligent; that indeed, when thinking, there seems to be an intermediate stage of peripheral muscular tension on the way to a stage indicative of more effective intellectual functioning during which muscular tensions are reduced or virtually eliminated. On the other hand, this intermediate stage of evident muscular tension may be "re-visited" by an individual when the material becomes increasingly difficult and complex.

Furthermore, available data make it apparent that the normal child or adult will learn to control excess amounts of activation upon repeated exposure to a task or situation that may initially elicit inappropriately high levels. On the other hand, individuals who are unstable, or who possess a nervous system in which certain mechanisms are defective, will often evidence continued and inappropriate levels of activation that will climb higher upon repeated exposure to stressful situations, individuals, or tasks. In other words, the adequate personality and physiology will accommodate to stress where the less than adequate will not only be unable to accommodate, but will at times evidence symptoms indicative of the fact that even less appropriate levels of activation may be present.

Levels of activation inappropriate to a given task, or classification of tasks, may interfere not only with the performance of new and complex motor tasks (because of the usually accompanying muscular tensions), but also with the perceptual acuity an individual may need to accomplish tasks that are more academic than physical.

There is further evidence to indicate that an individual's levels of activation are cyclic in nature, rising and falling within a single day, in a given month, and also on a yearly basis. Moreover, scores indicative of measures of activation are unique to each individual and relatively stable over a period of time.

Finally, there is a considerable amount of data supporting the positive effects on learning of medication, relaxation training, and reducing environmental stimuli. A section that follows will take a more thorough look at the specific effects of some of these interventions.

Activity Levels and Self-Control in Children

There are indications from more than one study that infants differ widely at birth in the amount of activity they evidence. In one investigation, infants placed on a force platform that recorded their wigglings produced data that indicated that some of the infants were more than 150 times more active than others.[4]

These differences in activity persist into later infancy and early childhood and may provide one of the more important early indices of later intellectual competence. For example, by about the sixth month of age, infants are visually inspecting some part of their environment for about 50 percent of the time, but again there are wide individual differences in this kind of measure. This type of attention and alertness, however, is found to be a moderately good predictor of later intelligence measures collected in late childhood and early adolescence. This is particularly true in the case of males, according to the findings from the longitudinal study by Bayley.

By the age of three and four, these same differences in activity level persist. Again, findings from a longitudinal study by Kagan and Moss indicate that the levels of activity in the pre-school youngster form an important predictor of later vigor, the type of occupation young adults enter, and the vigor and the onset of dating behaviors.

Accompanying changes in activity level, however, are other changes indicative of the extent to which youngsters are willing to exercise self-control. In a pilot study we carried out, for example, it was found that when asked to walk a twelve-foot long line, "as slowly as you can," four-year-olds took approximately thirteen to fourteen seconds to

---

[4] It is probable that infants at either extreme upon this "activation continuum" suffer from some kind of nervous system impairment.

do so; the six-year-olds in the same study took almost three times as long, from thirty-eight to forty seconds. The children of nine in the same study who were asked to demonstrate this measure of self-control spent almost a minute to travel the twelve feet. Changes in this measure of self-control in another study were marked and were accompanied by changes in academic competencies which were also encouraging.

Studies of hyperactive children also indicate that with age their hyperactivity seems reduced. However, the learning problems that may have confronted them during the time they were inattentive to their school work could have long-term effects of an emotional nature, which would interfere with subsequent academic efforts to a marked degree.

In general, there are several kinds of behavioral indices of what might be termed hyperactivity and the usually accompanying lack of attention on the part of children labeled "distractable." Such children may tend to spend a great deal of time moving their entire bodies, while others may remain seated for the expected periods of time, but engage in an inordinate amount of manual activity.[5] Still other children are seemingly passive when their bodily movements are observed, but their visual and, thus presumably their intellectual attention, too, frequently shifts from object to object and from event to event.

There have been several theories advanced to explain the existence of hyperactivity in some children. Some experts suggest that an extraordinary amount of motor activity is evidence of an immature stage of development persisting into later childhood. It is normal behavior, for example, for a child of one to two years of age to explore his environment via locomotor and manipulative behavior to a marked degree; he seems at this age to need to confirm and enlarge upon his perceptions of the world by collecting a great deal of motor information and correlating it with the visual information he obtains simultaneously. However, if this inordinate manual exploratory activity persists into middle and late childhood, it is usually considered pathological and is invariably accompanied by general and/or specific learning disorders.

A second theory, based upon psychological concepts, has been advanced to explain inordinate activity in children. It has been postulated that perceptual and central integrative mechanisms and the motor output in a normal child match exactly; there is little "spillover" of any of the three types of functions. However, on the part of a child with an inordi-

---

[5] The saddest case I have ever encountered concerned a boy who was reported as "hyperactive" by his mother, prior to being in a car accident that rendered him unable to walk. She also reported him hyperactive after the accident. When I asked the mother how he could be hyperactive in a wheel chair, she said that he would continually push it around the house, while seated, bumping into the walls and into anything else he encountered.

nate need to move and explore, there is evidence of a failure of the input, integrative, and output systems to integrate somehow and match up with each other; a motor "spillover" has occurred. Thus, a child or youth with some kind of nervous system disorder, according to this theory, cannot engage in perceptual, integrative, and motor behaviors with the same fluency as can a normal child.

Additional theories abound, some based upon psychological concepts and others upon biochemical and neurological constructs. During the 1950s and 1960s, with the publication of numerous works dealing with activity control mechanisms within the brain stem and other parts of the central nervous system (cortex), data have been produced which permit more precise causes to be attached to various forms of hyperactivity. Even more helpful has been information that has made various medicants more effective in the control of excess behaviors, a topic that will be covered later.

ACTIVATION AND LEARNING

In addition to the more frequent problem of hyperactivity, there are often children in classes for normal and for atypical children whose levels of activation are lower than optimum for effective performance in most academic tasks.

It is usual to see a number of obviously underaroused children in classes for the retarded, emotionally disturbed, and/or neurologically handicapped. These children simply sit, not attending to the work in front of them, seemingly oblivious to much of their environment. Often these children can be "moved" to higher activation levels through the use of various medications while other strategies that often work well involve introducing vigorous physical activities periodically into their school day in an effort to "wake them up." This underaroused child often poses an even more difficult problem to the teachers than one who is overactivated, for the latter obviously needs help, is seen by his teacher, and usually receives first the services of the diagnostic counselor. The lethargic child, on the other hand, posing no discipline problem, often receives either delayed or only cursory attention by his teacher and other professionals who might help him.

Strategies for Adjusting Levels of Activation and Self-Control

There are a number of ways in which professional workers may aid children to adjust unusual levels of activation to those more appropriate to classroom functioning. It is usually found useful to employ more than one of the techniques simultaneously in the control of this problem. Medication prescribed by the doctor may prove even more helpful if it is accompanied by efforts by the child's teacher to provide a learning environment containing various incentives for attention behavior, plus, perhaps, a quiet work area to which the child may go when distractions in the regular classroom prove too much for him. On the other hand, children who may or may not be on medication may also be aided by providing various relaxation and impulse control activities periodically during the school day.

The types of "de-activation" methods most often employed include the following:

1. The use of social incentives to enhance attentive behavior

2. The use of medication to adjust arousal levels, either upward or downward

3. The use of frequent extrinsic rewards, via a Skinnerian-like reinforcement schedule for behavior indicative of good attention and self-control

4. Various kinds of relaxation training borrowed from the physical medicine and physical therapy literature.

SOCIAL INCENTIVES

It is no secret that social reinforcement—praise of various kinds—is likely to modify the behavior of both children and adults. However, during the past years there have been studies that indicate that social rewards for attentive behavior in children will also change the amount of time they seem to spend looking at and dealing with the material on the desk in front of them.

In a clinic program we have conducted at UCLA for the past ten years, for example, we evaluated a nine-year-old boy whose attention span averaged somewhere between eight and nine seconds. We placed him in a one-to-one ratio with a male college student, a former football player, who praised him for doing *anything* longer than the few seconds he was initially capable of attending to a task. Within about six months, his ability to spend time on a problem increased to over five minutes and a parallel improvement was noted in his school behavior. The boy was periodically shown graphs of his improvement. The tasks involved those requiring him to draw various designs and to engage in big muscle activities, such as line-walking, ball-juggling, and the like, as well as more academic endeavors.

Similar data have come from a study by Allen and his colleagues. With the institution of frequent social praise for attentive behavior, they were able to raise a child's attention span from under one minute to over three minutes. On the other hand, when this type of social reward was then withheld from the child, his attention span diminished again to under one minute.

While it is often difficult for a teacher in a larger classroom to provide this type of frequent praise when appropriate, the data indicate its effectiveness when placed appropriately and when administered frequently.

In a study by Kagan and his colleagues, another interesting social strategy for controlling hyperactivity in children was researched. Essentially, an adult investigator convinced a child that in many ways they were alike (e.g., that they liked the same food, had the same number of brothers and sisters, and in other ways were similar in preferences and in life styles). Following this, the investigator engaged in constructive school behaviors that he hoped the child would imitate. In other terms, he attempted to create a *behavioral model* for the child to follow. It was hypothesized that the child would then behave in ways more acceptable to teachers and exhibit self-control and better attention. As a result of this type of social "modeling," it was found that impulsivity did improve significantly.

This same type of modeling was also employed by Ross with retarded children, but with different objectives. In this latter study, retarded children were taught rules and in other ways were introduced to more socially acceptable behaviors, as two or more adult figures acted out appropriate behaviors in game situations that the children then tended to model themselves after (Chapter 11).

EXTRINSIC REWARDS FOR ATTENDING

Several programs have been described in which an effort has been made, in rather precise ways, to reward children labeled "educationally handicapped" for continuing attention to their school work throughout the school day. In the programs described by Hewett and his colleagues, children were given cards upon which checkmarks could, at periodical intervals, be exchanged either for trinkets and candy rewards, or for privileges within the classroom that would fall under the label of enrichment, and could include engaging in various recreational activities as well. Children in both classes for the emotionally disturbed and for the more stable educationally handicapped were rewarded in this manner for merely trying to do their work, independent of the amount of success they may have encountered.

While improvement was measured and achieved in the expected classroom competencies under the conditions described, one of the primary factors measured in the latter programs of this type conducted by Hewett was attention span. This was clocked by observers, based upon "the time spent by a student maintaining eye contact with the task or assignment given him by the teacher." In tasks in which eye contact was not imperative, as when listening to a record, appropriate head and body orientation was assumed to constitute attentive behavior.[6]

The findings based upon at least 100 observations of each child were in the direction of positive change on the part of children within these "engineered" classrooms, when compared to similar children who were not exposed to the incentive reward system. By about one-quarter way through the school year, the differences in favor of the experimental group were highly significant when compared to the controls. These differences persisted and became even greater by the end of the school year. Other classes in this same study who were exposed to this reward system for attentive behaviors, midway in the semester also registered positive gains over and above that of control groups who engaged in classroom work without accompanying incentives. Although critics of this type of "operationalism" in learning and motivation often decry the use of extrinsic rewards, or what is sometimes termed "bribes," the data from these and other studies indicate that for some children they are not only highly effective, but at the same time produce in the child feelings of success that persist and are reflected in heightened academic achievement well after the more obvious rewards, such as candy and toys, are removed.

MEDICATION

As early as 1928 the use of medication to control excess behavior in mentally retarded and hyperactive children was being attempted with reasonable success. In the 1930s it was found, by accident, that often a stimulant would tend to calm a hyperactive child, while at other times drugs classified as "depressants" might somehow awaken one who was withdrawn or underactivated.

During the intervening years and particularly after 1950, a great deal of research has been carried out in which the use and effects of various medications have been studied as possibly influential of learning

---

[6] Two observers in one of the studies, spent two and one-half hours behind one-way mirrors clocking attention, via stopwatches, every morning during the entire year of the project. Each observer was assigned to four and five students whom they periodically evaluated during this period of time, taking five-minute samples of each student's attentive behavior. Ninety percent agreement was reached when observer scores were compared upon evaluating the same children.

behaviors. At the beginning of the 1970s, with the general concern for the use of drugs among youth and for other reasons, one can discern in some circles a kind of "backlash" against the use of medication for children with learning problems. Overall, the available evidence is quite promising, however. When medication is properly administered and supervised, hyperactive children can often be controlled, their attention spans increased, and parallel improvements in classroom efficiency can be seen and measured. With increased sophistication in use, children whose activation levels are inappropriate to productive work can be slowed down and at the same time their intellectual energies not dulled.

The teacher has several responsibilities when confronted with a child who may profit from medication. Included in these obligations are the following:

1. If a child's attentive behavior in class is so poor as to produce little learning and also so disorganized as to resist the best attempts of the teacher to restrain him and to aid him to zero in upon tasks at hand, it is often a sign that the teacher should confer with a school psychologist and school physician. They may then recommend to the parents directly, or to the child's physician, that an evaluation of him be carried out to discern whether medication might be warranted.[7]

2. Following the prescription of some type of medication, it is usually the teacher's responsibility to observe the child and report to the parents and/or physician various signs that the medication might be having some ill effect. Included among the signs to look for are excessive drowsiness or an increase in hyperactivity, particularly at certain times of the day when the effects of the medication might be wearing off or might be producing withdrawal symptoms.

3. The appearance of positive signs indicative of improved attention and learning are also important. At times, these are best reported in writing, but much of the time the physician and parent will seek the teacher's observations periodically, particularly during the early weeks that the effects of a given medication are being studied.

In general, the physician will prescribe only very small initial dosages of various medicants, starting with from five to ten milligrams. Also, the careful physician will seek frequent reports about the behavior of the child, as outlined above, from both the parents and the teachers. Physicians well-schooled in the effects of medication upon

---

[7] Stimulants seem to help such children slow down, it has been postulated, because when properly selected, they activate the centers of the brain within the brain stem that serve as regulators (inhibitors) of behavior, portions of the brain that may not be functioning well prior to the use of medication.

learning behavior will also be prepared to prescribe more than a single type of medication, if the first type prescribed does not have the desired effects.

To an increasing degree, teachers and therapists are seeing rather dramatic improvement in hand-eye control and in gross motor coordination, when children are given medication in order to increase attention span. Evidence of this improvement is seen in Figure 10.2, (a) and (b), taken about six months apart. During the intervening period, the child was not confronted with any program of motor training, but was given a medication to "slow him down," medication that also apparently aided him to attend to and control his hand while writing on a page. This improvement in hand-eye control was accompanied by a parallel improvement in other measures of balance and agility administered at these same times.

Opinion concerning the amount of time a child should be kept on medication varies. Some physicians will try a given dosage for a few weeks before changing dosages or types of medicants prescribed, even if no radical changes can be seen. Others suggest that the child should be placed on medication for prolonged periods of time in order to reverse the "failure syndrome" the child may have developed because of his inappropriate behavior in school.

RELAXATION TRAINING

In the 1930s, a text by a physician titled *Progressive Relaxation* outlined methods that seemed to make it possible, using a "muscular approach," to adjust levels of activation in children, youth, and adults. Other texts by foreign authors, as well as two other books by Jacobson, have expanded upon the initial concepts in this earlier text.

During the intervening years, educators, psychiatrists, coaches, and physical therapists have adopted and at times modified Jacobson's methods when attempting to work with school children, the emotionally disturbed child, and adults, athletes, and individuals suffering from a variety of neuromotor disturbances.

Generally, the principles followed in this training are as follows:

1. The aim is to aid individuals to reduce excess amounts of muscular tension over and above that needed to carry out life's basic activities. This tension has been termed "residual and muscular tension" by some.

2. This is accomplished by aiding the individual to gain a generally heightened awareness of muscular tensions and in specific body parts. This is carried out by instructions to "tighten and relax" muscle groups (or whatever language is suited to the individual's mentality and

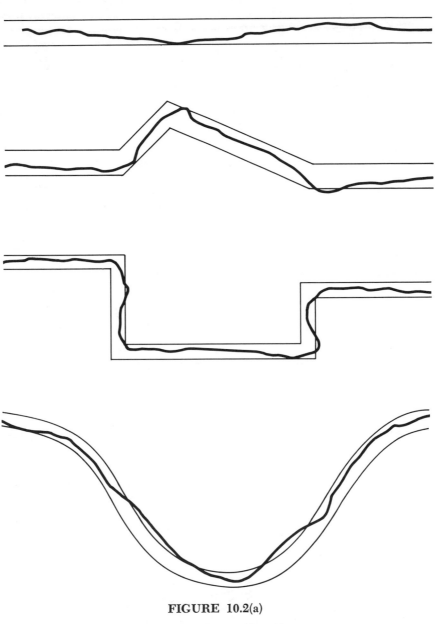

FIGURE 10.2(a)

Pre-Test Conducted October 23, 1969

The directions requested that the child carefully draw a line moving from
left to right, between each set of lines.

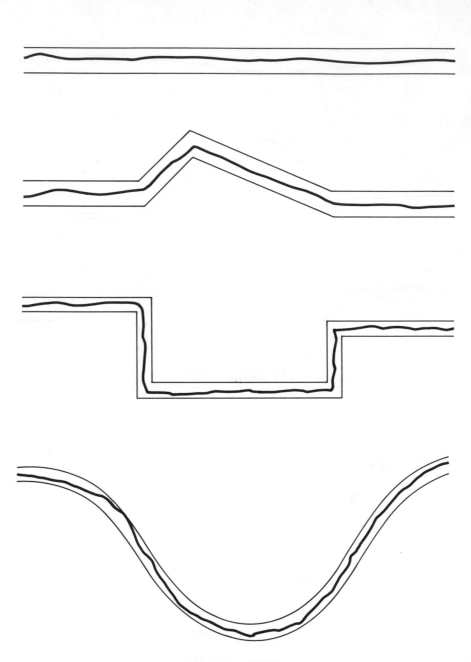

FIGURE 10.2(b)

Post-Test Conducted February 18, 1970.

maturity), interpolated by deep breathing and attempts to relax completely.

3. Refinement of the techniques involve helping the individual, or group, to feel varying degrees of muscular tension, such as "Tighten one-half that hard" (one-half as hard as miximum), and then perhaps one-half that hard (i.e., one-quarter of maximum). Other refinements, included specifically in the techniques outlined by Schultz, involve imagining that various parts of the body are warm, and introducing various kinds of mental imagery into the therapy (i.e., "Imagine that you are in a quiet place and by a lake", etc.).

Both clinical observations and statistical data available, which reflect changes of muscular and academic performance following such training, are reasonably encouraging. However, it is probable that techniques similar to these will not "work" for all people due to the highly specific nature of the muscular patterns accompanying activation in various individuals.

Bednarova in Czechoslovakia, however, reports highly significant changes in attentiveness in school children as a result of what he terms psychotonic exercises. Johnson and Spielberger found that various measures of anxiety were lowered as the result of exposing individuals to relaxation training, while Harrison and his colleagues found improvement in the self-help skills of retarded children after using relaxation exercises accompanied by music.

The findings from a study carried out in the central city schools of Los Angeles during the 1969-70 school year, employing children in the first through fourth grades identified as evidencing learning problems, contain further evidence supporting the effectiveness of relaxation training. Children were worked with in small groups for three days a week, one-half hour each day, and were given relaxation training and impulse control activities (i.e., finding out how slowly they could move following the movements of another child, and similar games and activities), together with games intended to improve academic skills, including letter recognition, pattern recognition, and spelling and phonics training. A measure of self-control was included in a test battery which was given periodically to the children in the experimental group. The measure was obtained by asking the child to "walk as slowly as you can" along a line, two inches wide, twelve feet long, placed on the floor. In Figure 10.3 it may be seen how this measure improved through the year, improvement which was accompanied by significant improvement in the academic competencies listed above.

Similarly promising findings were found when the data from an even more recent investigation were compiled. In this 1971 investigation,

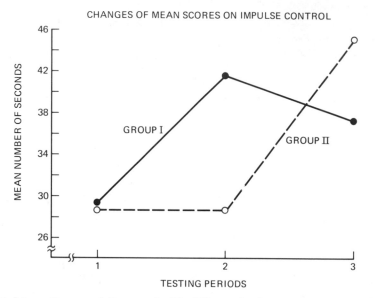

Reprinted from Cratty and Szczepanik, *The Effects of a Program of Learning Games Upon Selected Academic Abilities in Children with Learning Difficulties,* Part II.

FIGURE 10.3

Comparison of mean scores for impulse control, Group I (N-84), and Group II (N-73) for each of the three testing periods.

two groups were used: Group I was exposed to relaxation training together with a program of enrichment, composed of active games during the first one-half of the school year; Group II was not afforded help in improving self-control and learning via games during the first semester, but instead was given such special attention after the second testing, during the second half of the school year. By using the self-control measure of "How slowly will you walk the (12′ long) line?" it was found that marked improvement was seen in the first group, while the second, who remained in a classroom situation, had difficulty exhibiting self-control by the end of the first semester. However when relaxation was discontinued with Group I, and then begun with Group II, the mean scores reversed themselves by the final testing. Differences were statistically significant at both the second and third testing as shown in Figure 10.4.

This type of measure in which a child is asked to demonstrate self-control in some kind of gross motor activity was first explored in

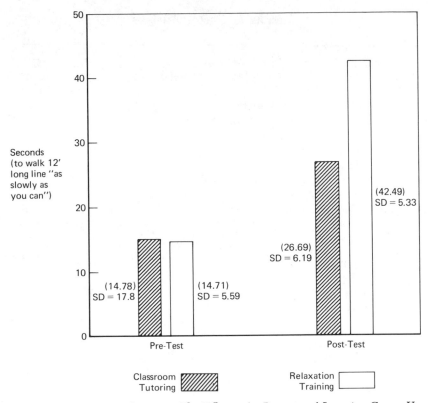

Reprinted from Cratty and Martin, *The Effects of a Program of Learning Games Upon Selected Academic Abilities in Children with Learning Difficulties.*

FIGURE 10.4

Improvement of self-control following a semester of relaxation training.

the 1930s. In more recent research by Maccoby and her colleagues at Stanford, it was found that moderate positive correlations were obtained when measures of this type (i.e., "how slowly can you draw that cart toward yourself?") and I.Q. were compared. In factorial studies we have carried out in the central city schools of Los Angeles, it was similarly found that scores from these impulse control measures correlated moderately well with general learning factors also contributed to by measures of spelling proficiency, serial memory ability, and letter and pattern recognition.

Results of Factor Analysis

FACTOR I
Perception and Identification of Figures

.91   Written Letter Recognition
.88   Verbal Identification of Letters
.83   Letter Recognition in Alphabetic Sequence
.81   Spelling
.69   Visual Serial Memory
.52   Body Part Identification
.38   Persistence (Self-Control in Line-Walking Task)
.36   Auditory Serial Memory
.33   Verbal Identification of Patterns

FACTOR II
Gross Motor Ability

.71   Gross Agility, moving in a vertical plane
.64   Static Balance
.63   Locomotor Agility, moving accurately when hopping, jumping, etc.
.30   Persistence (self-control in line walking)

FACTOR III

.93   I.Q. (Peabody Picture Vocabulary)
.39   Verbal Identification of Common Geometric Patterns

Source: Cratty and Martin

Activity levels in children are the result of a number of often interacting causes including emotional upheaval, neurologic dysfunction, and more temporary factors including immediately prior participation in a vigorous game.[8] At the same time, there are a number of strategies used together, or in some combination, that may be employed to arrest excess and disruptive amounts of visual and/or motor activity.

Moreover, factorial studies indicate that the ways in which overaction can manifest itself in measures of hyperactivity are numerous. In the study by McKinney in which eighty behaviors were intercorrelated, it was concluded that several discrete types of hyperactivity could be discerned including:

[8] In an unpublished study carried out in my laboratory, it was found that the measures of motor control in which larger muscles were employed, (i.e., "how slowly can you get up" from a back lying position) were somewhat slowed down following physical education, but measures of control involving writing, i.e., "how slowly will you draw this line?") were significantly faster.

1. Purposefulness, relating meaningfully to remote objects and people
2. Lack of restraining diversified, distractable behavior emphasizing touch, as well as bodily movment
3. Self-stimulation
4. Social interaction, seeking of social contact, touching others
5. Neuromuscular control, involving rocking and other behaviors associated with neurological deficiencies
6. Verbal behavior, meaningful or meaningless use of speech and language.

Summary

In the previous pages, I have attempted to outline material that suggests relationships between selected intellectual functions and human motor behavior. The concepts included activation, arousal, activity level, and self-control. The data suggested that there is an optimum level of activation-arousal needed for one to perform well in a given academic task(s) that, if not reached or exceeded, will result in performance which is less than desirable.

Data outlining the role of hyperactivity in learning were presented together with information about how one may aid in the adjustment of activity levels to those compatible with classroom learning and performance. These strategies included:

1. Social reinforcement for attending behavior
2. Creating models of attention for the child to copy
3. The use of distraction-free cubicles in which a child might work
4. Medication
5. Relaxation and impulse control training
6. Behavioral modification techniques

The final parts of the chapter contained data which bore upon the efficiency of various methods that the teacher might use within the classroom to calm inattentive children.

It is apparent from the research that bodily manifestations of arousal and activation are highly individual, but at the same time, within an individual, are very consistent. It is thus the job of a teacher to be able to judge whether specific children are either too aroused, or not aroused enough, to participate fully in classroom exercises, and then to apply various of the techniques suggested in order to bring about desirable change in the intensity with which a child approaches his school tasks. Moreover, helpful changes in children and youth are best achieved by cooperation between parents, a school psychologist, a physician, together with careful observation and sensitive handling by their teachers.

BIBLIOGRAPHY

ALLEN, K. E.; HENKE, L. B.; HARRIS, F. R.; BAER, D. M.; and REYNOLDS, N. J. "Control of Hyperactivity by Social Reinforcement of Attending Behavior." *Journal of Educational Psychology* 58 (1967): 231–37.

BAYLEY, N. "Behavioral Correlates of Mental Growth, Birth to Thirty-Six Years." *American Psychologist* 28 (January 1968): 1–17.

BEDNAROVA, V. "An Investigation Concerning the Influence of Psychotonic Exercises Upon the Indices of Concentration of Attentiveness." *Teor. Prax. Teles. Vychov.* 16 (1968): 437–42.

BURKE, KAREN. "A Survey of Selected Self-Control Measures in Elementary School Children." Unpublished study, Perceptual-Motor Learning Laboratory, UCLA, 1970.

CRATTY, BRYANT J., and SZCZEPANIK, SR. M. *The Effects of a Program of Learning Games Upon Selected Academic Abilities in Children with Learning Difficulties, Part II.* Washington, D.C.: U.S. Office of Education, Bureau of Handicapped Children. Printed at UCLA, 1971.

———. "The Adjustment of Arousal Level and the Improvement of Attention." *Motor Activity and the Education of Retardates.* Philadelphia, Pa.: Lea and Febiger, 1961.

CRATTY, BRYANT, J., and MARTIN, M. M. "The Adjustment of Arousal Level and the Improvement of Attention." *Perceptual-Motor Efficiency in Children.* Philadelphia, Pa.: Lea and Febiger, 1969.

———. *The Effects of a Program of Learning Games Upon Selected Academic Abilities in Children with Learning Difficulties.* Washington, D.C.: U.S. Office of Education, Bureau of Handicapped Children, 1970.

DUFFY, ELIZABETH. *Activation and Behavior.* New York: John Wiley and Sons, Inc., 1962.

EDFELT, A. W. *Silent Speech and Silent Reading.* Chicago: University of Chicago Press, 1960.

FREEMAN, ROGER. "Changes in Tonus During Completed and Interrupted Mental Work." *Journal of General Psychology* 170 (1930): 309–34.

HEWETT, FRANK M. *The Emotionally Disturbed Child in the Classroom.* Boston: Allyn and Bacon, Inc., 1968.

IRWIN, SAMUEL. "A Rational Framework for the Development, Evaluation, and Use of Psychoactive Drugs." *American Journal of Psychiatry* 124 (February 1968): 1–19.

JACOBSON, E. *Progressive Relaxation.* Chicago: University of Chicago Press, 1938.

———. *Anxiety and Tension Control: A Physiologic Approach.* Philadelphia, Pa.: J. B. Lippincott Co., 1964.

———. *Tension in Medicine.* Springfield, Ill.: Charles C. Thomas, Publisher, 1967.

JOHNSON, D. I., and SPIELBERGER, C. D. "The Effects of Relaxation Training and the Passage of Time on Measures of Static and Trait Anxiety." *Journal of Clinical Psychology* 24 (1968): 20–23.

KAGAN, JEROME. "Body Build and Conceptual Impulsivity in Children." *Journal of Personality* 34 (1966): 118–28.

KAGAN, JEROME, and Moss, H. A. *Birth to Maturity, A Study in Psychological Development*. New York: John Wiley and Sons, 1962.

KAGAN, JEROME; PEARSON, L.; and WELCH, L. "Modifiability of Impulsivity." *Journal of Educational Psychology* 57 (1966): 359–65.

KRONBY, BO. "How a Person's Numerical Ability Is Changed, During Different Loads of Physical Work on an Ergometric Bicycle." Report from Pedagogisk-Psykologiska Institutionen Vid GIH, Stockholm, October 1968.

LAUFER, M. W.; DENNOFF, E.; and SOLOMONS, G. "Hyperkinetic Impulse Disorder in Children's Behavior Problems." *Psychosomatic Medicine* 19 (1957): 38–39.

LYNN, R. *Attention, Arousal and the Orientation Reaction*. Oxford: Pergamon Press, 1966.

MACCOBY, ELEANOR; DOWLEY, E. M.; and HAGEN, J. W. "Activity Level and Intellectual Functioning in Normal Pre-School Children." *Child Development* 36 (1965): 761–69.

MAX, L. W. "Experimental Study of the Motor Theory of Consciousness Action-current Responses of the Deaf During Awakening, Kinesthetic Imagery and Abstract Thinking." *Journal of Comparative and Physiological Psychology* 24 (1937): 301–44.

McKINNEY, J. P. "A Multidimensional Study of the Behavior of Severely Retarded Boys." Unpublished Ph.D. dissertation, Ohio State University, 1961.

MORAY, N. *Attention: Selective Processes in Vision and Hearing*. London: Hutchinson, in press.

ROSS, DOROTHEA. "Incidental Learning of Number Concepts in Small Group Games." *American Journal of Mental Deficiency* 38 (1970): 718–25.

SCARR, SANDRA. "Genetic Factors in Activity Motivation." *Child Development* 37 (1966): 663–73.

SCHULTZ, J. H. *Das Autogenne Training, Konzentrative Selbstentspannung (The Self Training, The Concentrative Self-Relaxation)*. New York: Grune & Stratton, Inc., 1965.

STRAUSS, A. A., and LEHTINEN, L. E. *Psychopathology and the Education of the Brain-Injured Child*. New York, Grune & Stratton, Inc., 1947.

WHITSELL, LEON J. "Syllabus on Psychotropic Drugs: with Special Reference to Children." San Francisco, University of California Medical Center, 1969.

ZEAMAN, D., and HOUSE, BETTY J. "The Role of Attention in Retardate Discrimination Learning." *Handbook of Mental Deficiency*. Edited by N. R. Ellis, New York: McGraw-Hill Book Company, 1963.

IV

IMPROVING ACADEMIC AND INTELLECTUAL ABILITIES THROUGH MOVEMENT

11

Mathematics and Science
gaining quantitative concepts
and scientific information
through movement experiences

Introduction

Piaget identified three stages in the development of quantitative
concepts in young children. The first stage, lasting from about four
to five years, is marked by uncertainty and confusion when children
are asked to arrange objects according to size. The second, from
about five to six years, is characterized by a growing sense of order
and arrangement, and specifically by the ability to identify objects
correctly in quantitative sequence. The final stage, from about seven
years and above, is marked by organized plans of attack when
dealing with quantitative relationships. Objects are quickly and
accurately arranged in order of size, while more than one classification
of objects is arranged to correspond in a one-to-one relationship.
Moreover, underlying the operations achieved obviously at this age
are a number of conceptual operations, including the ability to
rehearse mentally various quantitative operations without the necessity to carry out the operations at the concrete level.

During these years obvious motor activity may be involved in
a rather subtle manner as a child forms quantitative judgments. It
is commonly observed that a young child must frequently use his
fingers to count out operations. A common clinical syndrome asso-

ciated with certain types of learning disorders (Gerstman's Syndrome) is characterized by poor perception of the fingers, body image deficit, and the inability to calculate well. A graduate student at UCLA recently found that teen-age children born without upper and lower limbs, while in other ways intellectually capable, seemed to lack the ability to engage in many mathematical operations with ease.

In general, it is usually believed that most reasonably complex mathematical operations are more conceptual than motoric. To translate arithmetic tasks to active games, and the concrete operations they entail, however, may be in line with Piaget's early observations concerning the need for concrete experience, as counting on the fingers to accompany early attempts to conceptualize about quantitative relationships.

Several writers have attempted to devise games in which various quantitative concepts are incorporated, either in direct and obvious ways or in indirect ways. One of these researched this approach with normal youngsters for brief periods of time, a second suggested this approach when working with children with learning difficulties, while a third has researched this methodology in the gaining of quantitative concepts in retarded youngsters.

In general, there have been several approaches to using active involvement of children to enhance quantitative concepts:

1. The children are used as units themselves, are added to and subtracted from, and are grouped in various ways to illustrate the specific arithmetic operation that needs improvement.[1]

2. A second way is to arrange numbered sidewalk grids, rocket ships, etc., on playgrounds, which the children may jump upon and in this manner to count, pose problems to each other, or to offer answers to problems written, spoken, or "jumped out" by another child or the teacher.

3. General self-testing operations in physical education are used as devices from which to obtain units that may then be added, subtracted, and the like. Standing broad jumps may be measured in inches and then second trials compared to first trials to arrive at the improvement attained. Relay runners' times may be added or subtracted from total time in order to arrive at "splits" each has achieved or to compute total elapsed time.

---

[1] Indeed the first historical reference to learning games was one apparently used by Maria Montessori, in which 12 children were lined up in the center of the room, representing a dozen eggs. They were then asked to divide themselves equally, count the number in the group to determine what half a dozen was, then divide into equal groups into the four corners, etc.

4. Incidental learning of numerical concepts has been incorporated into games for retarded children, generally with positive results. Children are shown the use of arithmetic and counting operations by keeping score, counting bases, and in other ways, and in at least one study positive transfer to tests of quantitative ability was achieved.

Accompanying this interest in the improvement of mathematics through movement has been a parallel interest in enhancing scientific concepts in young children. Essentially, at least three primary approaches have been employed:

1. Various abstract scientific phenomena are made vivid through concrete game experience; for example, the flow of electric current was translated into a ball moving between rows of children.

2. Motivating movement "rewards" are used for correctly identifying a scientific concept. ("You may move to the next base if you can properly identify the boiling temperature of water").

3. Bodily movements themselves are employed to illustrate basic laws of physics. Questions are asked, such as, "Why can you throw a ball farther with a windup?" or "What laws are operative when you have to push hard on the floor when starting to run?" and the movements are performed as a means to answering the questions and exploring some of the laws of physics.

Mathematics

Although research has been minimal, there have been several studies whose findings lead toward promising practices and toward further studies that hopefully will clarify the efficiency of a "movement" approach to learning quantitative concepts. In 1967, for example, Humphrey employed eight mathematics games in an attempt to enhance eight number concepts. The pre-post test changes in the experimental group were highly significant but similar to other studies of this nature. The duration of the program was only two weeks, no follow-up retention data were included, and little control was exerted for the effects of the extra attention accorded the children in the experimental group. Moreover, the number of subjects employed was only twenty.

In a second study reported a year later by Humphrey, a mathematics motor activity story approach was explored. Addition facts and subtraction operations were employed in games in which children were divided into groups in six different games. Again, the findings were positive but the subjects few in number and the duration of the study was only ten days [2] Humphrey's general approach to teaching mathematics and quantitative concepts, however, is highly original and creative. In general, he usually employs action situations in which the children themselves are units to be manipulated in a variety of ways. They may learn about the concept of sets by being asked "to group themselves into sets of three,'" while children themselves are counted in the various counting games he recommends.

Humphrey has divided his mathematic games into ten concepts: numbering, addition, subtraction, multiplication, division, fractions, decimals, measurement, geometry, and monetary system. Within these ten sections are fourteen additional sub-sections, and over one hundred games are described. This highly comprehensive program deserves careful attention by teachers and by researchers. It has been carefully thought out and with additional experimentation should find its way into most primary school curricula.

I have presented in several publications other kinds of counting and mathematics games using a slightly different format. In general, it has been my intent to retain the visual representation of the numbers in the game so that later mathematics operations might be expected to be directly affected. We have used grids containing numbers pictures, and mathematical signs such as equal signs. In this way, a child may either jump the answers to problems presented to him auditorily or visually, or can jump various problems in rather concrete ways (i.e., $2 + 4 = 6$; or, if pictures are included, 4 rabbits plus 6 rabbits = 10 rabbits).

In further refinement of this approach, movable numbers and signs have been employed. In this way, children can move the number in space, arrange them in order, be required to identify individual numbers without the presence of more than one or two numbers in front of them at a time, and in other ways have added more variety and flexibility to the activities. Thus, one or more children can arrange numbers in order, from one to ten, and then jump on them, counting as they go. Moreover, the arrangement of the numbers presents a more concrete expression of various quantitative concepts. The 2 is indeed one-half as close to the 0 as the 4 is, within this context, whereas when either Arabic figure appears on a blackboard, it is an abstraction.

Although this approach has not been accorded extensive research, it has proved helpful to teachers. Modifications have been made to ac-

---

[2] Humphrey reports a reluctance of schools to expose their children for prolonged periods of time to learning games in which proper comparisons could be made, just as I have.

Reprinted from Cratty, *Active Learning*. Prentice-Hall, Inc., © 1971.

commodate physically handicapped children, while these games and others, outlined in Chapter 6, dealing with reading and pre-reading abilities, are presently being employed by teachers of the visually handicapped.

Dorothea Ross has described an interesting approach to inculcating number concepts into retarded children through small group games. She describes her techniques as "incidental learning," and in a study with forty educable retardates, found that she could elicit significant improvement in a test of basic number concepts after nine months' exposure to various small group games.

Accompanying the recorded improvement in number concepts were increases in attention span: from two to twelve minutes of attention to the games was recorded in pre- and post-program observations as well as improvement in manifesting socially acceptable responses within game situations. Although the description of the research lacks details of just how the number concepts were integrated into the game, Ross states that five general categories of games were employed: table games, board games, active racing games, card games, and guessing games. Moreover,

Reprinted from Cratty, *Active Learning*. Prentice-Hall, Inc., © 1971.

Reprinted from Cratty, *Active Learning*. Prentice-Hall, Inc., © 1971.

unlike other researchers on this topic, she did attempt to control for experimenter effects by exposing her control groups to special attention by her "game controllers."

The game controllers exercised their influence in various ways. They were able to control, for example, the number of times an individual won or lost and to keep to a minimum a long string of victories or defeats on the part of any individual. Moreover, socially unacceptable behavior was acted out by the controllers in front of the offending child, without directly reprimanding the child himself, in a form of "modeling behavior" previously described in Chapter 10.

Each game began with the subtle insertion of from two to three number concepts. When a child proved not up to the task of utilizing the concepts, he was aided by the controllers, with no direct attempts made to teach the difficult quantitative idea. As the program progressed, some of the subjects were able to act as game controllers, while the regular controllers were also able to act out behaviors that reflected deficiencies in quantitative thought evidenced by the children themselves. Thus, the quantitative abilities of the children were molded in several ways within the experimental arrangements described:

1. A need for a concept arose in the game, which could only be resolved if the child correctly used a number idea.

2. Number concepts were regularly inserted into games, progressively made more difficult, and were corrected directly when found deficient in the participating children.

3. Deficiencies in number concepts were illustrated by the experimenter-controllers by "acting out" the problem in front of the children-subjects.

Although it is difficult to sort out the separate effects of each upon the final measures obtained at the conclusion of an experiment in which so many approaches are apparently being used simultaneously, the presence of adequate controls for experimenter effects and the valid and reliable nature of the testing instruments used render these findings and the accompanying experimental procedures helpful for clinicians, teachers, and others.

Science Concepts

Several writers have also devoted attention to discovering just how various basic scientific concepts may be instilled in children through an active game approach. Mosston, for example, has described lessons in movement that attempt to inculcate knowledge about physical principles into the participants' conceptual framework. To my knowledge, however, this approach has not been adequately researched.

In Humphrey's chapter on the subject, he lists six concept areas, including "The Universe and Earth," "Conditions of Life," "Chemical and Physical Changes," and "Light, Energy, and Health." Twelve separate sub-areas are contained within these six broad categories and over fifty games are described in this section alone.

Moreover, Humphrey and his students have carried out several pilot studies to explore the efficiency of these methodologies. In one research effort by Prager, for example, it was found that reinforcement of science concepts through movement resulted in significant improvement in eight concepts relative to simple machines. Although only a few subjects participated and the study lasted only about eight days, the author concluded that the games procedures were highly motivating to the children, especially to the boys, and that this type of work should be included in the science curriculum.

The games devised by Humphrey are extremely creative and potentially helpful. However, it appears to be important for the teacher to be acutely aware of the laws of transfer of training and to be able to apply them correctly. Particularly in the case of younger children, the concepts learned through active games must be carefully translated into their real meaning within a science lesson. A rolling ball is not the same as an electric current running along the wire, and the differences as well as the similarities should be carefully explained to the children.

On the other hand, movement experiences appear to have a positive effect upon gaining science concepts when used as reinforcement, in this context, as well as in those previously described. The two drawbacks in this arrangement appear to be possibly operative here as in other games described to improve reading, mathematics ability, and the like: (a) the game may be the total "thing" to the participating children, with little or no transfer to the concepts involved, and (b) hyperactive, difficult-to-manage children may be further distracted and overaroused in the exciting game situations.

At the same time, for children with slightly above normal tendencies for action—usually the young boys in the primary grades—this approach would seem to have a great deal of merit. Several of the findings emerging from more than one of the studies indicate that more benefit seems to be derived by the male subjects than by the females.

Summary and Overview

The findings from the rather superficially conducted research underlying the use of active games in the establishment of number and science concepts should be carefully considered. At this point, it would seem that such activities, rather than replacing traditional methods, should be used as adjuncts to them.

The motivating effects of these games would seem to be one of their main advantages. Expert teachers have been able to stimulate children to high levels of achievement without the sugar-coating provided by inserting a vigorous game into the lessons. It will probably be found with further research that games of this nature are not only useful to instill certain math-science concepts, but are specific to certain perceptual types among children. The relatively passive "augmenter" of stimuli, as identified by Petri in her research, for example, may be less amenable to learning through an active game approach than the more active, less perceptive and sensitive "reducer" of information that arrives at the sensorium.

Moreover, it will probably be found that individual personality trait patterns in teachers make some more accepting and thus, more effective, through such an active approach; while others, no matter how hard they try, simply cannot make an emotional commitment to the techniques, a reticence that will be easily discerned by the children. In any case, it is believed that further research exploring the effects of teacher personality, complexity of concept, and the perceptual tendencies of children should be productive.

BIBLIOGRAPHY

CRATTY, BRYANT J. "Mathematics." Chapter 6 of *Active Learning.* Englewood Cliffs, N. J.: Prentice-Hall, Inc., 1971.

CRIST, THOMAS. "A Comparison of the Use of the Active Game Learning Medium with Developmental-Meaningful and Drill Procedures in Developing Concepts for Telling Time at Third Grade Level." Ph.D. dissertation, University of Maryland, 1968.

GINSBERG, HERBERT, and OPPER, SYLVIA. *Piaget's Theory of Intellectual Development: An Introduction.* Englewood Cliffs, N. J.: Prentice-Hall, Inc., 1969.

HUMPHREY, JAMES H., and SULLIVAN, DOROTHY D. Chapter 6 in "Teaching Slow Learners Mathematics Through Active Games." *Teaching Slow Learners Through Active Games.* Springfield, Ill.: Charles C. Thomas, Publisher, 1970.

———. "The Mathematics Motor Activity Story." *The Arithmetic Teacher* 14 (1967): 14.

———. "Comparison of the Use of the Physical Education Learning Medium with Traditional Procedures in the Development of Certain Arithmetical Processes with Second Grade Children." *Research Abstracts,* Washington,

D.C., American Association for Health, Physical Education, and Recreation, 1968.

MOSSTON, MUSKA. *Teaching Physical Education.* Columbus, Ohio: Charles E. Merrill Publishing Co., 1966.

PETRI, ASENATH. *Individuality in Pain and Suffering.* Chicago: The University of Chicago Press, 1967.

———. *Piaget's Theory of Intellectual Development: An Introduction* (Ginsburg, Herbert and Opper, Sylvia). Englewood Cliffs, N. J.: Prentice-Hall, Inc., 1969.

PRAGER, IRIS J. "The Use of Physical Education Activities in the Reinforcement of Selected First-Grade Science Concepts." Master's thesis, University of Maryland, 1968.

ROSS, DOROTHEA. "Incidental Learning of Number Concepts in Small Group Games." *American Journal of Mental Deficiency* (1970): 718–25.

12

Speech, Reading, and Language Development

Introduction

Language, speech, and motor activity interact in both obvious and subtle ways. Speech itself is to some degree a motor act, and it is common to find a relatively larger percent of speech problems in youth who evidence other signs of motor dysfunction. Likewise, to some degree, speech therapy involves encouraging the child to perceive the manner in which mouth, tongue, and lip movements must correctly manifest themselves in the formation of sounds within the culturally sanctioned language.

Motor activity and communication also coalesce when various gesture and movement cues accompany the spoken word. The popular press, as well as scientific journals, to an increasing degree, have begun to explore the parameters of non-verbal speech, much of which involves movement cues emanating from the face, the limbs, and the trunk of the "sender."

From a developmental standpoint, one may also pair movement and speech. No less an authority than Piaget suggests that the earliest appearance of language understanding occurs in children in connection with movement activities. The youngster, prior to formulating language himself, learns to act correctly to various commands to move or to stop moving. The infant, shortly after his first birthday, learns to respond to such requests as "stop that!," "bring it here," "come here," "let's see you run," and similar verb phrases denoting action or cessation of action.

Luria proposes that the regulatory function of language over motor activities passes through a series of four developmental stages. These include:

1. An initial phase during which language may accompany and accelerate the appearance of motor activities

2. A second phase during which various motor activities are elicited by language cues

3. The third phase, which is marked by the appearance of language clues that may tend to inhibit as well as to elicit certain motor responses

4. The fourth phase during which language becomes internalized by the child and provides complex cognitive cues for the regulation of motor behaviors.

Most interesting are recent attempts to promote various kinds of language development through the use of bodily activities involving some of the larger muscle groups. This research has indicated that various kinds of motor activities, when paired with certain kinds of verbal communication, generally result in improvement of the latter abilities. These findings, together with the clinical practices that produced them, form the information that constitutes the bulk of this chapter.[1]

There have been several approaches to enhancing language functions (reading and written communication) through programs involving movement tasks. For example:

1. The Active Games approach has been used to instill language concepts in normal children. In one approach of this nature the rules of the game are written and discussed prior to playing the games, with the language lesson and the game taking place separately in time.

2. Foreign languages have been learned by pairing commands in the language with what has been termed "the total physical response," much as is done when young children learn their own language.

3. Pre-reading competencies have been incorporated into activities that involve hopping, jumping, and similar locomotor activities. Such basic abilities as letter recognition (by sight and by sound), pattern

[1] The reader might also wish to consult Chapter 13, "Communication Through Movement" in Bryant J. Cratty, *Movement Behavior and Motor Learning*, 2d ed (Philadelphia, Penn.: Lea and Febiger, 1967).

recognition, and serial memory ability have been the focus of this type of program.

4. Sight-reading exercises have been incorporated directly into games, with children able to move from base to base and engaging in similar activities by correctly identifying the word on flash cards held aloft adjacent to the game.

The use of this approach to language development has been justified in several ways. Some authors suggest that games are highly motivating to children, and when paired with language skills of various kinds are likely to "spread' their motivating effects to the often oppressive learning of reading and similar skills.

Others have implied that the abundance of kinesthetic input occurring as a child moves and learns language skills aids in the formation of reading and other communication concepts. While still others have implied that a kind of imprinting involving language skills is enhanced by pairing the total physical responses with some communication training.

In any case, the findings from some of these studies are quite provocative and have several types of implications for the teaching and learning of communication skills. In the discussion that follows, the information has been arranged into these categories:

1. Initially, information relative to *listening comprehension*

2. Techniques to enhance a *speaking vocabulary*

3. Various *pre-reading skills* and how they may be positively influenced in various movement situations

4. Various *reading skills* as paired with movement games

5. Techniques that have proved successful in aiding children to gain skills in *written communication* through games.

The information on this general topic is still expanding and has yet to be placed into a completely satisfactory theoretical framework. At the practical level, however, the findings are quite encouraging and present helpful teaching techniques that may be used by teachers of foreign languages, reading instructors, and those interested in expanding the vocabularies, reading comprehension, and creative writing abilities of children, youth, and adults.

Listening Comprehension

Before the normal infant engages in producing speech himself, he learns to comprehend the spoken words of others. As has been mentioned, this is often in response to various movement tasks and in conjunction with obvious actions.

A most interesting program of research has been carried out since the early 1960s by Dr. James Asher, through which he has explored the influence of what he terms "The Total Physical Response Approach" to gaining listening comprehension skills in foreign languages. His principles hold important implications for the training of language comprehension in the immature normal child, or the atypical child attempting to gain a beginning understanding of his native language. Additionally, Asher's findings contain helpful guidelines for the teacher of foreign languages.

Asher generally holds that the relatively small amount of time devoted to language teaching might best be focused first upon listening comprehension as this forms a basis for later spoken reproduction and written communication. The most important concept that Asher has explored, however, is the manner in which pairing a total physical response with language learning may enhance listening comprehension and retention of language concepts.

His initial hypotheses were derived from the common observation that young children apparently learn a foreign language more quickly than adults. Rejecting more traditional theories that have tried to explain this phenomenon, Asher suggested that this facility in the young appeared merely because most of their language learning occurred in action situations. Children, he points out, learn languages while playing. "Bring me that ball and put it here," is a phrase that is made vivid through action when a child plays with a foreign playmate, whereas their adult counterparts usually engage in language translations in more passive situations ("That is an interesting idea you are discussing.").

Stemming from these observations has been a series of over twenty-five experiments, carried out from 1963 to 1970, that has explored various parameters of the general approach to listening comprehension. Generally, the teaching techniques involve pairing a word and later increasingly complex phrases with immediate actions that describe the word or phrase. The learner is not asked to repeat the word or phrase verbally, but instead may either observe the action "jump," or participate immediately in the jumping action himself.

The greatest positive effects of this kind of language instruction (Russian and Japanese have been employed thus far) are seen in studies in which reasonably complex phrases are required to be recognized (i.e., "go to that table and bring me the book there") rather than retention of simple one or two-word phrases. Likewise, the approach is dramatically more effective when the learner must act out the meaning of the phrases during the re-test phase of the experiments.

In one series of experiments an attempt was made to determine just what components of the action teaching situation contributed most to the positive findings. Thus it was attempted to separate various components of the action situation, including whether the action occurred concurrently with the spoken phrase, whether there was somehow an anticipation of the next command by observing the previous one, whether the location of objects in the room provided cues concerning the nature of the command to be spoken later, etc. In general, these studies indicated that the efficiency of the methods was dependent upon a variety of cue-action-spoken combinations and that elimination of various components of the situation did negatively effect the total positive effects of the situation. As Asher states, "the intact kinesthetic event" apparently is important both when learning and when evidencing retention of a foreign language in the situations described.

Perhaps one of the most interesting experiments in this program compared the learning and retention of adults to those same qualities in children. For, Asher assumed, if the reason that children learn languages best is because they learn through action, might not generally more capable adults then learn better than children, if exposed to the same approach?

The findings from this study indeed confirm the fact that adults learn significantly better than do children within a total physical response situation. Upon comparing language comprehension of eight, ten, and fourteen-year-olds, with the same qualities in adults (college students), it was found that the adults learned best, and significantly better than the eight-year-olds and the ten- and fourteen-year-olds, while the latter two age groups were significantly more proficient during the re-testing phase than was the youngest group.[2]

The chart indicates the differences in the proficiency in the various age groups studied.

In general, it has been found that serious impediment to the method occurs if the students have to attend to more than comprehension function, i.e., if they have to speak or write the language while attempting to gain only comprehension. At the same time, the efficiency of the approach is enhanced if, during the retention interval, they must evidence a total bodily response; and retention is enhanced over intervals ranging from twenty-four hours through forty-eight hours to two weeks

[2] The children had above average I.Q.s (over 110) and although perhaps not as high as the college students with whom they were being compared, Asher points out the I.Q. usually does not predict language comprehension abilities. He does point to the possibility that differences in attention span between groups could have caused the differences in comprehension.

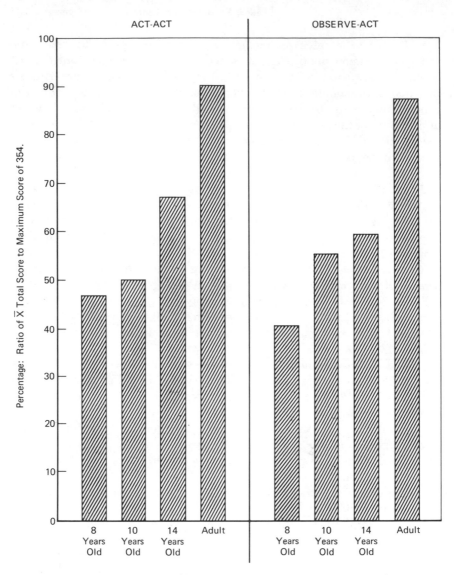

From James J. Asher, "The Total Physical Response Approach to Second Language Learning," in *The Modern Language Journal*, 53, January 1969.

FIGURE 12.1

Retention as measured by the total score from all retention tests.

and longer. Most important is the finding that the efficiency of the method is enhanced when the phrases to be recognized later become increasingly complex.

The general approach still needs considerable exploration. For example, it is not altogether clear just how initial learning of the listening skills via the methodology transfers to the ability to speak and write the language. Moreover, the methodology has not been investigated relative to more subtle types of communication not involving phrases that lend themselves well to action.

Several scholars have presented active ways in which children can be introduced to speech comprehension and vocal reproduction of their native tongue. Humphrey, for example, lists two games in which comprehension is purportedly enhanced, including a "Simon Says" game in which vocal directions must be correctly responded to when the prefix "Simon Says" is attached to them. A second game described, labeled "Do This, Do That," also attempts to enhance verbal comprehension. In his sequence of "reading games," however, Humphrey places these near the completion of the series, whereas, in truth, language comprehension developmentally predates reading skills and pre-reading skills (phonics, visual letter recognition, etc.) by several years in normal children.

The total physical response approach is potentially helpful in enhancing language comprehension skills in retarded children, but to my knowledge this application has not been tested at this time. The partially aphasic child may also derive benefit from this type of language teaching, and in the future scholars may hopefully explore this possibility.

Language Development

In the normal child, listening comprehension precedes actual speech production by the child, with the former beginning at shortly before the first year, while the child does not usually begin to speak himself until about midway into the second year of life.

Humphrey and others have suggested methods, through active games, for enhancing spoken communication and language development. Usually these methodologies involve games to enlarge vocabulary, as in the case of relays in which a child, given a word auditorily or visually, must then run and find a rhyming word among a pile of cards containing several possible choices. Other techniques, which have been suggested in a previous text of mine, involve requiring a child to describe one or more movements in correct series to a second child who has not had the opportunity to observe a previous demonstration of the movements.

Generally, the techniques attempt to provide a broader "auditory" base of comprehension prior to introducing reading in more direct ways. Moreover, some of the techniques aid in devising appropriate endings to words, i.e., by selecting, via a relay or in some other active situations, words that appropriately belong in the front of various word endings, such as *ed, ing, s, tion,* and the like.

Still another approach has been to present vocabulary development exercises while using direct and vigorous movement games as reward for correct performance. For example, in a base game, children may be verbally presented various words, which require action, i.e., *jump, run, skip,* etc., and the listening participants must then react in correct ways by moving from base to base via hopping, skipping, etc., or whatever is required. Most games of this sort, of course, involve the comprehension of action verbs and verb phrases denoting active movement, and thus to some extent are limited in the formation of a total program of language production and comprehension. At the same time, games of this type may provide important help in the education of children with minor to major hearing problems and who evidence the expected speech problems. However, at this point there has been relatively little research with this application in mind.

Reading Skills

PRE-READING COMPETENCIES

The observation that some children may be taught to read while playing was reportedly observed by educators in the 1600s. In more modern times, Humphrey and others have suggested that the kinesthetic sense may help children remember words they would take much longer to retain by simply observing the word shapes.

Although since the 1950s the literature has been replete with suggestions for enhancing reading with some kind of perceptual-motor enrichment, it does not substantiate most of the claims made. More encouraging, however, are studies in which reading and pre-reading skills have been incorporated into games in rather direct ways. For example, in studies we have carried out during the past four years in the central city of Los Angeles, within eighteen schools in the Catholic Archdiocese, it has been found that using active games to aid letter recognition, auditory-visual matching of letters to letter and letter combination sounds, and serial memory and pattern recognition proved more helpful than placing similar children in small-group tutoring situations within classrooms.

These games usually involved some kind of large visual stimuli, either a grid containing letters, painted configurations on the ground, or large geometric figures to which children would react by jumping, hopping responses, or by carrying the movable letters in various kinds of relay situations.

Some of the findings from these studies have been highly encouraging, particularly in the case of letter recognition, in which a significantly larger percent of the children (grades one to four with identifiable learning problems) learned to recite in order, to identify letters when presented either visually or auditorily, and to write their letters correctly in order or at random, when presented with this active way to acquire knowledge.

Our studies indicated that only when letter sounds and sounds of letter combinations are incorporated into the lesson does positive transfer to reading and spelling take place. The Open Court Method of Phonics training was used one year (1968–69), while the next year any phonics method preferred by each classroom teacher was employed in the enrichment lessons.

Moreover, it was quickly seen that blackboards should be stationed directly in the teaching situation in order for the correct transfer to occur from visual and auditory recognition skills to the more complex skills needed when writing letters and words correctly.

Pattern recognition was learned as well through an active game

Reprinted from Cratty, *Active Learning*. Prentice-Hall, Inc., © 1971.

approach using large geometric figures either painted or taped on a floor or playground, as when similar children were taught in more passive tutorial situations. However, it was seen that verbally attaching labels to the common geometric figures was not as helpful in itself, unless transfer was taught to common letter shapes. For example, it was found important to discover how triangles could be modified into the letter A, while also showing the children how half-circles could be formed into the capital letter B.

It was believed that practice in serial memory was helpful to the children in the games program described. In most of the activities of this type, observing children had to watch their classmates move in various ways through a series of configurations, perhaps a circle, square, cross, etc., placed on the ground in a semi-circle. The observing child then had to repeat the actions in the correct order, while the first demonstrator observed and corrected accuracy. Our findings included the fact that improvement in the memory for movements themselves improved from 2.75 to almost 6.0 in a single semester, but most important there appeared to be positive transfer to the serial memory of numbers presented verbally, and the serial memory of pictures (of animals) presented to the children visually. Significant improvement in spelling, in an unpracticed list, was also forthcoming in this research on the part of the games group when contrasted with the improvement in the same list on the part of a "classroom control group," afforded the same attention in small groups. Although further research in this area is needed to determine the efficiency of these methods versus the traditional ones in the preparation of children in pre-reading programs, the findings so far have been highly encouraging.

Humphrey has also outlined several types of games designed to enhance similar kinds of pre-reading competencies. For example, letter recognition games have been described in which children must ascertain correct alphabetical order by performing relays of various kinds. The visual recognition of letters is also contained in games in which letter patterns are matched, with upper-case to lower-case translation being the desired outcome. However, again relatively little "hard" data are available at this point confirming the efficiency in producing change in the pre-reading skills contained in these and similar games.

SIGHT READING, WORD COMPREHENSION, SENTENCE CONSTRUCTION

Reading is an extremely complex act involving the adequate control of eye movements, correct accommodation and convergence of both eyes on the nearby printed page and on a distant blackboard, as well as infinitely more complex processes involved in translating a visually perceived word-shape into a verbal and cognitive symbol. Moreover, words must be correctly ordered in spoken sentences and phrases with dispatch and accuracy by a child truly able to read well.

Remediation of reading problems has occupied armies of psychiatrists, psychologists, educators, physicians, and an even larger army composed of charlatans, quacks, and the misguided. A child may evidence a reading problem for a legion of reasons, ranging from some kind of ocular problem, an emotional upheaval in the family, some kind of neurological problem that prevents him from attending too long to the printed page, to more subtle problems involving short- and long-term memory and the correct matching of bits of verbal, visual, and conceptual information.

The correct approach to helping a child to read well, if he seems to be having problems, is first to engage in a thorough evaluation of his visual, perceptual, cognitive, auditory, and emotional characteristics and abilities. From this evaluation, a program, usually incorporating more than one approach, is then applied.

The findings from the few studies in which various reading skills have been incorporated, while generally encouraging, do not brand this type of methodology as an educational cure-all. Indeed, Humphrey and Cratty constantly exhort their readers to place their movement methods in proper context and to use them in conjunction with other methodologies that have traditionally proved helpful.

Our work on this topic has been primarily directed toward enhancing pre-reading competencies. In general, qualities of pattern recognition, serial memory, and letter recognition are highly predictive of later reading success and discriminate well between potentially poor and good readers. Moreover, serial memory that seemed to be improvable in general ways among primary age readers correlates positively with various measures of attention span and of perceptual span (the ability to enumerate what is seen following a short exposure to some visual information).

Humphrey, however, has researched the impact of the active game method upon reading skills in rather direct ways. In one short-term study, seventy-three fourth-grade children were pre-tested on eight reading skills and then placed in two matched groups. In one group the reading skills were reinforced for a period of eight days, while in the second the children were left to their regular classroom exercises. In fourteen of the fifteen matched pairs, the children in the experimental section scored higher on the post-test. Because this study was conducted for only a short period of time and failed to control well for the effects of extra attention given the children in the games group, further research on this question seems desirable.

In general, the reading games employed by Humphrey and outlined by Cratty and others fall into several general categories:

1. Those in which a correct response in a sight reading task is reinforced via some kind of movement response, (i.e., "If you read the next word you may shoot the basket," and "Make a point for your team or move to the next base," etc.).

2. Those in which a child must respond correctly to a more complex series of directions and then have his accuracy checked by observing children.

3. Reading lessons that are separate in time and space from the actual game situation. For example, a child must read the rules of a game and then go out and play it. Or, following a game, a resumé of the game is composed by the child or children participating.

Reading games seem to motivate children highly and, if not over-arousing, seem at least justifiable on the basis of current research as at least intermittent "breaks" within the weekly educational schedule for normal children. For certain types of children, notably the tough physically oriented children and youth of the ghetto, learning to read through games may provide one of the sole avenues through which to reach them.

It is not believed that the current reading games or an active approach to learning pre-reading skills are flexible enough to provide the sole manner of teaching reading and reading-related concepts and skills. However, future more creative activities, when devised and properly researched, may indeed expand the present role of activity in reading programs.

Written Communication

Written communication is the highest level of language-related communication engaged in by humans. Not until the ages of eight to nine do normal children give evidence of being able to engage in this complex process of translating thoughts to the written word. Deficits in written communication abilities are caused by factors that are as subtle and numerous as are the problems underlying reading itself, and they range from an inability to coordinate hand with eye properly, or less obvious problems involving the correct ordering of words to be written at the sub-vocal auditory level, to the inability to retain correctly the visual image of a word or phrase that is to be written later.

Several types of activities have been suggested to aid in more effective and accurate written communication using movement as a teaching channel.[3] Typical is the approach offered by James Oliver, using "logs" and retarded children. Essentially, he suggests that a "transfer of effect" will occur between the highly motivating and creative activities he has devised with "logs," cylindrical wooden pieces one tenth the weight of the child using them. Although at first, highly structured activities were employed using these devices, later a child exclaimed that he had "invented a jolly good exercise." Using this cue, the teachers began to have the children not only invent their own exercises, but also make drawings and then write out how they had decided to work with these strength-producing pieces of apparatus.

Their efforts, while at first crude, were indeed highly motivated. Long play is indeed a prestigious activity requiring strength and skill, and both attributes are highly prized by retarded youngsters.

The following is an example from a boy, chronological age of 13 and I.Q. of 61.

My Exercise

You muost kep the look under neath youre
legs olso you moust kep youre hans infrut
of youre head and walk fuwde wivf your
hands and kep your hend dhwn

The investigators were struck by the power of description the retarded boys were able to achieve and by the terms they employed (i.e., "shaped like a banana," "toes straight up to heaven," etc.). At the same time, they were intrigued by the possibilities inherent in the transmission of effort in long exercises to written communication, effort that conceivably could be re-directed in other tasks and in still new directions.

Summary and Overview

It has been the intent of this chapter to outline the admittedly sketchy research in which action has been combined in the remediation and teaching of reading, language, and other types of communication processes. In general, the approach is appearing to be a viable one; however, further work is needed to tailor sequences of activities to specified

[3] We are excluding methods to remediate hard-coordination problems in this discussion since we have covered them in other publications. For a thorough discussion of auditory and visual-perceptual problems that may underline problems in written communication, the reader is referred to Myklebust's text in the bibliography.

goals in the acquisition of reading and language skills. At the same time, significant steps in this direction have been taken. Humphrey, for example, lists three major classifications of goals: word analysis skills, sight vocabulary, and comprehension, together with seventeen sub-skills within these three classifications. Further, exploration of the efficiency of the principles derived by Asher in his work with foreign language learning seems important, together with the possible application of the principles to the remediation of language difficulties in children and youth.

Action, when combined with the teaching and learning of communication skills, appears to be highly reinforcing to the participating children, while at the same time requiring their rather total attention and involvement. When researchers and educators begin to structure more carefully and present the techniques they have researched, it is probable that most elementary schools in the world will begin to adopt at least some of the strategies that are beginning to be uncovered.

BIBLIOGRAPHY

ASHER, JAMES J. "Toward a Neo-Field Theory of Behavior." *Journal of Human Psychology* 4 (Fall 1964).
———. "The Total Physical Response Approach to Second Language Learning." *The Modern Language Journal* 53 (January 1969).
BEAUMONT, FLORENCE, and FRANKLIN, ADELE. "Who Says Johnny Can't Read?" *Parents Magazine,* June 1955.
CRATTY, BRYANT J. *Active Learning.* Englewood Cliffs, N. J.: Prentice-Hall, Inc., 1971.
CRATTY, BRYANT J. and MARTIN, M. M. *The Effects of a Program of Learning Games Upon Selected Academic Abilities in Children with Learning Difficulties.* Washington, D.C.: U.S. Office of Education, Bureau of Handicapped Children, 1970.
CRATTY, BRYANT J., and SZCZEPANIK, SR. M. *The Effects of a Program of Learning Games Upon Selected Academic Abilities in Children with Learning Difficulties, Part II.* Washington, D.C.: U.S. Office of Education, Bureau of Handicapped Children. Printed at UCLA, 1971.
CRATTY, BRYANT J.; IKEDE, NAMIKO; MARTIN, M. M.; JEANNETT, CLAIR; and MORRIS, MARGARET. "Total Body Movement as a Learning Modality, A Pilot Study." Chapter 4 of *Movement Activities, Motor Ability and the Education of Children.* Springfield, Ill.: Charles C. Thomas, Publisher, 1970.
HUMPHREY, JAMES H. *Child Learning Through Elementary School Physical Education.* Dubuque, Iowa: William C. Brown, Co., Publishers, 1966.
———. "Comparison of the Use of Active Games and Language Workbook

Exercises as Learning Media in the Development of Language Understanding with Third Grade Children." *Perceptual and Motor Skills* 21 (1965): 23.

———. "The Use of the Active Game Learning Medium in the Reinforcement of Reading Skills with Fourth Grade Children." *The Journal of Special Education* 1 (1967): 369.

HUMPHREY, JAMES H., and SULLIVAN, DOROTHY D. *Teaching Slow Learners through Active Games.* Springfield, Ill.: Charles C. Thomas, Publisher, 1970.

JOHNSON, GEORGE E. *Education by Plays and Games.* Boston: Ginn & Company, 1907.

McCORMICK, CLARENCE C.; SCHNOBRICH, JANICE N.; and FOOTLIK, S. WILLARD. *Perceptual-Motor Training and Cognitive Achievement.* Downers Grove, Ill.: George Williams College, 1967.

MYKLEBUST, HELMER R. *Development and Disorders of Written Language Vol. One: Picture Story Language Test.* New York: Grune & Stratton, Inc., 1965.

13

Levels of
Intellectual Achievement

Introduction

It is apparent to even the most casual observer that the content of the
programs of movement activities described in the previous chapters
(in particular, Chapters 3, 11, 12) differ markedly. These differences may
be compared on several scales. For example, some are highly "saturated"
with cognitive and/or academic elements, while others emphasize
movements in reactions to highly structured instructions (phrases that,
in some cases, seem almost to have been memorized by teachers). Some
contain activities emphasizing perceptual development, while others
are obviously intended to enhance academic operations.

In general, the literature seems to indicate that the efficiency of a
given program is directly dependent upon the congruence between the
objectives and the program's content. It appears that often the formu-
lators of the programs, in unrealistic ways, expect the tasks they recommend to transfer to too many or to too wide a range of other abilities.
In other words, the "theoretical explanations" that are offered encourage
those who practice these programs to expect too great a "transfer width"
to emanate from the various motor activities suggested.

I hope that the content of the previous chapters may aid the reader
to become more discerning when exposed to what are sometimes elabo-

rate claims by various writers for programs of perceptual-motor education. I also hope that the reader will exercise the same discrimination when covering the content of this chapter.

The material that follows proposes to suggest what types of movement tasks appear to correspond to selected categories of intellectual functioning. The categories of cognitive operations were arrived at by a survey of the literature, much of which was previously discussed. The selection of motor activities was similarly obtained from research we have carried out in my laboratory, as well as program content and data from the various perceptual-motor, "academic-motor," and cognitive-motor programs reviewed.

The reader should be cautioned that the matchings between motor activities and cognitive operations were arrived at without a great deal of empirical evidence. The following review could have several positive outcomes:

1. Some individuals may be encouraged to determine whether the activities suggested may serve to heighten the intellectual operations with which they have been placed.

2. Others may take more care when making claims for intellectual development through movement experiences without careful consideration of program content.

3. Still others may, upon reviewing the information, begin to expand their offerings of movement activities to include activities that encourage children to adopt a wider range of intellectual strategies than some of the program content presently appears to include.

4. Those who are qualified to undertake research on these questions may similarly be led toward fruitful hypotheses and studies after inspecting some of the material.

While it is believed that some of the more comprehensive models of human intellectual functioning reviewed in Chapter 2 are valid, I have decided to confine the discussion material to four intellectual "levels." Initially, movement tasks that appear to enhance *memory* are grouped together. Next, various activities that may aid the individual to *classify* better various kinds of information are considered. The third level of intellectual functioning involves processes of *evaluation*. Within the final category have been placed various movement tasks aimed at aiding the child and youth to engage in *problem solving* behaviors. Within each of these categories, however, I will attempt to conform in some ways to the more elaborate model of intellectual functioning espoused by Guilford. For example, I have attempted in several sections to suggest the manner in which movement activities may result in the acquisition of semantic, behavioral, figural, and symbolic content.

Memory

Memorization has been listed by several scholars, reviewed in Chapter 2, as one of the more basic intellectual operations. Indeed, speculation about the many ramifications of human memory has a rich and interesting historical background. The ancient Greeks and Romans, for example, postulated and practiced various types of memory aids that are found in contemporary programs of self-improvement advertised commercially. The Greek orator has been described as often pairing various parts of his speech with spatial reference points (i.e., rooms in the temple), and as he gave his speech he would "mentally travel" from room to room, upon whose walls he would imagine his words were inscribed.

There are many facets of the study of memory that have caught the interest of researchers. The order in which serially-presented material is learned has been a commonly researched learning phenomenon; the topic of more than one research project recently has been the tendency of an individual to "chunk" or imaginatively group large amounts of material in order to acquire it more easily.

Memory has also been studied within several time dimensions. Human factors researchers and others who have been struck with the similarities between the human mind and computers have suggested that information to be remembered may be "dropped" into the individual's long-term, short-term, and/or medium-term memory "storage bin." A second temporal dimension to the study of memory involves the processes important to mental rehearsal: How one can translate briefly presented material into forms that result in its retention over reasonably long-time intervals.

Two of the more basic processes involving human memory involve simple attention to a stimulus, and imitation or replication of it while it is still present. For a brief discussion of the role of attention in learning, the reader is referred to Chapter 10, while more detailed discussions may be found in texts by Norman and others. Imitative activities, reviewed below, are found within several tests, and in programs advanced by more than one contemporary educator.

IMITATION

It has been hypothesized by several writers that imitating the movements made by another individual may be a valid non-verbal test of body-image development (G.I.T.), and in another case may prove to be a helpful way of enhancing the child's perceptions of his body and its parts.

The gesture-imitation test of body-image development was constructed by two French scholars in child development, and norms for this ability have been constructed by giving the test to over 480 school children. Both simple (usually static) as well as complex gestures (usually involving movement) are employed in this test, and positionings of both the arms and fingers are presented for the children to copy. This test is not accompanied by training procedures, however, and the scores derived are based not only upon whether the child correctly imitates the examiner's gestures, but also upon whether he correctly reverses the gestures when they are bilateral in nature. Examples of some of the gestures to be imitated on this test are shown in Figures 13.1.

The Purdue Perceptual-Motor Survey also contains a section seeking to evaluate the ability of a child to imitate movements. Unlike the material above, Berges, Kephart, and his colleagues also suggest that imitation of the gestures and movements of another individual may involve either following (repetition after a time lapse) or immediate imitation. The material by Chaney and Kephart suggests that encouraging the imitation of the lip and tongue movements used in speech will enhance language development. McCormick and his colleagues also suggest activities involving the imitation of movements. In their program it is suggested that the child first inspect the movements to be imitated and then perform them while blindfolded.

SHORT-TERM MEMORY, SERIATION AND IMITATION

A number of programs, including one we have researched, contain tasks to enhance short-term memory via the imitation of various movements. These serial movements may require a child to execute one or more of several possible reactions:

1. Repeating in correct sequence a number of gestures, beginning with two, and then adding one at a time, after first visually inspecting the movements and then repeating them while blindfolded.

2. Reproducing two or more body positions, with the demonstrator fixed, after visual inspection and reproduction also with vision.

3. Reproducing a series of body positions originally presented via flash cards.

4. Remembering and repeating a series of movements through a maze constructed of boxes or similar objects.

5. Remembering and repeating, in the same order, a series of bodily movements made within geometric configurations on the ground.

FIGURE 13.1

Imitation of complex gestures: Hand and finger movements. 9 *items.*

a. The index and little finger of the left hand raised, the other fingers flexed, the back of the hand towards the examiner.

b. The same, right hand.

c. The two thumbs and the two little fingers touching each other, the other fingers flexed, the thumbs towards the examiner.

d. Two interlocking rings are formed by the thumb and the index finger, the other fingers slightly flexed.

e. The right hand is placed on the left hand, the palm of the right hand against the back of the left hand, the right hand completely concealing the left hand, the extended thumbs touching each other, palms turned towards the examiner.

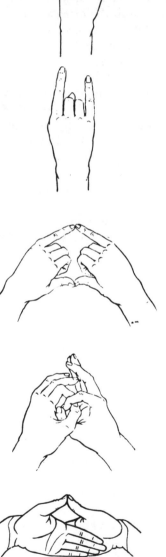

f. Same position except the little fingers are overlapped, the left-hand one underneath the right-hand one; the hands are flat, slightly turned towards the child; the left thumb is flat against the right thumb, hiding it.

g. The index fingers and the little fingers of both hands touch each other, the other fingers are flexed, the backs of the hands are turned towards the subject.

h. Continuing from the preceding position, the examiner rotates his left hand. The index finger of the left hand touches the little finger of the right hand, and the little finger of the left hand touches the index finger of the right hand.

i. The thumbs are crossed with the hands flat and the palms free. The left wrist is placed on the right wrist and the thumbs are turned towards the subject.

Reprinted from Jean Berges and Irene Lezine, *Tests d'imitation de Gestes,* © 1963, Masson & Cie., Paris. Trans. by Arthur H. Parmelee, Spastics International Medical Publications, London, 1965.

FIGURE 13.2

Imitation of simple gestures: Arm movements. 10 *items.*

a. The examiner extends his left arm to the left, horizontally with his hand open.

b. Same movement on the right side.

c. The examiner raises his left arm vertically.

d. The examiner raises his right arm vertically.

e. The examiner raises his left arm vertically and extends his right arm horizontally to the right.

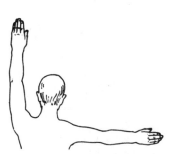

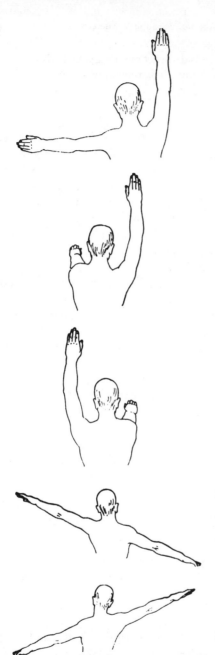

f. Reverse position.

g. The examiner extends his left arm directly in front of him and raises his right arm vertically.

h. Reverse position.

i. Both arms are extended laterally and obliquely inclined, the left hand high, the right hand low, the trunk remaining straight.

j. Reverse position.

Reprinted from Jean Berges and Irene Lezine, *Tests d'imitation de Gestes,* © 1963, Masson & Cie., Paris. Trans. by Arthur H. Parmelee, Spastics International Medical Publications, London, 1965.

(Reproduction may be done via verbal directions or by first visually inspecting the series of movements and then repeating them.)

6. Remembering and reproducing a series of locations to which a child has previously "traveled."

Several tasks involving serial memory ability are used in the various programs. McCormick et al., for example, suggest that ever increasing series of movements may be made over a jump rope, which is held or swinging in various ways (i.e., overhead or back and forth in pendulum fashion). A child may do something with a ball in two or more geometric configurations to afford further interest. Also it has been suggested that observational skills and descriptive language can be enhanced if a child is not permitted to see the original demonstrator, but must rely upon directions given verbally by a third child.

Other dimensions that have been outlined for short-term serial-memory tasks involve interpolating intervals between the time a series of movements are performed and the time when the inspecting child must imitate them.

Critical to the evaluation of these programs, which have been advanced to enhance serial memory ability, are two related questions: (a) How general or specific is serial memory? (b) Can practice in tasks involving serial memory of movements enhance the child's ability to remember a series of other kinds of stimuli (words, letters, information received auditorily, and the like)?

In an effort to answer the first question, scores on three tests of serial memory from 140 children in grades one to four were compared in a study published in 1969. The results of this comparison are shown below.

		1.	2.	3.
1.	Verbal identification of letters in alphabetical order	1.00	.37	.61
2.	Serial memory of pictures		1.00	.56
3.	Memory of gestures			1.00

Thus, it can be seen from the results of this pilot study that there is a moderate-to-high positive correlation between serial memory tasks in these young children, indicating that to some degree (from 30–37 percént common variance), serial memory ability taps some general quality in the young children. It is probable that serial memory tasks executed by older children and by adults involving two different input modes would not evidence the same high positive relationships.

In an attempt to answer the second question, the subjects, children in grades one to four, were not only given a test of how well they were able to repeat movements in a series, but also were given tests to determine how well they would retain a series of numbers given verbally and how well they could recite in correct order a series of pictures presented visually. The findings of this study suggest that the experimental group exposed to serial memory games involving movement imitation evidenced improvement in serial memory tasks involving the ordering of words in a series, in remembering the order of numbers presented auditorily, and in tasks involving the replication of the order of animal pictures presented visually. Although additional research on this topic is needed, the results of this study were highly encouraging.

Previous studies of movement tasks learned in a series, involving the blindfolded traversal of circuitous mazes, also suggest that the learning and retention of a series of movements is in some ways similar to learning a series of words. For example, it has been found that in both word and movement learning, first to be acquired are the initial parts of the series, next to be retained are the final portions, while most difficult to retain are the intermediate portions.

Tasks emphasizing the serial memory of movements are potentially helpful to educators and to the children because the quality of the child's memory ability is immediately apparent to all concerned. Moreover, data from other sources suggest that measures of serial memory are correlated both to measures of attention and to scores reflecting what is termed "perceptual span" (the ability to remember the nature of a group of stimuli when quickly presented via a tachistoscope.

Our observations of children engaged in serial memory tasks involving movements suggest that their attention is totally involved and that the games are highly motivating. Much of the time the children in our program requested additional games of this nature at the completion of a lesson; their additional participation formed a reward for their previous efforts on other tasks.

LONG-TERM MEMORY, SEMANTICS AND SYMBOLS

Other movement experiences have been suggested to heighten a child's ability to remember, over an extended time period, the shapes of letters, geometric figures, words, and similar symbolic and semantic content. Again, the types of experiences recommended have been varied and range from the grids and movable letters that may be jumped on, previously described, to the games suggested by Humphrey, which also lead toward the recognition of word-shapes and letter sounds and shapes.

These games have been applied to children of all ages and to those with varying degrees of intellectual capacity. Moreover, creative teachers have elaborated upon their content, aiding in the translation of the sound of words from viewing their shapes, and vice-versa. For example, one teacher has constructed a grid composed of various vowel sounds as shown in Figure 13.3.[1] Thus, a child must be able to jump not only in an E or I square, but must discriminate between the two possibilities placed on the grid, if given the instructions to "jump in the square containing the *I* sound in 'inside'." Numerous other games may be played to enhance this type of auditory-visual translation.

Improvement via games involving jumping and hopping responses in letter grids, on the part of children (ten in each group) who initially

FIGURE 13.3

(In)*	(ox)
U	U
I	O
(by)	(eat)
i	
Y	Ē
(able)	(up)
	U
Ā	U
(Use)	(pity)
	E
Ū	Y
(Open)	(Apple)
	U
Ō	A
(empty)	(Ice)
U	
E	Ī

* Words in parentheses are not placed on the grid; the grid may be enlarged, however, by placing both lower and upper case letters on it, like this A/a, etc.

[1] Mr. Leonard Geiger, Big Bear School District, California, devised the grid to be used by older children with learning problems. In this case, it has been employed with children from ten years of age and older.

scored lowest in tests of letter recognition, was recorded in one study carried out in the 1969–70 school year. Figure 13.4 compares scores obtained from a control group, given small-group tutoring in a classroom, to that of a group exposed to active games involving letter recognition.

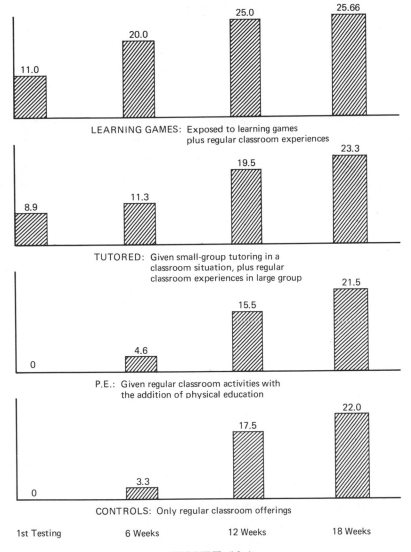

FIGURE 13.4

Progress through the semester of groups in a study by Cratty and Martin, representing the three children in each group who initially scored lowest on a test involving the ability to identify and to write the letters in the alphabet.

As can be seen, when the mean scores of the three children in each group who evidenced the inability to identify letters of the alphabet were compared and their progress recorded over a semester, the results were supportive of the use of activities involving learning games, when compared to the more traditional approaches. Most of the time, it is found that the movement approach to learning letters is most helpful to the children functioning within the lower academic and intellectual levels.

LONG-TERM RETENTION OF SEMANTIC CONTENT

Long-term retention of semantic materials also has been studied by various researchers employing a movement approach. Spelling involves not only the retention of letter shapes but the retention of letter series and word shapes. In the research previously alluded to, we have found that when using a phonics approach (The Open Court Method) to learning letter shapes via movement, significant improvement is seen in children when contrasted to the scores achieved by children receiving extra tutoring but in an environment that discourages overt physical activity. The improvement recorded was on a standardized word list, and the specific words on the list were not practiced during the semester.

Categorization

Listed on most typologies of intellectual functioning are abilities that involve making discriminations: placing objects, events, symbols, etc., into categories, and similar operations involving classification. The existence of this ability can be discerned in infants a few days old. For example, Fantz and others have found that infants evidence the inclination to spend more time visually inspecting unfamiliar and/or unusual stimuli than watching the familiar faces, shapes, and other events within close proximity. Additionally, Bower and her colleagues have found that infants from forty to sixty days of age can discern differences in three-dimensional and two-dimensional shapes, and can apparently discriminate between similar objects placed at two different distances away. Thus, during the first months following birth, infants have been able to categorize simple stimuli in various rudimentary ways.

As the infant matures, the improving abilities to make complex discriminations and to place objects, people, and events into increasingly discrete categories are important criteria upon which to base assessments of intellectual functioning. By the time the child reaches school, he must not only discriminate between the various letter shapes in the alphabet, but must additionally recognize characteristics common to the twenty-six

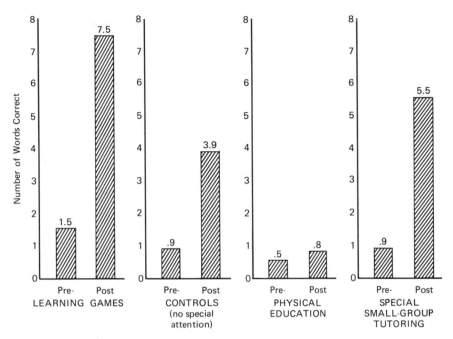

Reprinted from Cratty and Martin, *The Effects of a Program of Learning Games Upon Selected Academic Abilities in Children with Learning Difficulties.*

FIGURE 13.5

Comparison of first graders, pre- and post-tests, by group, in a test of spelling. All groups were given regular classroom work in addition to the special attention indicated.

letters even though they may appear in different sizes, print styles, and locations within his space field. If his efforts at reading are to be successful, he must also categorize word shapes into innumerable categories representing a multitude of meanings.

In several of his writings, Piaget discusses the maturing child's ability to classify and categorize. Testing children from two years of age and older, Piaget suggests that the ability to classify passes through three stages of development:

1. The pre-operational stage (two to five years) is the one in which children evidence difficulty placing geometric figures or representations of objects into "pure" categories. Often a "partial alignment" with some objects that are similar will be formed by the child during this age span.

2. In the second stage (five to seven years), children produce collections that seem to be true and valid classes. In one study, children were seen

by Piaget to arrange objects into two large categories, one containing all the polygons and the other containing curvilinear forms. Moreover, these same children could divide these categories further, placing all triangles in one pile and the rectangles in a second, while the curvilinear forms were similarly divided into those that included rings and those that were half-rings.

3. The third stage (about seven to eleven years) is marked by the ability to construct reasonably complex hierarchical classifications and to comprehend the qualities reflected by objects that determine their arrangement into various groups. Thus, pictures of flowers can be separated from pictures of plants; furthermore, the pictures of flowers can be divided into those of various types, while finally those within each name grouping may be further divided into those of various colors.

Movements and their meanings and uses must similarly be categorized by the growing child. Diffuse and discoordinate actions in the neonate become refined and specialized to meet life's many exigencies. Moreover, these actions must become paired with verbal meanings, which may be voiced silently and inwardly or put forth by others.

Various programs of education in which movement plays a part have not contained a great many types of tasks that could conceivably enhance the child's ability to classify and to categorize. The tasks that have appeared in the various programs might themselves be placed within the following categories:

1. Practice in pattern recognition in which various movement games and motor responses are encouraged while using large geometric figures placed on the playground. Using these techniques, the attempt seems to be to aid children to place verbal labels on commonly seen geometric figures. These activities are designed to enhance the classification and categorization of what Guilford would term "figural content."

2. The letter recognition activities described in the previous section, particularly if a wide range of transfer is sought (for example, lower-case, upper case, written letter, spoken letter, letter sound, etc.), represent another attempt through movement experiences to aid a child to form categories into which letters and letter combinations might be "placed."

3. In programs of movement education, a child may be asked to perform a movement within a given category, but at the same time may be permitted some latitude in his exact choice of movement. For example, an instructor may ask a child to "Move down the mat in a backwards way," or to "Show me a hopping way to get into the hoop," etc. Within this context a child is thus being encouraged to form categories of movement experiences and to demonstrate his acquisition of various categorical concepts by demonstrating various actions with his own body, or by observing and judging the efforts of another child to

demonstrate the same types of behaviors. These exercises are designed to enhance the classification of *behavioral content*.

4. Various spatial concepts may be learned through movement experiences. A child may be asked to do "something to the left" or "with the left side of your body" (or right side), and in a similar manner may be asked to go under (or over) a chair or other obstacle to enhance acquisition of the spatial concepts of up-down and left-right. For instance, division of movements into four categories, corresponding to up-down and left-right may be used.

5. Most of the reading games listed by various writers might be considered to be practice in categorization. A word shape (such as "look") must be classified, compared to other similar but different words shapes and word sounds, and in other ways categorized in order to be truly learned. Specifically, Humphrey lists two games in his 1970 text that are aimed at enhancing the ability to calssify letters; one involves arranging pictures of various kinds of animals (classifiable according to type, like "fish," or to function, "can fly," etc.) in a game in which children run to place the correct pictures in various cages with a risk of being caught by other participants. A second game, "Ducks Fly," is similar in purpose.

The data emerging from the programs in which these activities have a part are not extensive. However, in a study we carried out in which one of the objectives was to enhance children's verbal identification of geometric patterns (circle, square, half-circle, rectangle, and triangle), it was found that using a total-body movement approach was as successful as attempting to ingrain the same categorical concepts via small-group tutoring in a classroom environment. These results are shown in Figure 13.6.

In the study from which the previous data was obtained, it was found that the elementary school children could, without any appreciable errors, match common geometric figures by visually inspecting them at the beginning of the semester; the training seemed to enhance, however, their ability to place the various patterns into categories based upon the *verbal labels* attached to them.

Moreover, testing verbal pattern recognition was carried out with smaller geometric patterns, placed on cards, then contained in the training program. Thus, it might be assumed that the children had gained the *concepts* necessary to discriminate the geometric figures from one another, i.e., that triangles have three sides and angles, no matter where they occur, what size they may be, or how they are placed in the space field.

Thus, in summary, there is a little information to suggest that simple categorizations involving the verbal identification of geometric figures

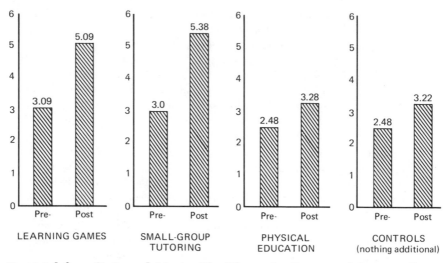

LEARNING GAMES　　SMALL-GROUP　　PHYSICAL　　CONTROLS
　　　　　　　　　　　TUTORING　　　　EDUCATION　　(nothing additional)

Reprinted from Cratty and Martin, *The Effects of a Program of Learning Games Upon Selected Academic Activities in Children with Learning Difficulties*

FIGURE 13.6

Comparison of pre-and post-tests in the verbal-recognition of geometric figures. All groups received regular classroom work, plus—as indicated. Total subjects—140.

may be enhanced through games;[2] at the same time, there seems to be no verification that learning to place movements in various categories (i.e., "move backwards," etc.) will enhance some general categorical ability among normal or atypical children.

Evaluation

Bloom places evaluative processes at the pinnacle of his taxonomy of the "cognitive domain." Similarly, his "affective domain" contains a level that he labels "Characterization by a value or value complex." Guilford has also found a quality that he terms "sensitivity to problems," which he feels is closely related to an evaluative ability; moreover, his

[2] In the study cited previously, no significant correlation was found between how identification of geometric figures via visual inspection was related to the ability to attach verbal labels ("triangle") to these same patterns ($r = .09$).

research has suggested that approximately eight different evaluative abilities exist, with the possibility of five more being uncovered as the result of further investigation.

Guilford suggests that evaluation involves the following sub-operations:

1. Comparing small differences prior to classification of combinations of letters, numbers, etc.

2. Deciding upon whether there is logical consistency in verbal statements and/or visually presented scenes.

3. Detecting imperfections or irrelevancies within various contexts.

4. Deciding which of two or more kinds of information come closer to satisfying a specific criterion.

More than one educator interested in enhancing cognitive processes has included exercises in evaluation in his workbook and in automated programs for children and youth. Evaluative processes have been inserted into the programs of education in which movement has also been inculcated. For example:

1. An observing child may evaluate the quality of the movements made by another child or children, in response to such directions as "Tell me if John performs his exercise well."

2. Quantitative aspects of movement experiences may also be evaluated by participation in programs of movement education: "How high did he jump?," "How many times did he do that?," "How fast did he run?"

3. Self-evaluation may be encouraged in "movement education" programs. To measure aspiration level and related measures of self-concept, a child may be asked to estimate his future performance in a task prior to its execution. He may then be permitted to perform and subsequently be asked to make estimates of predicted successes on the third trial and those which follow.[3]

4. A child may engage in the evaluation of relative success in making correct choices or responses within an academic program in which movement plays a part. One child may, for example, jump on squares of a grid containing the letters of the alphabet, calling them out as he

[3] Several types of lessons can be carried out using this type of approach, including those which aid a child to set realistic goals for himself, as well as helping him to modify goals when varying degrees of success or failure are apparent. Moreover, a self-estimation task may be employed as a diagnostic tool in the hands of the clinical or educational psychologist, relative to the assessment of ego function (See "Aspiration Level" in Eysenck's *Handbook of Abnormal Psychology*, p. 246, New York: Basic Books, Inc. 1961.

proceeds, while observing children may assess the degree of success he is realizing.

Mosston has perhaps paid the most attention to activities purporting to enhance evaluation within a program of movement education. In the section of his text dealing with "Reciprocal Teaching—The Use of the Partner," Mosston suggests that teaching by the "buddy system," in which one child acts as an evaluator while a second performs, has several advantages over the more traditional teacher-directed methods.

1. Most students are occupied; there is little time wasted waiting in lines. A student is either an active performer or an active observer.

2. The observer's self-concept is enhanced, particularly if the teacher is careful to work through the observer when seeking to correct performance.

3. Each pair is given the opportunity to move along as their individual needs and abilities permit.

4. The method gives the teacher more freedom to move around and to observe the class and what is really going on.

5. Immediate encouragement or correction is offered each performer by his partner, just after each trial, without waiting for the teacher to respond.

Mosston proceeds to give examples of how this type of partner teaching may be applied in programs of tumbling, basketball, and track and field. In order to structure the teaching situation better, he suggests the use of "task cards" on which objectives, task details, teaching points, and the like are placed. Using this teaching approach, Mosston suggests, not only will involve children physically in what they are doing, but will also tend to involve the emotional, social, and intellectual sides of their personalities.

In other phases of Mosston's "Spectrum of Styles," he also suggests that evaluation be carried out. For example, when "using small groups," he recommends that a student may be designated as an observer, another may serve as a recorder, while a third is engaged in performance. The individual program phase is also marked by opportunities for the performer to assess the quality and quantity aspects of his efforts.

Mosston does not suggest that some basic evaluative abilities may be enhanced in this way; instead, he suggests that by permitting a child the opportunity to evaluate himself and the efforts of his classmates in physical performance situations, the final result will be more vigorous physical effort, participated in by more people at the same time, together with more thoughtful consideration of basic principles of performance by both the active and observing member of the partnerships.

It is difficult to locate definitive studies in which movement experiences have been demonstrated to enhance evaluative abilities, based upon change in one of the several tests of this quality available. There are guidelines from such writers as Mosston and others that should serve to direct the efforts of the more creative and flexible teachers, as well as the energies of diligent researchers.

Problem Solving

Another (and overlapping) group of intellectual capacities may be termed "problem-solving abilities." This category, similar to the previous ones discussed, is rather amorphous and is composed of several sub-abilities, depending upon which author one consults. This classification, however, is considered by most to be the "highest" level of intellectual functioning, and may be studied with reference to several rather flexible scales.

For example, the problem posed to a youngster may require him to *synthesize*, to put together information and/or movements in some meaningful and perhaps original manner. On the other hand, the problem may pose a dilemma that may be solved through *analysis*, the taking apart of a more complex problem and/or situation in order to extract meaning. Some complex problems require, to varying degrees, both processes of analysis and synthesis. For example, within a sports situation the player must analyze his own as well as his opponent's weaknesses and strengths; at the same time, he must consider how the synthesis of his teammates' abilities and shortcomings, paired with these same qualities in his opponent, may interact when they clash in an athletic contest.

Another continuum upon which problem-solving behaviors may be studied, with reference to Guilfords work, is one at whose extremes the labels *"convergent"* and *"divergent"* thinking may be placed. A problem may be structured so that there are a limited number of correct responses possible, or even only one appropriate decision called for. On the other hand, the intent may be to prompt the learner to explore and/or make up a number of responses or conclusions. The former process would suggest *convergent* thought, one decision, while the latter suggests *divergent* thinking. It is unusual, however, to find that a problem-solving situation calls for either an unlimited number of responses or is restricted to a single one. Therefore, one may construct a scale upon which may be placed a given problem, movement problem or any other kind, relative to the degree of divergent or convergent thinking called for.

Divergent   Convergent
Thinking   Thinking

←———→

(A)   (B)   (C)   (D)

Examples of teacher-student interactions within programs of movement education that might fall at several points within the continuum pictured are as follows:

(A) Extreme divergent thinking would be expected to occur in response to the rather general directions, "Compose a dance routine."

(B) Less divergency would be expected if the directions, "using movements of the trunk only," or "to be carried out within four minutes," or "to take place within a 10′ by 10′ square area," were to be added to the directions given in example "A" above.

(C) Moving toward the middle of the continuum, we might elicit reasonably focused, yet somewhat unrestricted, movement choices by suggesting that a child "Find six ways of moving down the mat," or perhaps asking "How many ways can you start the 'trip' of a ball?" If the directions, "Move six *backward* ways down the mat," were given, still more convergence of response is called for.

(D) Several extremely thoughtful problem-solving situations have been described by writers that require the selection of a single "movement solution." These lessons impose a number of conditions that, when met, permit the individual only a single response or responses within an extremely narrow "band."

Mosston, for example, in a demonstration I witnessed in Wisconsin several years ago, led children toward the solution of a jumping problem in which individual differences could be accommodated, using a rope as the apparatus. After several attempts at solving the problem of permitting all the children to "have fun, (extend themselves without incurring failure), the children came up with one of the only solutions possible under the circumstances and conditions imposed. One held one end of the rope at ground level, while a second held it at an angle at the other end so that the rope inscribed an angle with the ground, as shown. Thus, all could jump over it when able and where capable.

There are other dimensions to problem solving behavior which involve moving a child from place to place along the divergent-convergent continuum. For example: one may arrange conditions, and or give instructions which require that the child's *movement (s)* must be carried out

in an ever restricted manner. Thus for example a child may be asked to move from line to line, with his back nearest the ground, backwards, using only one foot and two hands to aid him. Within this sub-category the instructor may again offer two types of alternatives: (a) giving instructions one at a time, and permitting trials between ever more restricting directions; or (b) giving all instructions at the same time and requiring a child to execute only one trial in an attempt to meet the conditions imposed.

In addition to posing problems, or arranging conditions so that only one or a few movements are "correct ones," the teacher may give directions, so that the child must arrange *items within the environment* within only one or a limited number of ways. Thus using a box, a rope, and perhaps a ball that doesn't roll very well, game rules may be devised, so that the implements may only be used in a single way to play the game invented by the teacher and to be discovered by the children. With a little thought the reader should become able to think of innumerable other ways in which these two types of convergent types of problem solving behavior might be initiated in children and youth.

Piaget suggests several dimensions of problem-solving behavior, usually not seen until adolescence, that are appropriate to consider for those dealing in movement as a learning modality. These include:

1. *Possibility-reality relationships.* While mature problem solving ability, according to Piaget, involves weighing what *might* be with what is, early in the child's life the mental manipulation of operations may only be handled in concrete terms. Piaget would probably approve the emphasis placed upon the encouragement of mental trial-and-error processes within various movement education programs, upon the seeking of alternatives that Bruner suggests and that Mosston reflects in the program he espouses. Thus, if one is to enhance this mature type of

problem-solving behavior, he should permit a child to weigh alternatives, to think, and to construct and manipulate reality without direct action prior to carrying out some movement task.

2. Combinatorial property. Piaget emphasizes that mature thinking, logical operations seen in adolescents, may involve the putting together of hitherto unrelated aspects of the individual's reality. Others would call this quality "creative thinking," or perhaps the ability to synthesize information as previously described. In any case, if one accepts the validity of this quality, he should aid a child to obtain "bits" of the total he may need to solve a movement problem, perhaps parts of a sequence of movements needed to traverse a vertical or horizontal distance and then permit the child to synthesize the "pieces" placed before him for consideration.

An example of a movement exercise of this nature was once explained during a workshop, by Richard Walker of the Gesell Institute.[4] He demonstrated how a child may be shown a number of footprints cut out of paper, some red and others blue. After placing these footprints in various combinations leading across the floor, the child may be then asked to respond via hopping, jumping, and similar behaviors on the footprints corresponding to the left (red) and right (blue) pieces of paper placed before him.

Walker also indicates that this represents practice in what might be termed "decoding," or deciding the movement "code" that corresponds to the placement of the footprints. This process, Walker states, is similar to some mental operations needed in reading. Furthermore, he suggests that the reverse process may be engagd in: a child may watch another child skip, hop, and/or jump in some order and then attempt to "encode" his progression by placing the proper blue and red footprints on the floor corresponding to the "trip" the performing child has just completed.

[4] Director of Perceptual-Motor Education.

3. *Flexibility* of logical thought is also emphasized by Piaget as he discusses higher level thought processes. He suggests that as the youth becomes able to remove himself and his thoughts from concrete operations, he also becomes more flexible in seeking alternative solutions. This quality is smiliar to Guilford's various divergent thinking abilities, which have been discussed previously.

4. *Reversibility.* Increased mental capacity seen in older children and youth, Piaget suggests, also permits them to perceive the manner in which logical and concrete operations may be reversed. An example of this was described in (2.) above, in which both encoding and decoding processes were encouraged. In the case cited, it would be interesting to determine whether the participating youths, after being given one of the operations by their teacher, could correctly predict the manner in which the tasks might be reversed.

Other examples of attempts to exploit this quality in programs of movement education might include seeking ways of getting down and getting up a ladder, or perhaps seeking to move from one point to another, moving both forward and backward.

At least two separate types of reversibility in problem solving behavior may be encouraged by the thoughtful teacher. A child may, using a movement task, be aided to perceive ways in which the spatial dimensions of a problem might be reversed if the teacher poses the question "How might you reverse the task?" after a child has jumped into the center of a hoop on the ground. The proper reverse movement response would be to jump from the hoop to a spot outside its periphery.

In other tasks the child may be encouraged to think of ways in which a *basic process* inherent in a movement task might be reversed. For example, after a child has begun to understand a code placed on a blackboard, by perhaps hopping every time he sees an X on the board, and jumping every time he sees an O, he might then be helped to seek the reverse of this problem—that is, the reverse of changing the signs X and O to movements. The reverse of this *process* would thus be to first observe a child alternately hopping and jumping in various combinations, and then transcribe the movement code to a written X, O code on the board.

5. *Theorizing—discovering principles.* Piaget and Gagne have suggested that the ability to discover a rule and to apply a principle to more than one situation constitutes rather high level intellectual functioning. Mosston, in numerous examples, outlines how in gymnastic lessons, basketball practices, and similar situations, students may be led toward the discovery of principles applicable to a wider range of situations than that one immediately encountered.

Mosston suggests the principle of "guided discovery," a kind of Socratic approach in leading children toward the acquisition of principles that may underlie their physical performance. In this manner, it is suggested, the teacher already familiar with the final appropriate principle or principles, through judicious questioning and creating the proper amount of cognitive dissonance, may aid students to uncover principles and rules with reasonably broad applications.

Relatively few studies have been carried out that demonstrate the efficiency of teaching toward principles versus teaching specific skills within the programs of movement education. An exception is the study by Whilden, who found that if skill specifics are taught in a basketball game situation, the skills are quickly mastered, whereas strategical concepts are more easily acquired with the more flexible approach suggested by Mosston and outlined by Piaget and Bruner.

Creativity

Several writers assume that promoting creativity in children and youth is one of the loftier goals of education, and specifically of programs in which movement activities predominate. Mosston lists it as the next step to reach after problem-solving behavior is achieved.[5] Other scholars interested in creative behavior have been quite active in recent years, however, and from their research have come guidelines helpful to the understanding of (1) the nature of creative thinking, (2) relationships between creative abilities and other abilities including intelligence, (3) the way to encourage creative behavior, and finally (4) steps in the process(es) which hypothetically lead toward creative behavior.[6]

Despite the emphasis upon the creative aspects within movement education programs during the past decades, relatively little data have been forthcoming confirming the widely held supposition that encouraging diversity and creativity in movement enhances creative inclinations in other situations. The few studies that have been carried out indicate that creative efforts in movement experiences may be highly specific and unrelated to scores on tests of creativity. Moreover, if any transfer between creative experiences does take place (movement-art, for example) it may be related to the sex of the participant; girls seem more likely to generalize, for example.

In any case, the available data indicate that measures of intelligence are only moderately related to scores that attempt to evaluate creative

---

[5] But then, unfortunately, he devotes only a page and a half to exploring creative behavior and its possible relationships to movement.

[6] For a detailed summary of this research, see Cratty, *Human Behavior: Exploring Educational Processes*, Wolf City, Texas: University Press. 1971 (Chapter 12).

abilities. Furthermore, the creative process has been described by several writers as consisting of at least four stages:

1. The collection of information.

2. An incubation period during which the information seems to "settle" within the individual's consciousness.

3. A period that seems to be marked by the sudden putting together of hither-to-unrelated information, facts, causes-effects, and/or events.

4. A period of time during which the resultant creative effort may be held up, studied, and evaluated.

Several authors suggest that with the conclusion of a period of time during which an individual has felt himself to be creative, there may be a period of psychological depression, a "let-down" during which the individual needs special handling by his teachers and during which he seems to be somewhat ill at ease or even guilty about the cessation of his inspirational efforts.

Some scholars suggest that the integral part of the creative process occurs when the individual feels some need, some strain, or some kind of ambiguity or dissonance; when this kind of disquieting psychological imbalance is resolved, the result is usually creative effort of some kind.

Whether an individual's output is judged creative or not depends upon a number of variables including the societal setting in which his creativity is manifested, as well as the bias of the test or individual judging his creative behavior. In a similar manner, opinions concerning the traits of creative individuals vary from writer to writer. In any case, there seem to be three general categories of traits that are seen most often in individuals judged creative.[7]

1. Creative people are tolerant and accepting of ambiguity and confusion. Not only are they more at ease with complexity, but at times may seek to create ambiguity in situations that are too bland for their liking.

2. Creative people, unlike the commonly held belief, are often found to be more psychologically stable than individuals who are not creative. They are able to control their impulses, to keep themselves balanced, and otherwise resist depression, except possibly when their creative efforts are at a standstill or have terminated.

3. Individuals who may be judged as creative often evidence the ability

[7] Some research has confirmed the existence of at least two types of creative efforts: scientific creativity in which technical skill is important, and aesthetic or artistic creativity that involves more sensitivity than technical skill.

to focus attention and to restrict their interests while marshaling energy toward the completion of a task.

Much of this information, superficially reviewed here, has obvious relevance to individuals working in movement as a creative endeavor. At the same time, "hard data" that might serve to confirm or to modify the goals many advance are largely absent.

Summary and Overview

As can be seen, there are relatively little confirming data that tie, in direct ways, intellectual operations to specific kinds of movement experiences. Much of the information contained in this chapter has been advanced in the form of unsupported hypotheses, rather than confirmed fact.

At the same time, deciphering relationships between the various intellectual levels reviewed becomes difficult insofar as there is a considerable overlapping between functions various scholars hypothesize as integral at the various levels. Certain sub-processes within the general ability level labeled "*categorization*," for example, are also found within the sub-division called "memorization." A similar overlap exists within various descriptions of *problem solving, creative thinking,* and other similar processes.

Further difficulty is encountered when attempting to synthesize behaviors as complex as the ones reviewed here, insofar as few authors and researchers agree upon similar classification systems. Different words are used to describe highly similar processes, or in other cases the same nomenclature is employed to describe processes that are dissimilar.

In any case, the available literature does indicate that if one has the objective of enhancing various intellectual abilities through movement experiences, more than one cognitive operation should be "built in" to the tasks to which children and youth are exposed. The complexity and nature of the cognitive operations that might be expected in youth of various ages are illuminated in the writings of Piaget in particular.

Moreover, the texts of scholars interested in cognition and movement make it clear that the encouragement of youth to think in movement situations might be engendered (a) by gradually transferring decisions to the participating children, and (b) by taking into account, when planning curriculum, the degree of diversity of response that is required when various instructions and situations are tendered to the students.

Studies of creative behavior as well as intellectual ability indicate that neither category of human functioning is an undifferentiated global whole. Rather, it seems as though not only are there several types of creative qualities and problem solving strategies, but also that the intellectual performance is multi-faceted.

Therefore, it appears that those who construct programs incorporating movement as a basic ingredient and whose aim is to elevate the participants' "higher" intellectual capacities should take into account the diversity of the qualities they hope to modify.

BIBLIOGRAPHY

BERGES, JEAN, et LEZINE, IRÈNE. "Tests d'imitation des Gestes." © Masson & Cie, 1963, Paris. Translated by Arthur H. Parmellee ("The Imitation of Gestures") London: The Spastics Society Medical Education and Information Unit in Association with William Heinemann Medical Books, Ltd., 1965.

BOWER, T. G. "The Visual World of Infants." Scientific American 215 (1966): 80–97.

BRUNER, JEROME S. Toward a Theory of Instruction. Cambridge, Mass.: The Belknap Press of Harvard University Press, 1966.

CHANEY, CLARA, and KEPHART, NEWELL C. Motoric Aids to Perceptual Training. Columbus, Ohio: Charles E. Merrill Publishing Co., 1968.

CRATTY, BRYANT J. Active Learning. Englewood Cliffs, N. J.: Prentice-Hall, Inc., 1971.

———. Human Behavior: Exploring Educational Processes. Wolf City, Texas: University Press, 1971.

———. "Comparisons of Verbal-Motor Performance and Learning in Serial Memory Tasks." Research Quarterly 34 (December 1963): 4.

———. "Recency Versus Primacy in a Complex Gross Motor Task." Research Quarterly 34 (March 1963): 3–8.

CRATTY, BRYANT J.; IKEDA, NAMIKO; MARTIN, M. M.; JENNETT, C.; and MORRIS, M. "Total Body Movement as a Learning Modality, A Pilot Study." Chapter 4 in Movement Activities, Motor Ability and the Education of Children. Springfield, Ill.: Charles C. Thomas, Publisher, 1970.

CRATTY, BRYANT J., and MARTIN, M. M. The Effects of a Program of Learning Games Upon Selected Academic Abilities in Children with Learning Difficulties. Washington, D.C.: Department of Education, Bureau of Handicapped Children, 1970.

EYSENCK, J. H. Handbook of Abnormal Psychology: An Experimental Approach. New York: Basic Books, Inc., Publishers, 1961.

FANTZ, R. L. "The Origin of Form Perception." Scientific American 204 (1961): 66–72.

GAGNE, R. W. "The Analysis of Instructional Objectives for the Design of Instruction." In Teaching Machines and Programmed Learning, II: Data *and Directions.* Edited by Robert Glaser. Department of Audiovisual Instruction, National Education Association of the United States, 1965.

GUILFORD, J. P. *Intelligence, Creativity, and Their Educational Implications.* San Diego, Cal.: Robert R. Knapp, Publisher, 1968.

HUMPHREY, JAMES, and SULLIVAN, DOROTHY. *Teaching Slow Learners Through Active Games.* Springfield, Ill.: Charles C. Thomas, Publisher, 1970.

McCORMICK, CLARENCE; SCHNOBRICH, JANICE; and FOOTLIK, S. WILLARD. *Perceptual-Motor Training and Cognitive Achievement.* Downer's Grove, Ill.: George Williams College, 1967.

MILLER, GEORGE. "The Magical Number Seven, Plus or Minus Two: Some Limits on our Capacity for Processing Information." *Psychology Review* 63 (1956): 81–97.

MILLER, GEORGE; GALANTER, EUGENE; and PRIBRAM, KARL. *Plans and the Structure of Behavior.* New York: Holt, Rinehart & Winston, 1960.

MOSSTON, MUSKA. *Teaching Physical Education.* Columbus, Ohio: Charles E. Merrill Publishing Co., 1966.

NORMAN, DONALD A. *Memory and Attention.* New York: John Wiley & Sons, Inc., 1969.

PARNES, S. J. *Student Workbook for Creative Problem-Solving Courses and Institutes.* Buffalo, New York: State University of New York at Buffalo, 1961.

PHILIPP, JOAN A. "Comparison of Motor Creativity with Figural and Verbal Creativity, and Selected Motor Skills." *Research Quarterly* 40 (March 1969): 163.

PIAGET, JEAN. *The Language and Thought of the Child.* Translated by M. Gabain. London: Routledge & Kegan Paul, Ltd., 1926.

———. *The Origins of Intelligence in Children.* Translated by M. Cook. New York: International Universities Press, 1952.

POPHAM, W. JAMES, and BAKER, EVA L. *Systematic Instruction.* Englewood Cliffs, N. J.: Prentice-Hall, Inc., 1970.

ROACH, EUGENE, and KEPHART, NEWELL C. *The Purdue Perceptual-Motor Survey.* Columbus, Ohio: Charles E. Merrill, Inc., 1966.

UHR, LEONARD, ED. *Pattern Recognition.* New York: John Wiley & Sons, Inc., 1966.

UPTON, A., and SAMSON, R. W. *Creative Analysis.* New York: E. P. Dutton & Co., 1963.

WHILDEN, PEGGY P. "Comparison of Two Methods of Teaching Basketball." *Research Quarterly* 27 (1956): 235–42.

14

Epilogue

Introduction

The previous material has attempted to reflect a wide diversity of view-points, scientific approaches, and programs that in some way link motor activity and so-called higher intellectual processes. As can be seen, some of the content areas are rather rich in ideas and research, while others contain more speculations than confirmations. Over-all, however, it is believed that the discussions of movement-cognitive relationships in various contexts reflect a growing interest in the numerous ways in which educational processes may be made more dynamic and effective through a consideration of the action capacities and inclinations of youngsters.

Behavioral scientists from numerous countries have begun to explore some of the ways in which motor activity and athletics are under-girded by intellectual processes and, conversely, how various cognitive and academic abilities may be modified through an action approach. Kiphard in Germany, LeBoulch in France, Oliver in England, Matsuda and his colleagues in Japan, and several Americans have provided conceptual bases from which more expanded programs, speculations, and research efforts might spring.

The several sections of this chapter are intended to summarize available information in order to provide the impetus for developing further creative movement-oriented programs, and to suggest new directions for research concerning the two components of the human personality that provide the focus of the book.

Motor Skill and Intelligence

It is believed that the research on the mental practice of motor skills and the varying factor structure of complex perceptual-motor functioning provide several guidelines for the more effective teaching and learning of motor skills. For example, when attempting to acquire skill or to inculcate the skill in others, it appears necessary to consider the following questions:

1. What are the various intellectual, perceptual, and motor components necessary to perform the skill well? Perhaps most important, to what degree are various of these factors important during the several stages of learning?

2. What are the individual differences in abilities necessary to adequate acquisition of the task that the learners bring with them to the performance situation? Are the learners relatively similar in abilities or divergent in their make-up? Which subgroups would be expected to show initial fast improvement? Which are likely to lag behind the others initially? Who may be expected to show relatively quick improvement at all stages of learning? Which ones might show initial lags and then faster terminal improvement?

3. What kind of performance pre-training might be engaged in with fruitful outcomes? Will verbal training relative to the exact manner in which the skill is performed be best, or will some kind of general training in the principles involved in the skill to be learned and in similar skills be most productive of best effort?

4. How might individual differences in values, attitudes, and motives affect acquisition? To what degree might some kind of preparation on the part of the teacher help erase negative attitudes? How might early success in skill acquisition aid in eradicating negative attitudes?

5. At what points in the acquisition of skill might certain helpful instructional interventions be inserted into the teaching-learning program? Will different kinds of instructions be effective at different times in the learning process? (This is usually the case.) How much time and emphasis should be placed upon formal instructions versus less formal trial and error on the part of the learner?

6. How much and what types of interpolated mental practice might be inserted between performance trials? How might this type of practice

best be encouraged? How is it best to deal with hypothetical individual differences in the type of imagery that may be preferred by various learners? Should mental practice be of a general nature, (for example, encouraging relaxation) or must specific types of mental practice be engaged in?

Coupled with these general principles are others that may be of help in enhancing performance of individuals at either end of a performance and/or intellectual continua. There seem to be helpful guidelines emerging relative to the more effective movement education of the intellectually superior and the intellectually stunted child and youth, just as other data serve to pinpoint axioms that may be directed toward the superior athlete and the child or youth who may be less adequate when attempting to exercise his movement capacities. For example:

1. While it appears helpful to afford superior athletes both specific and general instructions concerning the performance of the skill, there seems to be a tendency among more intellectually capable athletes to benefit more from inspecting data from personality trait tests and similar measures. The less intellectually capable, on the other hand, may reject the importance of this kind of information about themselves and/or be unable to interpret it in the light of their current needs, performance capacities, and contests in which they will be engaged.

2. Some recent studies indicate the importance of a great deal of intellectual pre-training prior to the practice of motor skills on the part of retardates. In one study, when this was carried out, the motor learning curves of the retarded youngsters approximated that of normal children with whom they were later compared.

3. Data afrom still other programs of research indicate that, if retarded youngsters are taught general principles which may govern their performance, the degree to which skill transfer will occur will be even more marked than will be found among normal youngsters. At the same time, of course, the degree of retardation will determine whether they will even be able to grasp principles common to two or more tasks.

Great difficulty will usually be encountered while testing retarded children in motor skills when trying to separate the influence of understanding from the effects of basic movement capacities in the production of the final outcome. Similar problems will be incurred when trying to separate attitudinal and emotional factors from cognitive capacities in the formation of the efforts of superior athletes. In any case, data from studies in which various atypical groups have taken part afford us views of the manner in which intelligence and movement are related within the average performer, and on the part of the intellectually normal child, youth, and adult.

Transfer

The concept of transfer was briefly alluded to in the previous paragraphs.[1] In general, most of the literature on transfer of training deals with the manner in which the performance and learning of one skill or concept influences the later acquisition of a second task.

Much of the information dealing with inter-task transfer attempts to explore the conditions under which the performance and learning of one task may either facilitate or impede the learning of a second. In some cases, it has been found that the performance of one task may *both* facilitate *and* impede the acquisition of a second: insofar as the first task contains both elements that are similar to the second, and thus facilitative, as well as components that are different enough to be confusing to the learner when attempting the second, thus causing negative transfer. The over-all effect on one task by prior practice of another will thus be the sum of the similar and positive elements within the tasks minus the negative effects of confusing variables in the two tasks that are likely to impede transfer.

This principle is thus likely to explain the improvement seen as the result of the application of a program of movement education within a home or school situation that is dissimilar to the findings of researchers carrying out well-controlled studies concerning the same effects.

The researcher, if his findings are to be accepted as valid, must control for extraneous and irrelevant factors that might elicit positive transfer. For example, he must insert into his study groups of children who are given only special attention without the special "ingredients" of the program he is investigating. In this way he is able to "purify" the findings he derives and support the contention that it was truly program content, not the emotional tone of the experimental environment or the rapport between the teachers-experimenters and the children, that caused the change elicited.

On the other hand, the teacher or parent who adopts a program of movement education has no such control over the situation, nor does he usually wish to exercise any. He is satisfied if the child improves, whether that improvement comes about because of better parent-child or teacher-child rapport or because of the intrinsic content of the activities. It is perhaps for this reason that programs which are apparently

[1] The reader is directed to the text by Ellis, *Transfer of Learning,* for a more thorough treatment of the concept of transfer with implications for education.

"mindless" may at times seem to enhance the intellectual abilities of children who are exposed to them.

It is for the reasons mentioned above that there are frequent communication problems between researchers and clinicians, teachers and parents. The latter group "know" certain perceptual-motor techniques "work" while the former are equally sure and can often provide objective scientific evidence to the contrary. It seems to me that the answer to this apparent conflict of perceptions is to attempt to optimize the influence of programs of movement education applied to children by paying close heed to the following principles:

TRANSFER WIDTH

One should not expect too much transfer to too many qualities from programs in which these same qualities are not clearly a part. This principle contains the concept of "transfer width." That is, one must ask the question when constituting a program and exclaiming its virtues, "Just how many kinds of abilities will this program content truly enhance?" Must the abilities to be improved resemble in exact, or at least closely approximate ways, the content of the program? It is believed that current literature, outlined in Chapters 11, 12 and 13, indicates that a close match between projected objectives and the nature of tasks within a program must be achieved! Mindlessly applied[2] programs composed of a few "basic" movements have demonstrated in several cases that they do not even improve movement attributes to any significant degree. Other programs in which primarily perceptual training is a part, have similarly not always been found to upgrade the academic skills that are purportedly undergirded by the perceptual abilities trained for.

Thus, when designing a program, one should carefully consider the goals proposed, and then collect a variety of tasks that resemble, in rather close ways, the abilities the program hopes to modify. Expecting too broad a transfer width, in other words, may result in a program that, while not offensive to the children or youth, will prove far from productive and generally wasteful of student time and, thus, of financial resources.

EMOTION AND TRANSFER

Movement education programs not only should be carefully constructed, but should be applied in a manner that is emotionally whole-

---

[2] Administered authoritatively by the parent or teacher, without any attempt to involve the child intellectually in the activities presented.

some to all concerned. Children are not animals blankly looking at their environment, but are constantly evaluating the pleasurable or painful components of the activities directed their way. If viewed as painful, a number of compensations, observed by many physical educators, may be evidenced, including increased hyperactivity, avoidance behavior in the form of various kinds of "acting-out" demonstrations, silent psychological withdrawal from the situation, or aggressive behavior. Thus, the available literature from psychiatric sources and from journals offering causal studies containing statistical data suggests that to optimize the effects of a program of movement education, one should take into account *both* the emotional content *and* the intellectuality of the total environment. In this manner, the positive transfer variables found in some clinical settings because of the parent or teacher concern for the child, plus the similarity of program content to hoped for outcomes, should combine to provide the most beneficial results.

COGNITIVE "BRIDGES"

Transfer between a program of movement education and other of life's tasks will be more pronounced if one accepts the premise I advance that children, youth, and adults possess the ability to make judgments, to think, and to evidence other intellectual qualities. That is, children must be given reasons for the tasks they are performing, and they should be afforded insight concerning relationships between the tasks performed in programs of movement education (or in any other type of educational program, for that matter) and the life functions to which it is hoped transfer will occur. Two examples may suffice to clarify the point:

1. A child, given the job of remembering a series of movements that a first child has performed, should be informed that this kind of task may help him to remember, with more clarity, the directions his mother gives him (if indeed it does!).

2. When jumping on grid squares containing letters and calling out the letters, a child should be shown the similarity between this exercise and the classroom equivalent. The teacher *knows* the obvious relationship between the two tasks, he or she *should not assume* that *the child* perceives the same relationships.

TRANSFERABLE EXPERIENCES

A second axiom important to the concept of transfer within an educational setting is concerned with the number of tasks containing a single concept or component within the training program. In general, the available data suggest that a number of transferable tasks should be engaged in, tasks that are intended to inculcate a single concept. For example, often seen in lists of goals for programs of movement education is the suggestion that the child be aided to perceive various spatial dimensions, including up-down and left-right. Purportedly, movement activities emphasizing either the integration of both sides of the body, and/or games with verbally administered directions emphasizing left or right, will aid the child to place letters into correct spatial contexts, to stop reversing the order of letters in words.

The information from current research, however, suggests that unless a number of left-right movements are engaged in, the child may only reflect acquisition of these spatial concepts when performing a rather limited number of tasks.

In summary, a thorough grounding in the principles of transfer of learning, provided by current summaries, should make the educator more effective when selecting activities for programs in which motor activities play an important part, and also will aid in the "spread of effect" of these activities into the child's life in school, at home, and after his school days have passed.

Individual Differences

Scientists from a number of disciplines have, within recent years, begun to discover the importance of considering individual differences when attempting to explain biochemical, physiological, neurological, and behavioral processes. Physiologists have largely ceased attempting to explain physiological phenomena by extrapolating from studies in which only a handful of subjects have been employed. Psycho-pharmacologists have likewise stopped classifying drugs as either stimulants or depressants, but rather are beginning to realize that the unique effects of medicants are often unique to an individual, some thought-to-be stimulants seem to tranquilize a large number of people, while reverse findings are often true when so-called depressants are administered to some individuals.

Individual differences in behavioral tendencies are most important to consider within the parameters of the content of this book. Several of these classifications important to the thrust of this text are covered in the paragraphs that follow.

ACTIVATION-AROUSAL

The information reviewed in Chapters 5 and 10 and in other parts of the book suggests that, while there is an optimum level of activation necessary in the performance of various intellectual tasks, muscular tension changes are only a portion of the indices of activation-arousal evidenced by an individual. Moreover, the available data make it clear that there are marked individual differences in patterns of activation within various people; thus, it is to be expected that some children will evidence marked tension changes during activation or overactivation within a given performance situation; others will appear to be muscularly relaxed, while, at the same time, other physiological indications of arousal may be markedly changed when compared to their normal resting state.

It is for these reasons that one might expect that programs of "deactivation," emphasizing muscular relaxation, may be quite helpful in the lessening of emotionality in some children, youth, and adults; while in other cases, little or no change may be forthcoming.

NEUROANATOMICAL DIFFERENCES

Another type of individual difference that is just now becoming apparent to neurologists is the common finding that about one-third of all children exposed to a given type of movement education evidence the expected changes, while the other two-thirds show either minimal or negligible changes. In general, the findings of Cohen and others suggest that there are marked individual differences in the manner in which peripheral movement and centered stimulation evoke even temporary changes in the central nervous system. The work done so far with animals indicates that similar peripheral movements (limb positionings and the like) of the same type in the same animals evoke highly dissimilar electronically measured changes in the central nervous system.

When it becomes possible to plot the nature of these individual differences in neural "connections," it may become similarly possible to design programs containing movement activities and other kinds of peripherally administered activities, including auditory, tactual, and visual stimulation to conform to the individual receptor-effector system. In this manner, children with severe movement and intellectual difficulties, the profoundly and severely retarded, may be matched with programs that more closely confirm the nature of their neural constitution.

INSTRUCTOR TRAITS

A summary of the manner in which teacher and experimenter expectations can modify the behaviors of children points to another important difference to be considered, particularly when studying the impact upon children and youth of a program containing movements.

More than one writer has, for example, suggested that in a true exploration of the value of the various programs of movement activities, one should study the nature of the placebo effects inserted. Even more important would be the exploration of the individual personality traits and emotional make-up of the children, versus the emotional needs reflected in modes of teacher behavior within the context of the movement education program. One need not watch an "action lesson" very long to discern the teacher's needs for authority, his liking for the children with whom he may be dealing, and their feelings about him and about the content he is presenting. Perhaps further research on this potentially important topic might reveal the complex dynamics of these personality variables.

INTELLECTUAL STRATEGIES

With the production of various models for the study of the intellect, notably that evolved by Guilford, researchers have become interested in the different manners in which people solve problems. These differences in strategy may consist of either attacking a problem as a whole, or piecemeal, dealing with concrete operations or cleaving more toward the abstract. In any case, this kind of individual difference could play an important part in matching a movement-oriented program to various sub-populations of children who might benefit.

For example, it is sometimes seen that children in ghetto communities, perhaps because of their rather pragmatically-oriented environment, tend to veer more toward the utilization of concrete operations when solving problems. They can deal best with the "here and now," with objects that can be seen, touched, and talked about. On the other hand, children in other socio-cultural groups, particularly those of parents who are professionally oriented, seem in many cases to be able to deal with abstractions at an earlier age than less privileged children. In the latter case, their basic needs for food, and shelter are usually met, so that their minds seem able to explore the possible, the abstract, and conceptual models, rather than being tied down to the concrete. It may be found, therefore, that problems in which operations are carried out via observable movement experiences may be more viable educational experiences for certain racial-ethnic groups than for others. It has been our experience to observe that the black child living within the central city enjoys the immediacy, spontaneity, and personal involvement inherent in programs of academic improvement in which he can move his total body and also observe his classmates in action. Additional research could certainly serve to illuminate these propositions more fully.

PERCEPTUAL ABILITIES

There are data from at least two researchers, Petrie and Ryan, which suggest that (a) certain perceptual attributes are found among more vigorous individuals, and that (b) individual differences in the inclination to move may serve either to blur information coming in through the senses or enhance its acquisition.

In general, these scholars contend that there seem to be two perceptual types identifiable according to the extent to which individuals seem either to "augment" or "reduce" stimuli. The augmenters, it is hypothesized, are the more passive individuals who perceive rather than "put-on," or move. They are usually found to be the more passive girl than the more active boy, and in general can be expected to do well within the more passive classroom environment. They have low thresholds of pain tolerance and seem to be more sensitive in tests of visual discrimination and in kinesthetic acuity.

The "reducers," on the other hand, may be found more often within groups of males on athletic teams, and are characterized by their tendency to move rather than to sit and look. They are relatively impervious to pain, seem to be reluctant to remain passive and "soak up" information, and in other ways might be expected to have problems adjusting their personalities within the usually more restrained classroom environment.

Thus, with further research, it may be found that this dichotomy, reducer-augmenter, may be a helpful one when assigning children to programs for academic enrichment in which movement activities play an important part. Teachers, particularly those in ghetto schools, receive daily confirmation of the difficulty of educating the more active boys in their charge; perhaps with further study, educational programs will be devised that more closely match these kinds of movement-perceptual inclinations with the vigor in which intellectual-academic offerings are tendered to children and youth.

ACTIVITY NEEDS

It is a common observation that children with high needs for activity tend to view vigorous and passive school experiences in different ways. Many boys and some girls can hardly wait to get out to the playground while the more passive boys and girls are content to sit for long periods of time and introspect, consider, investigate, read, and think. Moreover, these needs are seemingly in a state of flux during a school day and during the lifetime of a child.[3] There is more movement in

---

[3] Children of various ages whom we have tested in a recent pilot study on a task in which they were asked to draw a three-inch line "as slowly as you can," differed markedly. The four-year-olds took only about one-third of the time the six-year-olds spent on the same task, while the nine-year-olds were again 50 percent slower than the six-year-olds.

first-grade classrooms than in the third grade, while the well-controlled high school student is in marked contrast to the busier seventh grade child.

The research of Railo reviewed in Chapter 9 tends to suggest that children with high activity needs benefit less from prolonged classroom confinement than their less active classmates. This thwarting of vigorous children's "potential intellectual energies," to use Railo's terminology, may be one of the more serious crimes perpetrated by teachers upon their relatively helpless charges. Perhaps more careful consideration of the data emerging from studies of programs in which children are given an opportunity to move and think, rather than to sit and suffer, will lead to more enlightened programs in the future.

In summary, it is suggested that to assess truly the impacts of programs designed to improve intelligence, or any other qualities, one should consider carefully the individual differences in relationships between muscular tensions inherent in levels of activation, the personality make-up of the children and youth, as well as the needs, capacities, and inclinations of their mentors. Moreover, with more sophisticated research, differences in the neural make-up of various individuals may provide even more concrete principles to be followed when composing programs in which movement activities are important.

Future Directions

If, indeed, the writing of this text serves no other purpose than to stimulate research on the topics covered, the energy taken to complete it will be viewed as worthwhile. Not only are the available data scarce, but much of the information is from studies that lack proper controls or that contain sampling errors, statistical inadequacies, or logical fallacies.

Yet the apparent interest on the part of teachers in doing something with children via motor activity is incredibly high. If more sound research becomes available to guide their efforts, and the results of this research are communicated to them in usable form, more stimulating and useful educational programs will result. Children in the emerging nations of Africa, for example, may not be plucked from the natural movement-oriented village environment, confined to rigidly organized classrooms, and then expected to learn. Instead, they may be exposed to the naturalistic educational environment first suggested by Rousseau and Froebel; situations that are more compatible with their vigorous early childhoods. The black ghetto baby who is sometimes pampered, petted, spoiled, encouraged to move, given approval as he duplicates the rhythms of soul-music, and imitates the vigorous sports movements of his older brothers, may not be thrust suddenly into sardine-can-like classrooms during his fifth or sixth year, and expected to evidence a rather radical personality transformation, while at the same time attempting to assimilate reading, writing, and a number of other skills that may not be highly prized by members of his minority group.

With further investigation, the language differences in various children and youth may be helpfully combined with movement experiences. Children may be encouraged to engage in richer and more meaningful verbal mediation through the use of games in which speech and language play a part. At the same time, vocabulary development, and the seemingly dichotomized speech-language families sometimes needed by the central-city youngster, may be developed: one to join him in meaningful ways to his rich cultural heritage, and the second to aid him in becoming upwardly mobile within a language subculture that may be initially foreign to him.

Further thought and the consideration of some of the more sophisticated models depicting the numerous vicissitudes of the human intellect should prompt some to compose highly meaningful motor activity programs that truly impose a range of intellectual demands upon the participants. With additional data and attempts to translate findings into meaningful practical experiences, a rich range of activities should come to be devised, tasks that encompass the numerous types and levels of intellectual abilities that have been identified during the past twenty years. A beginning attempt at this pairing of intellectual levels with appropriate active tasks may be found in the previous chapter. Scholarly and creative readers are certain to expand and elaborate upon this general approach.

Whether one leads a child from the intellectually easy task by adding directions, or by transferring decisions to the child, is not easily decided, and perhaps depends to some degree upon the philosophy of the individual constructing the program. For example, one approach might be to create a situation initially in which extreme latitude of choice is offered: "Let's see you move down the mat any way you can," and then presenting directions that are, in a step-by-step manner, increasingly restrictive ("Move down backward," "Now go down backward with your back nearest the mat," "Now backward with your back nearest the mat and only your left foot and both hands touching the mats."). Such choice moves from eliciting actions which purportedly summon divergent thinking, to those which reflect a few alternatives, and then finally, to a single possibly "correct" choice or toward convergent thinking.

On the other hand, one might concentrate upon gradually removing restrictions, transferring planning and performance and decisions and/or evaluation to the learner as he seems capable of assimilating them.

Mosston has made inroads in this imaginative and operational approach. Perhaps with more time, he, his students, or those adhering to his basic philosophy will produce an even more useful methodology than is currently outlined.

More likely, it is hoped, a rather elaborate model will be formulated. To be a viable one, it is believed, it should incorporate variables of several kinds, including various levels and types of intellectual functioning, the manner in which movement tasks may be taught to match the levels, as well as some of the parameters suggested by Guilford, including differences in content. In any case, the outlines of such a comprehensive approach are barely discernible if one looks closely at the currently available literature.

Movement oriented programs of education have great potential worth because they provide observable evidence of a child's thought processes. With further refinement of groups of activities in which intellectual depth is combined with happy games, not only might children benefit, but their happiness and relaxation should transmit itself to their often harried mentors.

The guidelines for meaningful programs of movement activities, for the ways in which thought can be employed in the teaching of motor skills, and for other problems described within the pages of the book, have only scarcely been sketched in by a relatively small number of scholars around the world whose attention and energies have been attracted to these issues. It is hoped when the time comes to revise this effort, in four or five years, the superficial brush marks of information that are contained within these pages will coalesce into a clearer portrait of the ways in which action and thought may form more perfect marriages in a number of potentially important ways.

BIBLIOGRAPHY

BIRREN, JAMES, and HESS, ROBERT. "Influences of Biological Psychological, and Social Deprivations upon Learning and Performance," in *Perspectives on Human Deprivation,* Chapter II. Washington, D.C.: U. S. Dept. of Health, Education, and Welfare, 1968.

COHEN, L. A. "Manipulation of Cortical Motor Responses by Peripheral Sensory Stimulation." *Physical and Medical Rehabilitation* 50 (September 1969): 495–505.

CRATTY, BRYANT J. *Human Behavior: Exploring Educational Processes.* Wolf City, Texas: University Press, 1971.

ELLIS, HENRY. *The Transfer of Learning.* New York: The Macmillan Co., 1965.

GAGNE, ROBERT M. *Learning and Individual Differences.* Columbus, Ohio: Charles E. Merrill Books, Inc., 1967.

GUILFORD, J. P. *Intelligence, Creativity, and Their Educational Implications.* San Diego, Calif.: Robert R. Knapp, Publisher, 1968.

MOSSTON, MUSKA. *Teaching Physical Education.* Columbus, Ohio: Charles E. Merrill Books, Inc., 1966.

PETRIE, ASENATH. *Individuality in Pain and Suffering.* Chicago: The University of Chicago Press, 1967.

RAILO, WILLI S. "Physical Fitness and Intellectual Achievement." *Scandinavian Journal of Educational Research,* No. 2 (1969), 103–20.

RAILO, WILLI S., and EGGEN, S. *Physical and Mental Endurance.* Unpublished monograph, Norwegian College of Physical Education and Sport, 1967.

ROSENTHAL, ROBERT. *Experimenter Effects in Behavioral Research.* New York: Appleton-Century-Crofts, Inc., 1966.

RYAN, E. DEAN. "Perceptual Characteristics of Vigorous People." In *New Perspectives of Man in Action.* Edited by Cratty and Brown. Englewood Cliffs, N. J.: Prentice-Hall, Inc., 1969.

INDEX